Those We Forget
Recounting Australian Casualties of the First World War

David Noonan

MELBOURNE UNIVERSITY PUBLISHING
An imprint of Melbourne University Publishing Limited
11–15 Argyle Place South, Carlton, Victoria 3053, Australia
mup-info@unimelb.edu.au
www.mup.com.au

First published 2014
Text © David Noonan 2014
Design and typography © Melbourne University Publishing Limited, 2014

This book is copyright. Apart from any use permitted under the *Copyright Act 1968* and subsequent amendments, no part may be reproduced, stored in a retrieval system or transmitted by any means or process whatsoever without the prior written permission of the publishers.

Every attempt has been made to locate the copyright holders for material quoted in this book. Any person or organisation that may have been overlooked or misattributed may contact the publisher.

Typeset by J&M Typesetting
Printed in Australia by OPUS Group

National Library of Australia Cataloguing-in-Publication entry

Noonan, David C., author.
Those we forget: recounting Australian casualties of the First World War/ David Noonan.

9780522866674 (paperback)
9780522866681 (ebook)

Includes index.

World War, 1914–1918—Casualties—Australia.
World War, 1914–1918—Casualties—Research.
World War, 1914–1918—Casualties—Statistics.
World War, 1914–1918—Participation, Australian.
War casualties—Australia.

940.394

Contents

List of tables		vi
List of figures		vii
List of acronyms		viii
Acknowledgements		ix
Prelude		xi
1	Tracking the Sources of the Official Figures	1
2	Definitions and Statistical Methodologies for Assessing War Casualties	33
3	Counting the Diggers (1): Enlistments and Embarkations	50
4	Counting the Diggers (2): Specific Medical Conditions	64
5	Counting the Diggers (3): Multiple Examples of Harm	88
6	Those We Forget: Total Australian Casualties of the First World War	115
7	Some Comparisons in this Global War	150
8	The Post-War Impacts: Those We Forget	173
Index		200

List of tables

Table 1: Total casualties, 1921

Table 2: Total casualties, 1933

Table 3: Total battle casualties, 1919

Table 4: Enlistments and embarkations

Table 5: Official Sources © David Noonan, 2014.

Table 6: Sample Size

Table 7: Selected sample sizes © David Noonan, 2014.

Table 8: Analysis of results—MT1486/1 series © David Noonan, 2014.

Table 9: Examples of rejection—medically unfit © David Noonan, 2014.

Table 10: Actual enlistments MT series © David Noonan, 2014.

Table 11: Comparative total casualty statistics—Australia and other selected belligerents © David Noonan, 2014.

Table 12: Proportion of males in Australia's population, 1881–1921

Table 13: Comparative pension data of 1932 with other selected belligerents © David Noonan, 2014.

Table 14: Australia's total death toll from the First World War © David Noonan, 2014.

List of figures

Figure 1: Colonel A Graham 'Gertie' Butler © Australian War Memorial (AWM 8932).

Figure 2: Death by campaign © David Noonan, 2014.

Figure 3: Death from suicide and cerebro-spinal meningitis © David Noonan, 2014.

Figure 4: Death from Spanish Flu and pneumonia © David Noonan, 2014.

Figure 5: Prisoners of War © David Noonan, 2014.

Figure 6: Age at enlistment by year: officers and other ranks © David Noonan, 2014.

Figure 7: Applications for non-aged-based pension claims by year © David Noonan, 2014.

Figure 8: All applications for repatriation benefits post war © David Noonan, 2014.

Figure 9: The total impact of the First World War © David Noonan, 2014.

List of acronyms

AFC	Australian Flying Corps
AIF	Australian Imperial Force
AWGC	Australian War Graves Commission
AWL	Absent without leave
AWM	Australian War Memorial
CSM	Cerebro-Spinal Meningitis
DAH	Disordered action of the heart
GSW	Gunshot wound
NAA	National Archives of Australia
NCO	Non Commissioned Officer
NYD	Not yet diagnosed
NYDN	Not yet diagnosed neurosis
POW	Prisoner of war
PTSD	Post-traumatic stress disorder
PTSS	Post-traumatic stress syndrome
RSL	Returned and Services League
SNR	Soldier not required
SOS	Struck off strength
TB	Tuberculosis
TBI	Traumatic brain injury
TOS	Taken on strength
TPE	Termination of period of enlistment
USA	United States of America
VC	Victoria Cross
VD	Venereal disease
VDH	Valvular disorder of the heart

Acknowledgements

This book required an unusual mix of the mathematical analysis of a large amount of historical material, which is contained in the unique *online* collection of the NAA Australian soldier service records. As a result, I was fortunate to have considerable assistance from a wide range of experts in their fields. First and foremost, I must thank Professor Robin Prior of the University of Adelaide who provided me with broad guidance in the first instance and along the way in my research that has ultimately led to this book and its findings. Then there was Professor Joy Damousi, who set strict timetables, provided enthusiastic encouragement and invaluable support.

I must acknowledge the considerable help I received from the staff at various public institutions. First, from the National Archives of Australia, Andrew Cairns in Canberra and Andrew Griffin in Melbourne—the former in particular, for his professionalism and patience as I sorted out my sampling methodology. Then there were the enthusiastic staff at the State Library of Victoria who provided me with insightful additional material particularly on health definitions in Australia in the early 1900s. The staff at the Australian War Memorial were also helpful. The Baillieu Library staff at the University of Melbourne were of great assistance, in particular Caitlin Stone. I also wish to thank Associate Professor Mark Jenkins and in particular Professor John Hooper of the University of Melbourne Department of Population Health for their advice on how to address population health in an AIF context and to explore the statistical methods appropriate for its analysis. And so now to the staff at the Statistical Consulting Centre at the University of Melbourne: Ian Gordon and Sue Finch were of great help, but in particular Sandy Clarke, who alerted me to the power of the Excel spread sheet and Minitab. Thank you Sandy, you pushed me in at the deep end of the pool of statistical analysis but you did not let me drown. Thanks also go to Simon Clews at the Writing Centre for Scholars and Researchers at the University of Melbourne for guidance on how to turn a thesis into a book. And last on this list of contributed expertise was the considerable effort of clear thinking that was required in the copy edit of the manuscript provided by Julia Farrell.

I would also like to acknowledge the two professors who examined my PhD thesis—Professor John Horne at Department of

Modern History, Trinity College Dublin and Professor Jay Winter at the Department of History, Yale University—for their invaluable comments both positive and negative.

Finally, holding all of this together I acknowledge with love my soulmate Susan, for her patience, support, counsel and tolerance ('you're talking about the war again'), and for helping get me over the line after all these years so to bring my obsession to fruition. I dedicate this book to her, and Isaac and Violet Miller.

Prelude

They would often recall that distant day when they strolled after lunch in her parent's rhododendron garden, in the gentile Melbourne suburb of Elsternwick. It was Christmas Day 1915, the day that Isaac Pearce Miller had decided sometime previously that he would ask his sweetheart of eight years if she would become his wife. With an ominous, dreadful sign of the extent of their naïvety, he put another proposal to Miss Violet Ewart. Would she allow him to serve his country and join the Australian Imperial Force (AIF) to fight in the European war? He patiently explained that casualties from the great Gallipoli campaign were beginning to be returned to Australia from English and North African hospitals. Recruitment efforts were lifting, calling for more volunteers to make 'a good showing' for the young nation on the international stage. And besides, he would only miss one Christmas before he would be home to spend a whole lifetime with his wife. Violet said yes to both of his proposals, but on two conditions: he must avoid dangerous duties and stay out of harm's way, and he must give up the drink. He agreed to both, though he would subsequently fulfil only one.

Isaac had no idea what his proposal to enlist actually meant. At that time, Australia claimed (and in most quarters, still claims to this day) to be the only country with an all-volunteer army involved in this conflict. But to qualify for the status of volunteer, consent must be given when fully informed. The men of the AIF were not fully informed about that to which they were about to be exposed, and once they were on that ship, there was no turning back. The modern technology of artillery, machine guns and gas was about to deliver a devastating improvement to the previously established ability to slaughter in battle. In this context, the term 'volunteer Australian army' is a myth.

Isaac and Violet married early in the following year and, after a short honeymoon, Isaac walked into the South Melbourne army depot only to be promptly marched out to take a train to Bendigo on that same day, 14 March 1916. He had become part of the intake of the rural 38th Battalion being formed in the iconic country gold town. The next day the *Bendigo Advertiser* reported that another batch of 'well trained men had marched with precision' through the town to join the swelling ranks. White tents dotted the Bendigo showgrounds, and training consisted of marching and listening to lectures with shirt sleeves rolled up. Due to his clerical skills Isaac was promoted to the position of Quarter Master Sergeant of B Company. In that capacity he was to issue *real* rifles, as soon as they became available, just a matter of days before the 38th embarked in June 1916. His boys were headed for war, making farmyard animal noises below decks on the troopship each night after lights out.

Literally in the shadows of Stonehenge, they trained to dig trenches on the white, chalky plains of Salisbury. It was nothing like the black, gluey mud of Flanders in which men and mules later went missing. The fledgling word 'digger' took flight that year over the Salisbury Plains until it later became part of the lexicon of the AIF amid the mud and trenches of the Western Front. Isaac's battalion, now part of the Third Division, first saw action outside Armentieres in Northern France, shortly before the end of 1916. Regarded as a quiet theatre of war, Armentieres was known as 'The Nursery'—seen as ideal for the blooding of men for what was to come.

During the course of 1917 Isaac was joined on the Western Front by his three brothers, Donald, Harry and Norman. Extraordinarily, all four Miller boys returned to Australia, but not before Donald had been hospitalised with shell shock, promoted and sent back to the front, only to severely injure his leg in the field. In a series of interviews with Isaac's daughter, Joy, in 2003, she recalled that 'Uncle Donald' always limped. He was hospitalised for four months, promoted again and returned to the front, only to be gassed one month later and evacuated to England. He spent two more periods in hospital: two weeks for scabies, and four months for his leg. In May 1919, he was discharged medically unfit upon his return to Australia. Shortly thereafter, he left his wife and children and moved to Sydney.

Harry Miller received gunshot wounds to the buttocks, a common wounding among soldiers as a result of having to crawl flat on one's face in no-man's-land, in an effort to stay below the web of bullets and shrapnel ripping across the torn-up landscape. He then spent four months recuperating in England. He subsequently returned to France in September 1917 for eight months, this time sustaining severe shrapnel wounds to his legs. He was hospitalised for five months and shipped back to Australia to be discharged medically unfit. 'Uncle Harry' also limped for the rest of his life, but he was not around much, preferring to live a reclusive life in the Dandenong Ranges outside Melbourne.

Norman, the eldest and last to enlist, was to fare the worst. Within days of reaching his post on the Western Front, on Christmas Day of 1917, he was hospitalised for two months with 'colic'. Six months later, he collapsed with muscular pain and a blood infection that covered him in boils. Stress had destroyed his immune system. On 11 November 1918, he was declared medically unfit for service, diagnosed with myalgia, and shipped back to Australia in 1919 where he was promptly discharged. He returned his medals in 1923 to the Victoria Barracks in Melbourne, was diagnosed as dipsomaniac and set about the lonely task of drinking himself to death over the next twelve years.

Isaac *and only one other man* from his 250-strong B Company that departed Australia in 1916 were to return with B Company in 1919. They had been lambs to the slaughterhouse that was the Western Front. Violet was to later tell her daughter that Isaac returned 'a changed man', and *never* spoke of his experiences. His legacy was the 125 letters he wrote to Violet over this period, some forty pages long. Her legacy was that she kept them all. That distant day of Christmas 1915 was longingly referred to many times in those letters, as was the blissful ignorance of their pre-war shared experience, now lost forever. Isaac Miller was my grandfather.

In total, the four brothers were hospitalised fourteen times; three were discharged medically unfit. The 38th Battalion, in which Isaac served, had thirty-two officers who departed together on that ship. Only two of them, one of whom was the Commanding Officer, would return with the battalion. The rollicking history of the 38th Battalion was published in 1920, and honoured with a foreword by none other than Prime Minister Billy Hughes, extolling the efforts of the men of the 38th who, as part of the Third Division, had been under the celebrated command of Sir John Monash, from their arrival in England until the end of the war. The list of officers' names who served in the 38th is included in an appendix to this official history. A staggering 140 men would hold those thirty-two officer positions over the twenty-two months during which the battalion saw action—a turnover of five times. The widely shared post-war construct of mateship sustaining our forces is tested here when we consider that if one had visited that battalion around *every sixteen weeks* throughout the course of its twenty-two-month period of engagement in the war, apart from the two officers who served throughout (one being the Commanding Officer), on average, *none* of the officers would have been the same as the last time one visited. Mateship would hardly have had time to flourish, let alone sustain or succour the men.

As for the 1000 men who originally comprised the 38th Battalion as a whole, the casualties were such that 2000 men would eventually serve among its ranks. What remained of the battalion was withdrawn from the front in the first week of October 1918, no longer at fighting strength. Its sister battalion, the 37th (originally of 1000 men), had only ninety men capable of taking the field by that time.

These appallingly high numbers of casualties are simply not supported by the official statistics of the AIF, which record the deaths of 60 000 men and 155 000 hospitalisations for wounding sustained by the 331 781 Australian soldiers who, officially, embarked to serve overseas. Were the Miller boys unlucky? Was Isaac's battalion overexposed? Where are the instances of injury and illness recorded? Was shell shock counted at all? When did they stop counting after the fighting had stopped? After all, men would still continue to die after the celebrated *cessation of hostilities*.

To answer these questions, for the first time since the end of this worldwide conflict, the official histories' of Australia's casualties in the First World War are to be reviewed and reassessed to answer the simple question: what really did happen? The only way to do this requires a painstaking forensic recount of random samples of over 12 000 individual First World War soldier records using sophisticated statistical analysis to accurately determine the real extent of the pain, suffering and death of the men of the AIF. The results are startling, providing a new level of appreciation of the cost to this young Dominion country never before contemplated.

It can now be revealed for the first time that, by any major measure, the official casualty figures of the AIF are seriously inaccurate. In terms of the total number of hospitalisations alone, they are wrong by *a factor of five*. By any major measure, the men of the AIF were decimated. The mask of the post-war construct of *the spirit of Anzac* has shrouded the ghosts of untold suffering. It was, for Australia, a tragic, pyrrhic victory; a victory gained at too great a cost.

Before the facts behind this claim can be explored in detail, we must first address the question of how Australia's public official casualty figures for the First World War came to be so inaccurate and incomplete, and why they have remained so understated today, despite the voluminous historical analyses published since. Was there a conspiracy to cover up the true numbers? Or was this the result of the gross incompetency of our official historians? Or was it simply, the unquestioned past acceptance of the official historical record?

Chapter 1
Tracking the Sources of the Official Figures

The publication of the official Australian casualty figures for the First World War began with CEW Bean in 1921, with the *Official History of Australia in the War 1914–1918, Volume I: The Story of ANZAC from the outbreak of war to the end of the first phase of the Gallipoli Campaign, May 4, 1915*.[1] Sometime later, figures were recorded by Professor Ernest Scott, Professor of History at the University of Melbourne, who was responsible for *Volume XI* of the same official history, *Australia During the War*, published in 1936.[2] The official *medical* statistics were compiled and analysed by AG Butler in his three volumes of medical text, analysis and statistics, entitled *Official Medical History of the Australian Medical Services, 1914–1918*, the last and most significant volume of which was finally published in 1942. As Editor-in-Chief of Australia's official war history, Bean published his last volume, *Volume VI*, later in 1942. These three authors are universally accepted as the authorities on the human cost of this conflict for the men of the AIF. Remarkably, their contributions have essentially remained unquestioned. This book invites the reader on a journey of discovery to firmly establish the extent to which the men of the AIF suffered and, with various levels of success, how they struggled to endure. Indeed, this is a journey to find the truth about what really did happen to these men and thereby fulfil our national commitment: to remember them all, lest we forget.

Recent decades have seen a significant rise in the volume of historical analysis of the social and cultural consequences of the First World War, exceeding the previous number of what were essentially military orientated examinations. Within this recent body of work, Bean's tome and, to a lesser extent, Butler's medically based works have been used as fundamental starting points. For example, Joan Beaumont's book *Broken Nation: Australians in the Great War*, published in November 2013, relies extensively on Bean's material. Both Scott and Butler recorded the *post-war* costs with reference to the repatriation pension system, highlighting the extent of human suffering as the number of pension recipients—and their dependants—continued to increase over time, and veteran deaths were occurring at a rate of three per day by the outbreak of the Second World War. By way of example of the more recent examinations of post-war consequences, Marion Larsson's excellent *Shattered Anzacs*, released in 2009, relies on the official histories. In it, she points out that by 1920 about 90 000 Australian ex-servicemen were receiving war disability pensions, and that over the next two decades the total number of pensioners fluctuated between 25 and 33 per cent of the returned soldier population. At the outbreak of the Second World War, over 77 000 veterans were still living with a war disability.

However, along with the total reliance on the data provided by these official historians for all subsequent examinations of this conflict come serious implications, if Bean's and Butler's works are deficient. Contrary to the widespread belief that a review of the casualty data was practically impossible, there is a way forward whereby this official casualty record *can* be tested. This can be achieved by using the mine of information contained in the unique and extraordinarily detailed AIF individual soldier Attestation Papers. A review and recount of these records enables us to challenge the prevailing understanding of Australia's casualty figures, indeed to question the understandings of the medical basis of these First World War statistics. It can also assess, for the first time, the true and measurable *post-war impacts* contained in and implied by the individual's AIF service record, which have only been guessed at to this day. In the process, this record review can present a new social history canvas, as individual soldier experiences are brought to light. This approach therefore has the potential to rewrite this part of Australia's Anzac history.

But, first, we must revisit how the accepted official casualty record was created and how, as now claimed, it got it so wrong.

As mentioned above, Australia's foundation author of the history of the First World War is CEW Bean, through the twelve volumes of the *Official History of Australia in the War of 1914–18*. Bean was not the sole contributor to this definitive work. In the preface of the final work, *Volume VI*, published in May 1942, Bean acknowledges the extraordinary work of Colonel A Graham Butler, who in his three-volume *Official History Of the Australian Army Medical Services, 1914–1918*, 'is sacrificing not only his livelihood but [also] his health in order to provide his countrymen with a history of their Army Medical Service (…) and is largely drawn on in these pages'.[3]

Bean's mention of Butler's health in this manner is odd; yet its significance becomes clear when we later consider the inaccuracy of Australia's casualty statistics. It should be noted that Bean had little to do with compiling or publishing overall casualty statistics. The only references to such are found in a small footnote in his first volume, referred to shortly. And in his last volume, *The Australian Imperial Force in France during the Allied Offensive, 1918*, published in 1942, several months after Butler's last work, there is a large table of data on recruitment and British Empire casualties, incorporating the Dominion of Australia, which he cites as extracts from *Statistics of the Military Effort of the British Empire during the Great War 1914–1920*, consisting of data effective as of 31 December 1920. But where are Butler's medical data on injury and illness? Bean only cites *military* statistics of death and woundings. In a note to these data in the final volume he directs the reader to further statistics available in tables in Scott's *Volume XI* and Butler's *Volumes II* and *III*. Extraordinarily, and in contradiction of his earlier quoted reliance on Butler's work, Bean ignores Butler's updated casualty figures in his own table. This seems at odds with Bean's role as editor of Butler's work—an issue that will be examined in detail later. However, initially, all of the work of *official* casualty statistical summarisation rested with Scott when he published in 1936.

Bean invited Scott to finish *Volume XI*, dealing with Australia at home during the war, which remained unfinished. It had been started in 1925 by TW Heney, formerly an editor of *The Sydney Morning Herald*, who had taken ill after three years of working on the volume and died soon after. Scott perhaps reveals a little of his character when he suggests in his preface that the pressure Heney faced in having to produce this volume had something to do with his untimely death.[4]

Scott decided to start again. Although known as a prodigious worker, Scott took eight years, albeit part-time, to complete the volume. A personable man, staunch defender of the British Empire but not necessarily a friend of Bean, or holding him in high regard, Scott was unusual in that he had previously been a journalist himself for the *Herald*, when he was invited in 1913 to apply for the position of chair of history at the University of Melbourne. He was appointed, his research and personal qualities seen as outweighing his lack of academic qualifications and experience.[5] He was empirically minded and hostile to the very concept of the theory of history. In the context of the prevailing view of the 'mighty Empire', he was a fine choice, albeit someone with a journalistic background. Indeed, it was the acclaimed Australian historian Ken Inglis who stated that Scott's was the only volume of the twelve in which serious historians should take any interest.[6]

Bean's role, as far as Butler was concerned, was that of an overseeing editor of text only. It was Bean who insisted on the introduction of marginal headings into Butler's work, which Bean used himself occasionally. These marginal headings were single words inserted into the text in bold at the beginning of a paragraph describing the subject of the section or even just the paragraph that followed. The frequency of their use in Butler's volumes gives us early warning of what was to come.

Under pressure from Bean, Butler finally finished his work on the official medical services history in 1942,[7] thus allowing Bean to publish his final volume of the official war history, twenty-one years after the First World War had finished and two years after the Second World War had started. This delay in publication was exacerbated by the confused and variable results produced by Butler, which will be dissected shortly. It is to be noted here that in his final preface Bean, while acknowledging Butler's contribution, did not acknowledge Ernest Scott. This is significant because it is Scott's volume of the official war history, *Volume XI*, published in 1936, in which the first 'official' reference to Australian casualties is made, and these figures, shown below in Table 1, are dated 'as corrected in 1921'.[8] (It was the practice to numerically add the incidence of deaths to the incidence of wounding to express total casualties.)

Table 1: Total Casualties, 1921

Total embarkations 331 781	Total casualties 215 585	Percentage 64.98

Source: Ernest Scott, Official History of Australia in the War 1914–1918, Volume XI, Angus & Robertson, Sydney, 1936, p. 874.

In the footnote to the casualty table above, Scott explains that he has made a correction for 'participating forces' (which has the effect of elevating Australia's percentage *contribution*) to a table published in Bean's *Volume I—The Story of ANZAC from the outbreak of war to the end of the first phase of the Gallipoli Campaign, May 4, 1915*.[9] This volume was first published in 1921, and republished unaltered in 1933. A footnote to Bean's table sources reads: 'The following are the British official figures (as cabled to Australian newspapers)'. These figures are presented in Table 2.

Table 2: Total Casualties, 1933

Enlistments 413 453	Total casualties 215 585	Percentage 52.14

Source: CEW Bean, Official History of Australia in the War 1914–1918, Volume I, Angus & Robertson, Sydney, 1941, p. 548.

Thus, until Butler and Bean published in 1942, these data presented in Scott's *Volume XI* formed the basis of the Australian official casualty figures for the First World War, as published by Bean in 1921, and 'as cabled to Australian newspapers'. Or did they? And what did he mean by his reference to British official figures?

It is Scott who leads us to even earlier work and provides insight into the apparent disregard at the time for the real meaning and impact of casualty figures, as they were almost celebrated as some measure of achievement. In a preface written by Scott for a book published in 1919, entitled *Australian Campaigns in the Great War: Being a Concise History of the Australian Naval and Military Forces 1914 to 1918*, written by Lieutenant The Honourable Staniforth Smith, Scott, revealing his total allegiance to *all* that is encapsulated by the British Empire, refers to an already large body of literature concerning Australia's part in the 'Great European War':

There are books about the Australians in France, in Egypt, and in Palestine, and there is an especially thrilling collection of narratives of the splendid adventure of Gallipoli. In due course, we may expect to have an ample official history of the Australian share in the war, based upon the authentic records, and covered by official sanction.[10]

Scott was unaware in 1919 that he would later play a role in the production of an official war history.

In Smith's book, Scott notes in the Introduction that he:

> ... was fortunate in having information obtained for him from the War Office, as to the casualties suffered by the troops from various parts of our far-flung empire, and from the foreign legations in London particulars, not previously published, of the casualties of our allies. This, with details gathered regarding the Central Powers, has enabled tables to be compiled, and for the first time published, of the casualties of the whole of the belligerents.[11]

Here, then, in 1919, is the first list published in Australia of the British Empire's First World War casualty statistics, including members of the AIF, predating anything, however small, published by Bean or any other official Australian historian. This is important because as the source is the British War Office, these statistics are in a purely military form and injury and illness are excluded. Such medical statistics had not even begun to be compiled at that time.

Table 3: Total Battle Casualties, 1919

Enlistments	416 809
Embarkations	331 781
Total deaths	58 132
Wounded, gassed, POW	156 228
Total battle casualties	214 360

Source: The British War Office, *Statistics of The Military Effort of the British Empire during the Great War 1914–1920*, London HM Stationary Office, London, 1923, pp. 759–770.

The official compilation of these 'military' figures—as at July 1919, then reviewed as at 31 December 1920—was later published by the British War Office itself in 1923.[12] And to this day all Australian 'official' historical casualty analyses have remained embedded within these figures. The most frequently cited figures are presented in Table 3.

In relation to the above, the question arises: from where did the British War Office source these statistics? The answer is the Australian War Memorial (AWM), which contains a document entitled 'Australian Imperial Force, Statistics of Casualties, Etc.'.[13] The record's release is indicated by its dating: 'Compiled to 30th June 1919'. The Records Section, AIF Headquarters, London issued the record. This is the source of Smith's figures. It was compiled by members of the AIF Records Section, initially at its location in France, and then later in London to where it relocated in 1916. Updated figures were presumably provided to Smith for his publication and to the British War Office for its official publication in 1923. Two important observations need to be made at this time. First, the numbers that do not change are those for enlistments and embarkations. Second, and most critically, the numbers are defined solely in military terms—they cover death and wounding or prisoners of war (POWs). There is no record presented of injury or illness. This was considered to be the responsibility of *others* in the medical services and this task did not commence in Australia until 1923. But was there an independent verification of these military numbers? Have they been subjected to scrutiny? In a partial sense, they have.

Early in 1918, Australia's fighting force was facing a desperate shortage of men. At the behest of Prime Minister Hughes, a Royal Commission was hastily declared requiring one commissioner, Sir Samuel Griffith, Chief Justice, to enquire into the Department of Defence records. The Royal Commission officially ran from 6 March to 4 April 1918, although Sir Griffith signed off on his report on 14 March—giving it the dubious distinction of being the shortest running Royal Commission in Australian history. Its aim was to report to a special conference convened by the Governor-General, Munro Ferguson, on 11 April of that year.

The purpose of the conference was to examine the subject of securing reinforcements under the voluntary system of recruitment for the AIF force then serving abroad. Attempts to introduce conscription by way of referenda had failed twice, opening significant divides in the Australian community, at a time when voluntary enlistments were falling dramatically. The thirty-seven delegates from across Australia, from political representatives from both sides of politics, and business and union representatives, attended a seven-day 'summit' and were treated to an impassioned opening address by the Governor-General, imploring those present to set aside their differences as the situation was 'of sufficient gravity to justify the sinking of public differences and personal antipathies in one supreme united effort to find an issue from the impasse'.[14]

The first item to be voted on after the Governor-General spoke was the decision over whether the press should be allowed to attend. The vote was split 19–16, with two abstentions, reflecting how divided Australia had become over this war, which was also seen in the close outcomes of the two referenda on conscription. The Royal Commission's report to this conference provides an excellent insight into the official figures, from which the data shown in Table 4 are drawn, effective to 31 December 1917.

Table 4: Enlistments and Embarkations

	Enlistments	Embarkations
1914	52 561	31 881
1915	165 912	96 984
1916	124 352	139 592
1917	45 101	42 396
Total	387 926	310 853

Source: Australian Royal Commission on The War—Australian Imperial Force and Sir Samuel Griffith, The War: Australian Imperial Force: Report by the Royal Commission (His Honour Sir Samuel Griffith, Chief Justice) as to number of members fit for active service and number of reinforcements and enlistments required, Government Printer, Melbourne, 1918 (also published as a Parliamentary Paper, 1917–19 session, vol. 4).

If one consults Scott (dated 1936) and an unsourced table in his volume showing enlistments, for the year 1918 the number is 28 883,[15] which when added to the Royal Commission's total results in the *exact* same total of 416 809 as that cited in the British War Office statistics (of 1923), Bean and Butler (both 1942), and every other historical publication since.

However, the precise match among these cited figures is simply not credible in light of other data variability and therefore it must be challenged. But it does tell us that a single source for all *battle* casualty (death and wounding) and embarkation statistics exists. In other words, if this single source is correct, our efforts to identify the extent of the human cost of the war are concluded. It also indicates that the ramifications of such a source being wrong are highly significant, not least of all because the basis of this number withstood the examination of a Royal Commission inquiry. If the figure is wrong the whole basis used to calculate the human cost of the war must be called into question.

The 1918 conference proved a failure in being able to significantly improve recruitments, as evidenced by the low number of enlistments for that year of fewer than 29 000 men, when the Royal Commission had called for 75 000. This was mainly because the conference's only positive proposal, the Voluntary Ballot Enlistment Scheme,[16] could not be implemented before the end of the war. But as LL Robson, Professor of History, University of Melbourne, stated in 1982:

> The enlistment of the AIF, and the War, revealed both splendid and deplorable aspects of Australia: thoughtlessness, cruelty, unswerving devotion to the suppression of opposition; great courage, shining sincerity, high and proper ideals and mindful sacrifice.[17]

Robson also asserted that Prime Minister Hughes and his supporters were prepared to do anything to ensure that Australia *appeared* to meet its commitments to the supply of soldiers to the war effort. Hughes had relied on a census conducted in September 1915 of all males aged between 18 and 60 years, from which he wrongly concluded that Australia had 600 000 potentially eligible soldiers. He failed to take into consideration their health and physical capacity to be a soldier. Some of the means used to promote enlistment included paying police ten shillings for each man that they managed to enlist, compulsorily calling up unmarried men between the ages of 21 and 35 years for military service inside Australia (they could not legally be called up for *overseas* service),[18] employers dismissing eligible males on the pretext that returned soldiers should be given precedence in selection for their job positions, and withholding the results of the soldiers vote in the conscription referenda because they might influence the general public's opinion (the soldiers voted against conscription).[19] Robson claimed that:

> The struggle in Europe was the best example to that time of the suppression of facts that might conceivably be useful to the enemy, and of the feeding to the public of half truths, and sometimes utter lies. This was recognised early in the war: in June 1915 Lieutenant-Colonel Sir Albert Gould told the Senate that one of the great troubles the nation had to contend with was the erroneous belief that the allies were doing well.[20]

Based on these considerations, we might ask: were Australia's official enlistment figures one of these half-truths or 'utter lies', not for the consumption of the Australian public, but to support the wider political agenda of maximising Australia's perceived contribution to the war effort in the wider international forum?

In the questioning of the accuracy of enlistment figures, it is worth reviewing a *single* page in Butler's history, as it serves as evidence of a developing picture that Butler was out of his depth. This single page is *not* exceptional in that it contains a multitude of errors, but it does encapsulate, in one page, discrepancies in Butler's work that are spread over multiple, non-sequential pages. On page 882 of *Volume III*, under the heading 'Problems and Services', two tables are presented—Table 11: Australian Forces and Enlistments and Embarkations, and Table 12: Destination, Ultimate Disposal of Recruits. If one closely examines the figures therein *three* different enlistment numbers are quoted or inferred: 416 809 (Table 12); 416 604 (Table 11: Australian Army Nursing Service [AANS] personnel were never counted in the AIF and Royal Australian Navy [RAN] personnel were already serving); and when those that were rejected are deducted from those that were medically examined during the course of the war (Table 12), one is left with 411 147.[21] The clear implication contained in Table 12, apart from two different numbers, is that many more men attempted to enlist than were accepted for service (Medically Examined 589 947; Rejected 178 800), leaving the unambiguous category of 'enlisted'. (The politics of the time are on display here as a medical examination for war fitness became compulsory—it was another pressure point in the relentless efforts at recruitment.) Butler's table was clear—these men had enlisted. Related to this point of an 'enlisted' statistic, the 1918 Royal Commission's report also clearly referred to those who had enlisted but *not embarked* as follows. The commission reported that at the end of 1917 '68 937 were discharged or deserted or died before embarkation'. There was no ambiguity in the definition of 'enlistment'; these men had joined the AIF and were clearly defined as such in both publications of the official medical services history and the report of the Royal Commission. Further discussion of what constituted 'enlistment' follows in Chapter 2, as the need for accuracy on this point is fundamental to understanding the country's level of involvement in this conflict and hence its ultimate human military cost.

The next dubious number to be assessed is the consistently quoted embarkation number of 331 781 which Butler uses in one table[22] but on the *same page referred to earlier* in another table he also uses 330 714, that he sources to Scott (who in turn does not cite a source). Bean cites yet another number, 331 814,[23] which he sources to British War Records. On the face of it, the number of embarkations should be accurate, as soldiers were presumably counted as they boarded a ship to leave Australia. However, another source of data on men serving overseas—*Census of The Commonwealth of Australia, 30th June 1933: Volume III—Statistician's Report*, in its section on 'War Service'—reveals that the oft-cited number of 331 781 embarkations *overstates* the number of men who served overseas, as it includes those who returned to Australia and later embarked for a second time.[24]

As the Censor noted, the official records stated that 265 000 members of the AIF were disembarked and discharged in Australia upon returning from service overseas, but those persons who enlisted on more than one occasion were discharged on more than one occasion. More frequently, re-embarkations involved men who returned to Australia for medical treatment and were then sent back to service. A special detailed examination of the AIF records at the Defence Department offices in Melbourne was carried out in 1936, in response to the Commonwealth Censor's request, to ascertain the *net* number of individuals who were discharged upon return. By deduction of the numbers generated a *duplication* of approximately 7500 (7481) disembarkations and, therefore, embarkations was identified.

What did Bean make of all this? It appears that he chose to effectively ignore the Censor's finding, preferring to maintain the status quo and the British War Office 1921 incorrect embarkation number shown in his main table. In the main appendix of Bean's last publication, *Volume VI*, citing enlistments, embarkations and casualties of the British Empire and its Dominions, in the last footnote on the last page, which has no numerical reference to it and is indented as if it is somehow unique, it is stated:

> Note by Australian Official Historian. It is now estimated that the figure of 331 814, representing embarkations from Australia, includes some 6000 embarkations by men who had already once embarked, and who returned and re-enlisted.[25]

But Bean did not correct his main table, let alone explain the role or significance of the 'Australian Official Historian'. Bearing in mind that this information had arisen when the *Statistician's Report* of the 1933 Census was later published in 1938, we might ask: what did Butler know of this?

His view is expressed in one page near the end of his third volume.[26] He states his disappointment that the census study was not more broadly based because it could have been more valuable. As it was, he argues, the discrepancy was negligible, and furthermore that it can be reduced if a few adjustments are made, which he presents in his 'correcting table'. But for a historian like Butler, who presumably sought to pedantically record statistics in inappropriate detail of single units or several degrees of decimal points, to dismiss this discrepancy as *negligible* surely raises doubts about the validity of his work. Furthermore, in his *correcting* table in which he presents these new data in a *clearer* form, Butler erroneously reduces the discrepancy to 6000 by including nurses who are not normally included in AIF data.

In this same correcting table, Butler also records 'soldiers who returned' as 258 011, adding 492 men who had returned but died *prior* to discharge to the number arrived at by the census enquiry of those who had returned to Australia and were discharged. In other words, Butler is asserting that the Censor would not have counted those men who had returned to Australia because they had died before they were discharged. Yet it is *highly* unlikely that this was not accounted for by the census enquiry. Further loss of confidence in Butler arises when we examine another of his tables (Table 14) in the same *Volume III*, on page 884, which contains data on the 'Returned to Australia' category. On the previous page he states the number returned as 264 373, not 258 011, as he cites on page 957. And in Table 14, he cites the total number of men who 'Returned to Australia' as different again, at 266 300.

These are not the only conflicting figures to be found in Butler's work. Another discrepancy appears in relation to the number of men who embarked that 'Died, [were] discharged, etc.' overseas, which is cited on page 883 as 66 341. Butler had earlier cited that 7030 were discharged overseas[27] (and in another place, 7311),[28] a number also quoted in the census review. Therefore, this produces a figure for those who died overseas of 59 411 (he claims in a footnote on page 894 that *all* soldiers had been accounted for by 1921, including those missing and 'illegal absentees'). This number does not agree with his statement on page 894 in which he provides a *third* number of soldiers who died overseas, of 58 853.

These discrepancies—some minor, some major—appear regularly in Butler's *Volume III*. And while they can perhaps be explained by author exhaustion, or illness, or the time pressures limiting editorial corrections, they nevertheless underscore the lack of scrutiny to which the official record has been subjected to date and reinforce the need for a recount of the figures. It is hoped that the detail presented here is not too overwhelming to absorb. But this level of detail is deemed necessary to support the claim that the official medical historian has shown himself to be unreliable. The sad story of Butler the person will be examined shortly, explaining Bean's reference to Butler's failing health.

However, Butler is not alone in regards to discrepancies. Table 5 below, which contains data compiled together for the first time,

Table 5: Official Sources©

	1	2	3	4	5	6	7	8
	Smith[1] (War Record)	Butler/Bean[2]	Parliamentary Library[3]	Australian War Memorial[4]	National Archives Australia[5]	Australian War Graves Comission[6]	Australian War Memorial Encyclopaedia[7]	Statistics of Military[8] 31.12.20 July 1919
Enlistments	413 608	416 604	425 000	416809	–	416809	416809	416809
								416809
Embarked	330 000	331 781	340 000	Approximate 330000	330000	331 781	353 600 Implied @ 65%	331 781
								331 781
Killed	59 038	60 650	61 520	Over 60000	Nearly 60 000	61 720	58 961/61 513	59 330
								58 132
Wounding	166 817	155 133 Not incl. POW	–	156 000 Incl. POW	152 000 +4000 POW	155 000 +4044 POW	166 811 +4098 POW/ missing	152 171 +4084 POW
								156 228 POW(4057) Included
'Total Battle Casualties'	226 048 missing 193	215 783 Not incl. POW	–	Implies over 216000 Incl. POW	Implies nearly 216000 Incl. POW	–	Implies 229 870	215 585
								214 360
'Non-Battle' Illness/ Injury	–	431 448	–		–	–	87 865	–
								–

Source: Compiled by David Noonan from cited sources.

1. Miles Staniforth Smith, *Australian Campaigns in the Great War: Being a Concise History of the Australian Naval and Military Forces, 1914 to 1918*, Macmillian & Co, Melbourne, 1919, p. 196.
2. Numerous, in official histories and covered elsewhere, but includes tables 26 and 27 in A Graham Butler, *Official Medical History of the Australian Army Medical Services, 1914–1918, Volume III*, Australian War Memorial, Canberra, 1942.
3. Parliament of Australia, 'Section 8: Statistics, links and other reading Australia's wars and warlike operations', <http://www.aph.gov.au/library/pubs/anzac/stats.htm>. Introduces another unspecified variable citing that the figures represent army and navy, but so does 416809, so it may also include nurses and those Australians serving with the RAN who were a permanent pre-existing 'at sea' force (appearing in Butler, Official Medical History of the Australian Army Medical Services, Volume III, p. 882 and not treated as a new enlistment by him), and no authority treats *these members of the military and support personnel (nurses) in this way.*
4. Australian War Memorial, 'First World War 1914–1918', <http://www.awm.gov.au/atwar/ww1.asp>.
5. National Archives of Australia, 'Conflicts', <http://www.naa.gov.au/collection/explore/defence/conflicts.aspx>
6. Australian War Graves Commission, ANZAC Day, 'Selected WW1 Statistics', <http://www.anzacday.org.au/history/ww1/anecdotes/stats01.html>.
7. Australian War Memorial, Encyclopedia, 'Enlistment statistics and standards, First World War', <http://www.awm.gov.au/encyclopedia/enlistment/ww1.asp>, 'Deaths as a result of service with Australian units', <http://www.awm.gov.au/encyclopedia/war_casualties.asp>.
8. The British War Office, *Statistics of the Military Effort of the British Empire during the Great War 1914–1920*, London HM Stationary Office, London, 1923, pp. 237, 759, 769.

draws on a selection of official sources of Australian First World War casualty statistics. With the first column showing data from the first record published by Smith, the columns present the different, most often quoted sources of Bean and Butler, the Australian Federal Parliamentary Library, the AWM, the National Archives of Australia (NAA), the Australian War Graves Commission (AWGC), a second site of the AWM, and finally the British War Office, the original source of battle-only statistics.

The table is intended to be viewed as a snapshot of the huge variability in Australia's official casualty data, which has over the decades provided us with a confusing and completely unreliable picture due mainly to its omissions.

First, attention is drawn to the Australian Parliamentary Library data in column 3.[29] The number of enlistments cited is unsourced and therefore open to question. It is probable that the staff of the library did not engage in original research to establish this enlistment figure, but it differs from the major primary sources—that is, Butler and Bean.[30] Besides this exception, it is noteworthy that the consistency of all other enlistment figures reaffirms a single source. The inconsistencies among the figures for deaths have much to do with the variability in the effective cut-off date used. In relation to the wounding data, some historians treat wounding numbers as the number of men wounded, while others base this figure on the incidence of hospitalisations from wounding as some men were wounded more than once. The latter is the correct measure,[31] but the proposed review of the records will assess its accuracy. With regards to this common question of whether the word wounded means a man wounded or the incident of wounding, this book will use the term *woundings* to mean a hospitalisation due to being wounded. While this is grammatically uncomfortable, it is done in order to emphasis that it represents an admission to hospital. The counting and treatment of POW casualty statistics is also variable and confusing.

However, the most striking feature of the data shown in Table 5 is the glaring absence of the coverage of 'illness' and 'injury'. In 1942 Butler produced a non-battle 'illness and injury' figure that highlighted a shocking aspect of war casualties that is rarely mentioned in Australian historical war analysis, despite much recent examination of the 'aftermath' of war. This figure became public halfway through the Second World War but has effectively now been forgotten. An unsupportable statistic exists in the official sources in the public domain, which is based on the proposition that if a soldier died of illness or injury he was to be counted, but if he became ill or injured and recovered, he was not. Australia and Canada are alone in this misleading treatment in their official, easily accessible *public* records. A comparison with the common practice among the other belligerent countries of Britain, Germany, France and the USA of citing *all* hospitalisations of wounding, illness and injury is presented in Chapter 7.

The AWM has not helped to clarify this confusion as it has a number of contradictory statistics on death, illness and injury on its website. The statistics found on its 'encyclopaedia' page reference Patsy Adam-Smith and her 1978 publication *The Anzacs*.[32] However, the figures cited do not match that reference. Adam-Smith does not mention 'died, wounded, missing or prisoners of war' in her publication, but does mention illness and injury admissions to field ambulances for the period April 1916 to March 1919 in France, quoting the total number as 136 799. While Adam-Smith does not cite any source for her data, the form in which she presents the material suggests that her source was Butler and the timeframe she uses is identical to that used by Butler for data collected for the Western Front. The figure of 87 865 sick men cited on the AWM website originates from Jeffrey Grey's 1990 publication *A Military History of Australia*.[33]

It is worth discussing Grey further in this context. His military history was published in a *third* edition as recently as four years ago. It includes the previously mentioned data on illness, but does not disclose a source for these data. Indeed, the data shown in the AWM encyclopaedia column in Table 5 above are taken from page 118 of Grey's work, and as a consequence the figure on illness that is provided has no source. It is a matter of some wonderment that the AWM is so reliant on Grey for its statistics (although it claims that one part of these figures at least was sourced from Patsy Adam-Smith). In *A Military History of Australia*, Grey's total casualty figures are given as 214 360,[34] which happens to be 15 700 (or 5 per cent) less than the figure the AWM provides on its 'encyclopaedia' web page and is more in line with the other web page reference which cites 216 000 (which appears to be sourced from Scott). How this discrepancy arose is uncertain. The proposed review and recount of these soldier Attestation Papers records will seek to redress these ongoing discrepancies.

The AWGC referred to in column 6 of Table 5 relates to a website sponsored by the Australian War Graves Commission, called 'Anzac Day', which cites the usual sources. However, the British War Graves Commission website goes a little further. On an education page entitled 'Remember Me, First World War, A Commonwealth Nation', the following statements are made on Australia's involvement in the war: 'In 1914, Australia's population was less than 5 million. Nearly half a million people enlisted. Two out of three men sent overseas were injured (most more than once).'[35] The bracketed comment is correct, but the other statements are not even close to the truth.

In returning to this book's search for the truth on these statistics, at the centre of our enquiry lays Butler. It is therefore necessary to examine Butler the person, and the findings are indeed revealing and highly significant in terms of his impact on the assessment of Australia's First World War casualty rate.

An excellent work already exists which comprehensively reviews Butler's personal circumstances and is therefore worth citing extensively here. Much of the following descriptive narrative on Butler borrows from this work. In a 1988 article for the *Journal of the Australian War Memorial*, entitled 'Butler's Medical Histories', Brendan O'Keefe, a historian at the AWM, wrote of Butler's work. According to O'Keefe, Butler, at the time a 42-year-old medical doctor, immediately enlisted in the AIF at the outbreak of the First World War and was appointed to the position of regimental medical officer of the 9th Infantry Battalion. Says O'Keefe: 'his demanding sense of duty, manifested as a finicky attention to detail (...) greatly irritated the soldiers [who] came to regard him as an old woman and nicknamed him "Gertie".'[36]

However, Butler eventually gained respect for his renowned tirelessness in the performance of his duties, receiving a Distinguished Service Order (DSO) at Gallipoli, and was mentioned in dispatches in France. His work ethic was such that he often drove himself to exhaustion, so much so that the Director of Medical Services Major General Neville Howse, appointed him Collator of Medical Records at the Australian War Records Section in London in November 1917, after prompting by Bean and Captain JW Treloar, the unit's commanding officer—a decision made in part for the sake of

Butler's health. By this time Bean, together with Brigadier General Brudenell White, an AIF senior staff officer, had drawn up plans for an Australian medical history, for the purpose of providing information on which improvements in methods of medical treatments could be developed, adopting a highly pragmatic, educational framework for the medical history.

According to O'Keefe, early in 1918 Bean introduced an inspirational theme to the project, and hence the medical history was intended to serve both an inspirational and an educative purpose presented in a chronological form. Butler was uneasy about this approach, but it was a fait accompli by the time he became involved.

Figure 1: Colonel A Graham 'Gertie' Butler

Source: Australian War Memorial (AWM 8932).

Later that year the war ended and so did the Department of Defence's interest in funding a medical history. Butler returned to medical practice in Brisbane. Yet Howse persisted with planning for the medical history, and drawing on his rising political influence (he later became a member of the House of Representatives, holding the seat of Calare for the ruling National Party, and held the appointment of Minister for Defence and Health for the period 1925–1927), at the end of 1922 he secured funding for a two-year project. And together with Bean, he secured Butler for the task of writing it.[37]

O'Keefe proffers that Bean greeted Howse's suggestion of using Butler enthusiastically, a response he tempered, however, with the observation that a curb needed to be placed on Butler's prolixity as 'his main defect'.[38]

Butler pushed himself to the limit in an attempt to keep his writing of this volume on schedule, but given the combination of the huge task, his prolixity and his gift for becoming absorbed in detail, the deadline passed, resulting in Butler suffering what Bean later described as 'a breakdown through overpressure'.[39] An investigation by the Department of Defence into the failure to complete the project on time resulted in an extension of funding for a further two years. As the second deadline approached with an alarming lack of progress, Bean wanted Butler sacked. However, Howse refused to let Butler go, so Butler and his wife were moved to Canberra where he worked under the direct supervision of Bean, and his salary was halved. In 1928, it was apparent that the lengthy treatment of Gallipoli and Palestine in the book would necessitate a second volume. Butler's salary was reduced again and Thomas George Tucker, Professor of Literature at the University of Melbourne, Bean's own editor, was appointed to help with the work. However, this never occurred as Tucker fell ill. Butler was told to finish the second volume by mid-1932, or all payments would cease at that time, and he would need to finish it at his own expense.[40]

In mid-1929, when the first volume was finally nearing completion, General Brudenell White, who was at the time still a member of the Medical History Advisory Board, subjected the draft manuscript to severe criticism.[41] He claimed that the work was confusing, disjointed and many chapters lacked precision, and went so far as to question the factual basis of the book's medical conclusions. Bean, too, was having difficulties with editing the book, describing one chapter as 'easily the most difficult editorial effort I have ever undertaken'. Butler's tardiness in amending the drafts was also causing Bean considerable concern.

The effect of White's criticisms on Butler was near shattering; for the first time he thought of quitting the project. Bean, however, defended Butler's work to White, minimising the lack of precision White had detected as minor inaccuracies and assuring White that he need 'have no fear of inexactness or superficiality in medical matters'. With regard to the disjointedness of the work, Butler attributed this to the chronological structure adopted for the medical history, the decision for which he took full responsibility. Yet it was Bean and White who were actually the authors of this method.

A further problem arose due to a lack of interest in forward sales; Bean's publishers, Angus and Robertson, were not interested in taking on the book, so Bean convinced Treloar—who had previously promoted the appointment of Butler when head of the records section during the war and was now Director of the AWM—to have the AWM undertake publication. In 1930, Tucker resigned due to ill health; Howse, the project's original champion died; sales of *Volume I* fell rapidly; and Bean walked away. Payments to Butler ceased in mid-1932.[42]

Over the next few years Butler and his wife found themselves desperately short of money, so short in fact that they were forced to subsist for weeks at a time on nothing but porridge. Butler's health began to decline, as he contracted amoebiasis—a form of dysentery and 'a relic of Gallipoli'[43]—and cataracts affected both of his eyes.

In late 1936, with concerns rising over the instability in Europe, officers of the Department of Defence became interested again in the medical history of the previous world conflict. Bean was consulted, and the Director-General of Medical Services, Major General Rupert Downes, lent his support to a refinancing of a First World War official medical history.[44]

The amount of remaining material to be written indicated the need for a third volume. So in mid-1938, funding for Butler for a further three years was granted. Bean unsuccessfully endeavoured to get medical specialists to collaborate with Butler, whose health was failing. Severe sinusitis and a bout of double pneumonia were taking their toll and, according to O'Keefe, by the end of 1940 Butler, then sixty-eight, was 'blind in the left eye, and seeing double with the right. He could only continue to work on the medical history with the aid of a large magnifying glass'.[45]

Volume III was finished in 1942 and appeared in mid-1943, too late to be of much use to serving military medical officers. Sales of *Volume III*, arguably the most useful as it covered the period of Australia's involvement in the conflict on the Western Front, were supported by an Army *order* that medical officers buy it and read it on departing troopships. Yet sales remained poor. Of the print run of exactly 1006, some 250 were given away as review or presentation copies and only 650 had sold by the end of the war. Butler died in 1949.

O'Keefe's excellent work, cited extensively here, provides a most valuable window through which to view and assess the material contained in Butler's official medical services history for the First World War. It perhaps explains the many inconsistencies mentioned earlier, and certainly lends weight to a reappraisal of the AIF medical history of the war.

The post-war data contained in Butler's work were sourced from the Repatriation Commission and Department and should be more reliable, as they was administered under strict criteria and definition, albeit altered somewhat by the Royal Commission's determinations in 1924 on pension eligibility. This material will prove useful in the assessment of the total post-war impact of death and suffering, but more will be said on this later.

At this point it would be of benefit to take stock of the trail travelled so far. By the early 1940s, statistics of death and woundings only, had been in the public domain for nearly a quarter of a century, with Bean yet to publish his final volume. Butler lay at the heart of the delays in the publication of the official medical history and was delaying Bean's final volume. And it has been shown that when Butler's work was eventually published halfway through the Second World War it was full of inconsistencies; not even Bean cited Butler's material. We have explored the background of a man vested with the responsibility of writing Australia's official medical services history for this nation-changing conflict, yet whose health, and mental and physical state, was simply not up to the task. Butler was a peripatetic pedant. But what if his methodology was flawed also? What material data *was* Butler working with when analysing these wartime medical statistics? In answering such questions, it is appropriate that we explore, in Butler's own words, his chosen approach to the task. To do this we must backtrack a little.

The records to which Butler turned, in the absence of the now destroyed individual soldier medical cards, were approximately 2350 Admission and Discharge Books supplied by the British Ministry of Pensions, via War Records.[46] It is worth highlighting that Butler states in the opening of Chapter XVII, 'Statistics of the War', that:

The figures here do not pretend to be an exact statistical study. Owing to the accidental destruction of part of the Australian records by the British Ministry of Pensions and Office of Works many results have had to be arrived at by computation from sample counts. Great labour—running into several years of patient toil—has been expended by the small unspecialised staff of this history in the endeavour to repair that loss.[47]

Butler complains of the 'amazing ignorance' of the importance of medical statistics, from commanding officers in the field to those responsible for the 'pension problems' at home. This is said in the context of his important role as the AIF Collator of Medical Records (to which he had been appointed by Major General Howse), through which he was vested with the task of identifying medical information not only on the type of injury but also on preventative issues like sanitation standards at the Front, transmission avenues of disease, and information on repatriation pension costs, as well as other medical issues.

After the First World War, there were fundamental conflicts of interest among those responsible for determining a casualty for the purpose of pension eligibility: those who were representing the interests of returning soldiers, and those whose position led them to minimise the forward estimates of the financial cost of the war. This conflict appears to have been profound, even within the medical profession responsible for defining pension eligibility, particularly of men suffering from mental trauma.

It is somewhat at odds with the view of Howse's relationship to Butler painted by O'Keefe as that of a benefactor, champion and defender, that Butler himself scathingly refers to the inaction (and implied ignorance) of Howse in failing to carry out Butler's recommendation to have the exact Australian medical records (individual medical cards) held in London returned to Australia. He goes on to say in a footnote:

> The immediate decision of pension claims is based chiefly on *direct* evidence not on clinical (aetiological) principles or hypotheses. Gen. Howse refused to accept this principle and when recommended to procure the completion of the

tabulation of the medical clinical records in 1919, expressed the view that they would be of no practical value, since the decision of pension claims would be based on the men's condition interpreted in the light of clinical principles and aetiology.[48]

These sentiments were written sometime after Howse's death in 1930, probably around 1939 or 1940. Given Butler's apparent past indebtedness to Howse, this requires to be reconciled as it, prima facie, reflects badly on Butler's character and his failure to accept at least some responsibility for the loss of these records. He had been in a position to save these records himself, as will later be demonstrated.

But what were these 'exact' records to which Butler refers? The basis of these records held in London consisted of Field Medical Cards[49] which were pinned to a soldier's clothing upon admission to a field medical unit and stayed with him until he was discharged from care in France or upon evacuation to England for hospitalisation (a similar card system commenced upon admission to hospital). These cards were then sent to the Medical Research Committee of the War Office in England after the soldier's discharge from care. The basis of the statistics maintained by the British Army was a combination of this card data, the Admission and Discharge Books (regarded as less accurate, imprecise and transitory in diagnosis) kept by each field treatment centre, and Medical Case Sheets.[50]

In September 1919, Butler had again raised the issue with General Howse of a return of the AIF-specific cards to Australia. Further procrastination led to the British War Office advising the Australian Government in early 1920 that the cards for 1914–1915 were ready for dispatch, but that the cards for 1916 onwards were only half sorted, and that the office was not prepared to finish that work unless a payment of £850 were made. In his account of this time, Butler makes no reference to Howse's efforts campaigning behind the scenes to obtain funding for an official medical services history,[51] nor the fact that he, Butler, had actually started work on the project in Melbourne in November 1922. He claims that no formal response was provided by the Australian Government to the request for payment when, on 26 April 1924, the Ministry of Pensions informed the War Office that all of the cards related to AIF servicemen had been destroyed. Butler implies that this delay is the fault of Howse and accepts no responsibility, although he was employed full-time to collate this material. The destruction of these records came about following a request from the Canadian Government to destroy the Medical Record Cards of Canadian soldiers as they were unwanted. Her Majesty's Office of Works inadvertently destroyed the Medical Record Cards *of all* Dominions, including those of the Australian forces. The British War Office advised the Australian Government that as an alternative source of data the Admission and Discharge Books from AIF medical units were available. Accordingly, in July 1924 some 2350 Admission and Discharge Books were sent to the AWM in Melbourne, which included books for some British medical units that were believed to have handled Australian wounded.[52]

Butler believed that he had no choice but to turn to a substitute analysis based on the data in these books. He states:

> By colossal labour extending over a number of years the small staff of the Australian Medical History extracted and classified statistics of disease. The results appear in statistical tables later in the chapter.[53]

Fortunately the Australian Medical Case Sheets, being no longer required by the British statistical authorities, had been removed to Australia on the representations of Colonel Butler in 1919.[54]

In a further comment, unconnected with the above quote, almost as an afterthought and out of context, he refers to the individual soldier Attestation Papers. He states:

> The personal records of the AIF gave a comprehensive history of each member of the force. They showed the movements from day of enlistment until discharged or death, and contained the details of casualties, promotions and reductions, honours and rewards, crimes and punishments, etc. and in fact were a collection of personal histories, which during the war period were available for war purposes and later for post war use in connection with repatriation, reinstatement in civilian life and pension claims—in justice to the claimant and tax payer.[55]

In the reassessment and recount to be presented in this book, it is *these* Attestation papers that will be assessed, *not* the Admission and Discharge Books that were the basis of Butler's work. Butler did not use these personal records, presumably because he preferred to source the purely 'medical' hospital records as contained within the Admission and Discharge Books of medical units through which Australian casualties passed.[56] However, it is contended that this was a fundamental mistake.

In his account of events, Butler goes on to say that, in consultation with the Commonwealth Statistician, he analysed approximately one third of all admissions for the period 1 April 1916 to 31 March 1919, and that various measures of 'weighting' were then used to bring the count to approximate totals for each category.[57] But in a revealing footnote he states that, *at best*, his statistical analysis is *generally* accurate and thereby significantly diminishes the impression of accuracy implied in the minutiae presented in his statistical tables. This revealing admission deserves a quotation in full:

> A question of great importance in connection with medical statistics of the War concerns the accuracy with which the diagnosis as entered in the 'A. and D. Books', and even as finally identified in the 'statistics card', expressed the actual morbid condition or clinical syndrome. Concerning a set of tables compiled by him on somewhat similar basis, Col. A B Soultau, RAMC, in the Journal of the RAWC for August 1920, page 152, says in relation to diagnoses 'PUO' and 'Myalgia', 'the pyrexia or muscular pain so frequently obscured the real issue that the final statistics of the War will not present in the real indication of disease in the Army.'
>
> He believed however that with modifications to provide for certain epidemic diseases, especially Trench Fever and Influenza, his own figures might be taken as 'representing proportional wastage in sickness in the Army concerned, and in the main were probably correct for the whole of the armies at this period'.
>
> It is believed that the statistics prepared for the present work have a similar value. More than this is not claimed.[58]

Here, Butler uses passive and negative expression (for example, 'more than this is not claimed') in a footnote, borrowing from the words of another, to define the limits of the accuracy of his work. In other words, his results are at best general and may be inaccurate due to misdiagnosis. Thus, it can be argued that Butler's character had a profound impact on the historical analysis of Australian casualty statistics. His choice of the Admission and Discharge Books as the source of his raw data was a fundamental error, as was his treatment of them and this will be discussed in Chapter 2 in which Butler's approach is compared with that taken by the British medical historian.

The individual AIF soldiers' records to be researched and analysed here contain a large amount of information as Butler rightly indicated. Of particular relevance here is Form B103, headed 'Statement of Service', used to record the units in which the soldier served, their promotions, demotions and period of service in each rank; embarkation, and date and place of disembarkation; hospitalisation for wounding and illness, often alongside a brief description of wound such as a gunshot wound to the left leg ('GSW left leg'), or illness, nearly always defined (for example scabies, trench fever, trench foot); hospital transfers; leave taken; absenteeism; and the outcome of disciplinary proceedings, in addition to other minor notations necessary to define the soldiers' whereabouts.

Another form of medical documentation maintained was the hospitalisation form entitled 'Table II—Only for Admissions to Hospital or to the Sick List in the case of Warrant Officers treated in Quarters'; however, these records were not as rigorously maintained and are often blank or omit the details of hospitalisation from wounding. A four-page pro forma document entitled 'Medical Inquiry' appears in many soldiers' files, recording examinations and symptom descriptions for the purpose of determining an individual's sickness or any other condition that may necessitate their being discharged medically unfit.

Another form, known as B103-II, which often ran to several pages, was contained in all soldier records and was entitled 'casualty form—active service'. This form records, in quite some detail, all of the soldier's movements, admissions and discharges to hospital, offences and punishments or forfeitures, and in more detail than the B103 form.

Unappreciated until now, documentation also exists in these soldier files that are critically important for a quantitative *assessment of post-war suffering*. This documentation is correspondence between Base Records, Victoria Barracks, Melbourne, and the Deputy Commissioner of the Repatriation Commission requesting or providing a soldier's medical records, often years after the end of the war. The response nearly always involves the sending of a copy of the B103 form, and occasionally a list of dates of movements, promotion, punishments and hospitalisations and discharge and the reason for such, or details of the diagnosis of an illness. It is contended that each appearance of this particular type of correspondence constitutes a record that the soldier concerned has *applied for a pension*. This information will prove invaluable in relation to ascertaining how many soldiers were at sometime on a pension or importantly *believed* they were entitled to one. The pension records that we have today only show the total number of men who were on a pension at any one time, which is of course quite different to the total number who successfully applied, because as one pension is withdrawn another may be given. In the analysis presented in this book, the year of this record was collected. These data representing individuals who applied for a pension will portray a very different picture of the post-war impact on the men of the AIF to that which currently relies on gross successful pension data alone.

The interrelationship between the three 'official' historians of the First World War who were responsible for the publication of casualty data—Bean, Butler and Scott—had a significant influence on the omissions within and inaccuracy of Australia's current official casualty statistics we are left with today. Based on the facts that are known, the prefaces these three men wrote, *and omitted to write*, in their last (or only, in the case of Scott) publications on this matter, the following scenario is presented as probable.

In 1936 Scott did not make reference to Butler in his volume because Butler had failed—he had not been paid for four years, he was no longer 'official', and he was not producing anything remotely useful.

Bean does not use Butler's statistical material in his final volume, published in 1942, although it was available. This should be viewed in light of the history of their relationship, including Bean's desire for Butler to be sacked in the late 1920s, and Bean's fruitless efforts to bring in experts in editing and medicine to assist with the project. The last deadline of 30 June 1932, when Butler ceased to be paid, must have been the final straw for Bean, who had his own reputation to safeguard. After all, he and Howse had recruited Butler; and, according to O'Keefe, they had devised the structure for the official medical services history as well. Bean himself had promoted Butler's talents in wide and important circles. When Butler failed to deliver yet again in 1932, Bean could turn to no-one but Scott, who was working on the volume dealing with Australia at home during the war.

It is proffered that Bean asked Scott to include some material on war casualties and *post*-war pension demands up until his publication deadline, which was 1936. Scott, a great supporter of the British Empire, would have had no hesitation in delivering military war office casualty statistics that did not incorporate illness and injury. In any event, data on illness and injury were unknown at that time.

According to O'Keefe, Bean was not the instigator of the project's revival in late 1938 and early 1939. In 1938, Bean would have had his lack of faith in Butler reinforced by the Censor's finding of overstated embarkations that Butler had not identified. In fact, it was the overstated numbers of soldiers returning to Australia that Butler and officials (at varying levels) often used that led the Censor to request a Department of Defence review.

It is therefore conceivable, and entirely understandable, that Bean had washed his hands of Butler and so had Bean's publishers. Butler's data appeared in numerous places so disjointed and inconsistent that Bean did not include any of Butler's data in his own last publication, instead simply referring to Butler's declining health in his preface.

More widely, it seems that Butler's work was not highly regarded, as evidenced by the silence with which it was received and the official adoption it did *not* receive. It was too late, too confused and too unreliable, the last point further evidenced by Butler's sad failure to maintain any type of schedule and, when the detail is examined and cross-referenced, there are many discrepancies in his work. Butler acknowledges that his analysis of the Admission and Discharge Books is to be treated as generally correct, but offers no guidance as to which parts are generally correct and which are generally wrong. Indeed, he appears to have made very few decisions regarding his data, presenting them in a level of detail that is clearly inappropriate.

Dealing with Butler and his idiosyncrasies must have tried the most patient of editors. His failures to deliver must have tested the reputations of those around him. His writings were regarded as incomprehensible by his peers. Butler failed to deliver *officially adopted and reliable* casualty statistics.

And so we must start again and attempt to recount all Australian wartime and post-war casualties of the First World War.

Lest we forget.

Notes

1. CEW Bean, *Official History of Australia in the War 1914–1918, Volume I*, Angus and Robertson, Sydney, 1941.
2. Ernest Scott, *Official History of Australia in the War 1914–1918, Volume XI*, Angus and Robertson, Sydney, 1936.
3. CEW Bean, *Official History of Australia in the War 1914–1918, Volume VI*, Angus and Robertson, Sydney, 1942, p. vi.
4. Scott, *Official History of Australia in the War 1914–1918, Volume XI*, 1936, p. xiv.
5. Kathleen Fitzpatrick, 'Scott, Sir Earnest (1867–1939)', in *Australian Dictionary of Biography*, National Centre of Biography, Australian National University, 1988, see <http://adb.anu.edu.au/biography/scott-sir-ernest-8367/text14683>. This article was first published in hardcopy in *Australian Dictionary of Biography Volume 11*, Melbourne University Publishing, Carlton, 1988.
6. Ken Inglis, 'The Anzac Tradition', *Meanjin Quarterly*, vol. 24, no. 1, 1965, pp. 25–44.
7. A Graham Butler, *Official Medical History of the Australian Army Medical Services, 1914–1918, Volume III*, Australian War Memorial, Canberra, 1942, p. vi.
8. Scott, *Official History of Australia in the War 1914–1918, Volume XI*, p. 874.
9. Bean, *Official History of Australia in the War 1914–1918, Volume I*, 1941, p. 548.
10. Miles Staniforth Smith, *Australian Campaigns in the Great War: Being a Concise History of the Australian Naval and Military Forces, 1914 to 1918*, Macmillian & Co, Melbourne, 1919, p. vii.
11. ibid., p. viii.
12. The British War Office, *Statistics of the Military Effort of the British Empire during the Great War 1914–1920*, London HM Stationary Office, London, 1923, pp. 759–770.
13. Australian War Memorial, AWM 27, control symbol: 4/11.
14. Commonwealth of Australia, conference convened by His Excellency The Governor General, paper presented at the 'Securing of Reinforcements under the Voluntary System for the Australian Imperial Force now Serving Abroad' conference, Melbourne, 1918.
15. Scott, *Official History of Australia in the War 1914–1918, Volume XI*, p. 871, Appendix 3.

16 Graham Donley, 'Voluntary Ballot Enlistment Scheme, 1918', *Journal of the Australian War Memorial*, see: <http://www.awm.gov.au/journal/j38/vebs.asp>.
17 LL Robson, *The First AIF: A Study of its Recruitment 1914–1918*, Melbourne University Press, Carlton, 1982, p. 4.
18 The government had the powers of conscription for service in Australia only.
19 The soldiers in France voted against conscription.
20 Robson, *The First AIF: A Study of its Recruitment 1914–1918*, p. 71.
21 In 1916, under the provisions of the Defence Act (whereby every male Australian between 18 and 60 years of age could be called upon for military service *in Australia*), all men between the age of 21 and 35 were required to report for the medical examination in what Butler refers to as 'largely a political move in a bitter political campaign'. This resulted in a further 180 000 men being medically examined.
22 Butler, *Official Medical History of the Australian Army Medical Services, 1914–1918, Volume III*, p. 882, Table 11.
23 Bean, *Official History of Australia in the War 1914–1918, Volume VI*, p. 1098.
24 Commonwealth of Australia, *Census of The Commonwealth of Australia, 30th June 1933: Volume III—Statistician's Report*, Commonwealth Government Printer, Canberra, p. 397.
25 Butler, *Official Medical History of the Australian Army Medical Services, 1914–1918, Volume III*, p. 1099.
26 ibid., p. 957.
27 ibid., p. 957.
28 ibid., p. 891.
29 The Parliamentary Library has recently changed its website, but not this figure, see: <http://www.aph.gov.au/About_Parliament/Parliamentary_Departments/Parliamentary_Library/pubs/anzac_day/stats>.
30 It is speculated that they have added all services. Over 10 000 were permanent members of the navy and therefore not treated as enlistments. To date, they have not responded to an enquiry.
31 Butler, *Official Medical History of the Australian Army Medical Services, 1914–1918, Volume III*, p. 894.
32 Patsy Adam-Smith, *The ANZACS*, Thomas Nelson, West Melbourne, 1978, p. 360.
33 Jeffrey Grey, *A Military History of Australia*, Cambridge University Press, Melbourne, 1990.
34 ibid., p. 119.
35 Commonwealth War Graves Commission, 'Remember Me, A Commonwealth Nation', see: <http://www.cwgc.org/education/imp_pop/cw_nation.htm>.
36 Brendan O'Keefe, 'Butler's Medical Histories', *Journal of the Australian War Memorial*, no. 12, 1988, p. 25.
37 ibid., p. 27.
38 ibid., p. 27.
39 ibid., p. 27.
40 ibid., p. 28.

41 Regarded by Robson as one of the greatest officers of the AIF, White, together with Brigadier-General W T Bridges, was responsible for the establishment of the AIF. Robson, *The First AIF: A Study of its Recruitment 1914–1918*, p. 22.
42 O'Keefe, 'Butler's Medical Histories', *Journal of the Australian War Memorial*, p. 29.
43 ibid.
44 According to O'Keefe, Downes confided to Bean *at that time* that he found the first volume 'confused and un-understandable' and quoted two eminent medical colleagues who thought the same of draft chapters of the second volume.
45 O'Keefe, 'Butler's Medical Histories', *Journal of the Australian War Memorial*, p. 30.
46 Butler, *Official Medical History of the Australian Army Medical Services, 1914–1918, Volume III*, pp. 862, 925–926.
47 ibid., p. 846.
48 ibid., p. 925, footnote. Oxford University Press, 'Aetiology: Cause of disease', in *Oxford Concise Medical Dictionary*, Elizabeth Martin (ed), Oxford University Press, Oxford, 1998, p. 12.
49 ibid., p. 851. The Field Medical Card referred to on p. 851 was designated as document AF3118.
50 ibid., p. 859, footnote.
51 ibid., p. 862.
52 ibid., p. 926, footnote.
53 ibid., p. 862.
54 ibid.
55 ibid., p. 863.
56 ibid., p. 926.
57 ibid., p. 926.
58 ibid., p. 928, footnote 64.

CHAPTER 2
Definitions and Statistical Methodologies for Assessing War Casualties

There is one consistent definition used in both Australian and British *medical* statistical analyses of war casualties from the First World War—that an *admission to hospital* is used to count as a casualty resulting from wounding, injury or illness.[1] This may seem self-evident but unfortunately it is the *only* consistent approach taken in this field of study, one in which there is much confusion about terms and findings. At the 2006 launch of a book by Professor Robin Prior, *The Somme*, General Peter Cosgrove, the then Commander-in-Chief of the Australian Armed Forces, referred to casualties cited in that book as deaths, when in fact the word was, *in its context*, a standard military term which referred to the combination of the occurrence of deaths and the incidence of wounding. In 2013, at a talk on the Battle of Fromelles presented by Ross McMullin at the Shrine of Remembrance in Melbourne, he described the episode as the worst 24 hours for casualties in Australian Armed Forces history, referring to casualties as the total number of men killed and wounded. When asked about the potential to mislead by adding together two entirely different measures of the loss of men, he responded that he did not use the term 'killed', but rather 'casualties', as an appropriate measure to define the loss for the forces. A member of the audience commented that, besides, in dealing with casualties a lot more effort is required to care for the wounded (than the dead), as if to somehow justify this definition of the term 'casualty'. Australia is not alone in the use of this definition. The Dutch historian Leo van Bergen, commenting in 2009 on the variability of numbers related to French and German casualties at Verdun, stated: 'The first and perhaps primary cause of all these mysteries lies in the Word "casualties". Sometimes it is used to refer to the dead, sometimes the dead and wounded, sometimes the dead, missing, wounded and sick, and it often includes prisoners of war as well.'[2]

The AWM seems to skirt around the issue by providing the following definition in the encyclopaedia section of its website.

> In its military sense, the term casualties includes all those who are killed in action or who died of wounds as well as those who are wounded, listed as missing, or taken prisoner of war. Casualties are often wrongly confused with deaths, but in fact, as this definition suggests, casualty is a broad category.[3]

This raises a fundamental point, which is highlighted here. The casualty category implied by the AWM's definition is wider still as one that not only includes *battle* casualties but *all* casualties of the war, and it is unsupportable to limit the official human cost of this war to a purely military version. Injury in the trenches and hospitalisations for trench feet, scabies, trench fever, malaria and so on incurred from exposure to war cannot be left out of any accurate appraisal. And these categories are not left out of the tabulations of other belligerents' official war casualties; indeed, the data produced by other countries involved in the war go further than battle-exposed illness and injury to include *all* hospitalisations. This lies at the heart of the confusion over the accurate definition of casualty statistics. Is the intended audience meant to be the military historian or the public at large? Nearly 100 years on, it is the latter this book sets out to inform.

The practice of counting all hospitalisations of servicemen during the war does raise the challenge of differentiating the public health levels among civilians during the war years. (The eminent war historian Jay Winter argued in *The Great War and the British People* that civilian health actually *improved* during the war as ration coupons introduced a more balanced diet.) Yet no country applies a deduction for civilian levels of health to arrive at a *war-only* calculation of the human cost of the war. This is simply because comprehensive public health records are not available until after the advent of a truly public hospital system decades later; until that time, health treatment, for those who could afford it, was practised in the home. Obviously, civilian deaths arising from involvement in the conflict is another outcome of war—a factor to which Australia was not exposed.

This limited nature of the military definition of casualty which covers those men killed plus hospitalisations for wounding suggests the need to consider the various audiences for casualty categorisation because their perspectives differ markedly—a fact that has been responsible for much of the confusion. First, as said, there is the military historian, whose interest is in the campaign and the battlefield level of casualties incurred. The emphasis is on casualties defined as wounding and death, and the subsequent availability of men, and perversely the term 'wastage' is often used. Terminology such as 'lightly wounded' confounds the picture, generating numbers that relate more to calculations of wastage, reserves and reinforcements. Such an approach introduces the element of time, and whether the soldier will return to strength, stay in the field, or require replacement within the duration of the battle or campaign. The incidence of illness may play no part in this definition, as in the main it takes place off the field and the soldier is unfit for duty or to be 'taken on strength' (TOS). In 1931, a further split in the categorisation of casualty came with the British medical historians' introduction of the terms 'battle' and 'non-battle'. Mitchell and Smith, in their *Medical Services Official History of the War: Casualties and Medical Statistics of the Great War*, introduced the following classification:

> In dealing with casualties a classification has been used which is as yet unfamiliar, but which seems to be the most suitable. They have been divided into 'battle' and 'non-battle' casualties, and each group has been further subdivided into 'permanent' and 'temporary' losses 'for military purposes in the field'. The term battle casualty includes killed, missing, prisoners of war, and those who suffered injury caused by or arising from enemy action.

'Non-battle' casualties include all cases of sickness or injury independent of any act of the enemy. From the point of view of the military commander in the Field, permanent losses include the killed, missing and prisoners of war, for although a certain number of missing or prisoners are returned to the Army at the close of the campaign, until then they are lost to the force. So the expression 'permanent losses for military purposes' has been adopted.[4]

Butler decided to place more emphasis on the *medical* aspects of casualties. In the *Official Medical History of the Australian Army Medical Services, 1914–1918, Volume III*, he writes:

The general policy adopted in the present work in presenting the casualties of the war is a compromise between the usage which adheres strictly to matters of purely medical concern, and that—adopted in the *British Official Medical History*—where the writer sets himself deliberately to serve the requirements of the General Staff. In this work while these latter are kept in mind, and 'missing' and 'prisoners of war' are included in the figures for battle casualties, the responsibilities of the medical service have the first consideration. This policy is illustrated by the place allotted to 'died of wounds': in the American statistical volume they are not mentioned; in the British they are placed with killed (i.e. 'killed and died of wounds'); here, except where otherwise indicated, they are put with wounded ('wounded and died of wounds').[5]

Then there is the use of the term among other historians, who, in the review of an event, record statistics of death, wounding, and all illnesses and injuries incurred during and after the cessation of hostilities. The main difficulty with this approach concerns how to determine the period of time after the event after which records should end. Yet its value lies in its more accurate measure of the total human cost to the fighting force. As such, it is this definition, in accordance with international practice, that will be adopted in this review. Each incident of death and in the main, its cause, plus the hospitalisations for wounding, injury, illness, and other factors indicating damage such as discharge medically unfit, needs to be recorded in order to accurately assess the true level of death and suffering inflicted on these men.

Third, there is what I call the socio-political use of the term 'casualties'. Mainly used for news at home, to disseminate misinformation, to improve troop morale, to promote conscription/enlistments, or to raise popular or political support, this interpretation is often biased, involving censure, censorship, understatement, glorification, simplification, and so on. More recently, a term like collateral damage would align with this use of terminology.

The fourth approach is a socio-cultural one, which uses the word 'casualty' in its broadest sense to incorporate loved ones and carers of servicemen, and even the public through pensions, medical services, mental health services, and those impacted by the casualties inflicted on others.

Until Butler published in 1942, Australian post-war historians used a *militarised* definition of casualties (which was deemed to be 60 000 killed and 155 000 wounded, with a 65 per cent casualty rate). The military focus of this perspective could be seen to align with the socio-political definition used for propaganda purposes, but in reality it was predominantly due to the absence of available hospitalisation statistics on illness and injury up until that time. This book sets out to demonstrate that the flawed nature of Butler's medical casualty data has left Australia with the legacy of a limited definition of military casualty statistics for the First World War, which is out of step with international practice.

Very few historians have addressed this omission. Statistics including some references to illness only began to appear in the 1970s, with the work of Bill Gammage in 1974, *The Broken Years: Australian Soldiers in the Great War* (which recorded casualties of 152 422, and reported sick of 332 901),[6] and Patsy Adam-Smith's 1978 book, *The ANZACS* (which counted non-battle casualties including primary infections of 136 799).[7] However, examples of such work are rare indeed. Butler's statistics purportedly represented the enormity of the suffering, with his 1942 publication of 427 061 hospitalisations due to illness, and 4287 injured (deliberate and accidental), to amount to a total of 431 448 hospitalisations.[8] Yet, even in recent times, it is extremely unusual to see the 'illness' category reported at all, let alone accurately, only to be repeated in later editions. (Jeffrey

Grey, in *A Military History of Australia*, reported the number of 'sick' as 87865 first in 1990, and again in a revised edition in 2008.)[9]

When we seek to understand why historians who have investigated the phenomenon of Australian casualties of the First World War have failed to incorporate illness and injury into their analyses, a number of factors become evident. No larger is the failure of Butler's contribution. Following the Second World War, there was little interest in reviewing his data as historians' attention was drawn to more recent events. The shocking numbers of hospitalisations that Butler finally produced were obscured by a new war and effectively overlooked, as their reliability was not well regarded by those close to their publication. Primarily, the person with overall responsibility for the delivery of the official medical services history and its associated statistical data was the official war historian, Editor-in-Chief Charles Bean, and he chose to ignore them. And in so doing, he did a great disservice to those we forget. His publication of only 'military' casualty statistics has become enshrined within Australia's war history through its unquestioning acceptance since.

Furthermore, there is another issue resulting from this acceptance of the data that limits the full appreciation of Australia's war casualties. A shift in focus on the assessment of *post-war death and suffering* is required, as such death and suffering did not suddenly stop at the official end date for the war, marked by the disbandment of the AIF on 31 March 1921. Men continued to die of war-related injury and illness, and pension applications climbed, peaked, and then surged again in the early 1930s as men succumbed to their nightmares or failing lungs. As noted earlier, Butler and Scott worked independently of each other and both collated pension data. But pension data on their own are inadequate to assess post-war consequences, as they only reflect one element of the administration of returned servicemen and a measure of the standards that this administration chose to apply to those men seeking support from the public purse. The full assessment of post-war suffering needs to incorporate a recording of the individuals who had contact with the pension system via a lodgement of a claim for assistance. In order to define the nature of this contact, we can refer to the Attestation Papers, which show correspondence from the Department of Repatriation requesting medical records, indicating that the individual or their next of kin had approached the department for the purpose of applying for pension support. Recording the year of this contact will provide a new valuable and more comprehensive measure of post-war suffering. However, two elements of these raw data will need to be removed. The pension entitlement based on age and the entitlement of next of kin to seek funeral expense support can be practically culled from the raw data to leave only those applications by ex-servicemen for support.

But the problems with the reliability of the official histories do not end here. Aside from the variability of definition confounding an accurate assessment, further difficulties arise from the official medical services histories of the war produced by Butler for Australia, and Mitchell and Smith for Britain, who both based their data on the assessment of a percentage sample of available records. This approach was unnecessary and reveals an ignorance of proper sampling methodology. The critical factors that determine the accuracy of any given sample are that the sample taken *must* be random and that it is taken across the *full range* of the population being analysed. While this may be self-evident, surprisingly it was not accurately applied in the calculation of the number of war casualties by either country's official medical services historian. In light of the critical importance of the randomisation of the sampling method, it is of benefit to briefly review the methods of sampling employed by the official British statistics analysts (a method Butler described as 'promiscuous') and that utilised by Butler himself in his count of Admission and Discharge Books. This review exposes the extent of the unreliability of this war's official casualty record for both Britain and its Dominion.

In the British *Medical Services Official History of the Great War: Casualties and Medical Statistics of the Great War*, a description of the method employed arose when it was calculated that thirty clerks would take three years to process the entire 5.9 million soldier casualty cards from 1916 onwards held at the war records.

> Two sets of sample cards, representing 1 043 653 cases, or about 18.5% of the total cards for the years 1916 onwards, were taken as closely as possible in proportion to the approximate strength of the various arms comprising the British Army, and as the record cards were filed under regiments and in regimental numerical order, the samples

were taken one-third from the beginning, one-third from the middle, and one-third from the end of files. The tables in this chapter are the result of the scientific analysis of these two sets of samples. They cover the period from 1916 to 1920, and therefore include the transition stage from war to peace, a time when men were not required for active fighting, and it was desirable to have them demobilised and reinstated in civil employment.[10]

Several issues arise here that suggest distortion of the analysis. The sample is taken from a range of population that *extraordinarily skews the result* to a focus on peacetime (1916 to 1920), such that the representation of wounding is diminished and illness is misrepresented as half of it occurs under peacetime conditions. Moreover, the method of sampling from the British Army regiments, ordered in sequence by drawing from one third from the beginning, one third from the middle and one third from the end, is open to considerable criticism. Does a higher regimental number mean less exposure to war service as that regiment may have been created later in the war? Were entire regiments selected, or were units arbitrarily chosen from among those regiments? Additionally, it is not clear how 'two sets of sample cards' were taken. The British and Dominions suffered 11.1 million casualties,[11] yet only 5.6 million cards (if 1 043 653 cards equated to an 18.5 per cent sample size) were sampled. And the overlap of dates, 1914–1918 and 1916–1920, further confounds the analysis.

Butler, as noted previously, did not have access to card records, and resorted to analysis of Admission and Discharge Books, some of which included British and American soldiers as they were processed through the nearest ambulance, casualty clearing station and subsequently base hospital. He decided that, as the AIF units started to arrive in France at the end of March 1916, for the purposes of identifying the statistics for Australians, he would cover the three years from 1 April 1916 to 31 March 1919. He then placed the books in four categories: Field Ambulance, Casualty Clearing Station, Expeditionary Base, and Hospitals UK. For each of the three years, in each of the four categories, he tabulated figures for Total Admissions (approximately), and an Admission and Discharge Book count.[12] The totals were 594 547 and 277 265 respectively, amounting to an approximate sample of 46 per cent.

However, the sampling proportions he used varied widely across the years (for example, for the Expeditionary Base category he used 38 per cent for 1917–1918 but 62 per cent for 1918–1919) and among the categories (for example, for 1918–1919 he sampled 56 per cent for Field Ambulance, but 36 per cent for Hospitals UK). And no adjustment is considered for the same soldier being counted in each of the four categories as he is referred on to England. It is possible that a proportion of admissions to the Field Ambulance (more than 42 per cent of Butler's total sample) would have stayed in the field or at least suffered a less serious casualty. Moreover, the sample population is drawn only from men on the Western Front, to the exclusion of all other theatres and campaigns. The omission of the Gallipoli campaign has material impact on the assessment of total numbers. Similarly, service in Palestine and the Light Horse Brigade indicates a skew towards disease over wounding, and illness aboard troopships is ignored. The 'weightings' Butler claimed he applied to his sample count were simply a multiple he applied to each of the four sampling categories, for each of the three years, to obtain the total up to 100 per cent of what he believed were the 'approximate' totals in each category. For example, if he counted 50 per cent, he multiplied by two; if he counted 25 per cent, he multiplied by four. A properly sampled count of *the entire* number of individual soldier records of men in the AIF will provide a measure of accuracy against which to determine the validity of Butler's sampling methods.

In order to achieve this, a physical count is necessary of a statistically significant sample of soldier records of the AIF, held by the National Archives of Australia (NAA) in its Canberra and Melbourne stores. The records held in Melbourne are the MT1486/1 series, which until recently were described as containing AIF records of soldiers who did not embark for overseas service. The other series, B2455, housed in Canberra, contains files for enlisted AIF soldiers who predominantly served overseas.[13] The B2455 files can be accessed in full online, a unique feature in the world, of which we should be proud.

This book proposes to use a method for the analysis of these soldier files drawing on statistical theory developed in the late 1700s, when sample surveys were developed in England as a means of measuring the rural economy. This method declined in importance during the nineteenth century due to the emergence of comprehensive census data and the theory of population statistics.[14] But the inter-war period in the twentieth century saw the popular adoption of this method in the polling techniques used by George Gallup in 1935, when it received significant attention for accurately predicting American election outcomes and is discussed shortly. The use of this sampling method is widespread today, but has not previously been applied to First World War soldier records. Its application in historical research could become more widespread *provided* that fundamental criteria are met—namely, that the population of historical data to be analysed is large, that the sample taken is random and that the sampling is drawn from across the full range of the data population under analysis. Analysing a segment or a cohort within a population will only provide an assessment of that segment or cohort and therefore potentially presents a bias of the population as a whole.

In statistics education the following example is widely used as it underscores the importance of random sampling and sample size. In 1936, Franklin Roosevelt was facing his second election, this time as incumbent President of the United States. The Republican candidate was Governor Alfred Landon of Kansas. At the time, the second most popular magazine in the United States was the *Literary Digest*. The country was emerging from the Great Depression and Landon was campaigning on a program of economy in the government. Most observers believed that Roosevelt would be an easy winner, but the *Literary Digest* thought otherwise. Quoting from the magazine's 22 August 1936 edition:

> Once again, the Digest was asking more than ten million voters—one out of four, representing every county in the United States—to settle November's election in October. Next week, the first answers from these ten million will begin the incoming tide of marked ballots, to *be triple checked*, verified *five times*, cross classified and totalled. When the last figure has been totted and checked, if past experience is a criterion, the country will know *to within a fraction of 1%* the actual popular vote of forty million.[15] [Emphasis in original]

At the time, this was the largest survey ever undertaken in the world. The magazine mailed 10 million questionnaires to people whose names and addresses were sourced from telephone books and club membership lists.[16] In 1936 there were 11 million residential telephones, and 9 million unemployed. The magazine received 2.4 million responses and loudly proclaimed that Landon would win in a landslide victory of 57 per cent to 43 per cent. The *Literary Digest* had called the winner in every presidential election since 1916.

In 1936, George Gallup was setting up his survey organisation. Using the sample lists published by the *Literary Digest*, Gallup sent a simple questionnaire on the election to only 3000 people from these lists. This produced a result almost identical to that reached by the magazine, which he also published, indicating that Landon would win 56 per cent to 44 per cent. Gallup then used another sample of his own of 50 000 people (unnecessarily large), and reached a result that suggested *the exact opposite*, that Roosevelt would win by 56 per cent to 44 per cent. The actual result of the election differed slightly more than Gallop's prediction, with Roosevelt securing 62 per cent of the vote; and so began his second term as president. Gallup's fame and fortune took off while the *Digest* folded the following year. The magazine had sampled the wrong people. The economy was a major issue and poor people did not have telephones or belong to clubs. Poor people did not respond to questionnaires. And the size of the sample only made the wrong answer worse.

So, how do we do it? In sampling from very large populations, the statistical formulae used are such that population *size* has very little effect; indeed it is negligible, on the proportion of elements being sampled, provided that the sample is *random*. The finding that it is the absolute size of the sample, and not the proportion of population sampled that essentially determines sampling precision, is difficult for many people to accept intuitively.[17] To put it in another way, the interesting principle that emerges for cases in which the populations are large relative to the sample is that the absolute amount of work done (sample size), not the amount of work that might conceivably have been done (population size), is important in determining sampling precision.

The confidence with which a sample of a large population accurately represents the proportion of the element that is being estimated will obviously be 100 per cent, or certain, if *all* elements in the population are sampled. But if an acceptable level of confidence, adequate for the purpose at hand, is generally adopted at a level of, say, 95 per cent confidence, then *random* sample size takes over as the sensitive criterion *if* the population is large. Furthermore, the level of accuracy of a prediction arising from the sample, adequate for the purpose at hand, may be expressed as a percentage width plus or minus, or above or below, the predicted number. Hence the statement 'I am 95 per cent sure that the true proportion of the population is contained in the interval, +/– 1%'.

Table 6 shows the sample sizes required to estimate a proportion, based on specifying the width of the 95 per cent Confidence Interval.

Table 6: Sample Size

'Width' of 95% Confidence Interval	0.02	0.03	0.04	0.05
+/– %	1.0	1.5	2.0	2.5
Sample size required	9 604	4 268	2 401	1 536

Source: David Freeman, Robert Pisani, and Roger Purves, *Statistics*, WW Norton & Company, New York, 1980, p. 302.

As emphasised earlier, critical to the accuracy of random sample methodology is the randomness of the sampling across *the complete range* of the population being analysed. Anything short of this coverage will introduce bias or skewed results. However, this is easier said than done, so it is important to outline in detail the method proposed by which a random sample can be achieved.

In assessing practical methods of random sampling in the context of the present record review, the need to limit moving from one soldier's record to another is critical. It would be impossible to count thousands of records, whether available in a digitised format online (as is the B2455 series) or stored in boxes containing anywhere from between fifty and ninety-five soldier records each, as are the records housed in storage in the NAA in Melbourne (the MT1486/1 series) if *individual* randomly chosen records had to be assessed. For example, using randomly chosen soldier serial numbers, aside from the practical reality that soldier serial numbers were often duplicated, the time needed to move from one to another would extend the time taken for sampling to impossible lengths. However, it is entirely acceptable to sample by relatively small batches of records, so that a number of sequential records could be accessed and assessed, and then the next batch accessed and so on, thereby minimising the time taken to move from one soldier's file to the next. In adopting this approach, the means by which these *batches* are randomly identified then becomes critical.

At first, a trial or pilot count was undertaken, to determine a consistent approach to the variety of data that would then be applied from the outset to the main sample count. The pilot count proceeded by choosing a surname and then counting the first 250 *acceptable* records (that is, being soldiers who actually enlisted) by alphabetically filed sequence of first names for those files digitally available under the NameSearch function on the NAA website. The surnames that were chosen, for no particular reason, were Miller, Smith, Jones and Murphy. The similarity of the results for each of the four surnames was striking and implied randomness and much valuable information was obtained, including in regard to additional factors that needed to be assessed and the expansion of categories to be included in the review. There was only one feature that varied significantly among the surnames: it was found that men by the name of Murphy were twice as likely as men by the name of Jones to be hospitalised with venereal disease (VD). In order to maintain high levels of rigour for the proposed record review another, more mathematically based method of sampling was sought, rather than the arbitrary choice of a surname.

The sampling method adopted for the MT series lay with the method of storage that staff at the NAA in Melbourne had used when the series was re-boxed in 2007. The entire series was sorted and stored alphabetically by surname into 1151 sequentially numbered boxes. A list of randomly generated numbers was provided by the University of Melbourne's Statistical Consulting Centre of the series one to 1151, and the first few thus produced numbers were used to select a box, the contents of which were used in the count. The numbers of records in each box varied but boxes were sourced by the random sequence numbers until a sample in excess of 1536 individual soldier records were counted, thereby providing a Confidence Interval of 95 per cent +/– 2.5 per cent. The results of this sample will be presented in Chapter 3.

The digital record of the B2455 series proved more problematic. The algorithms used to list the records digitised online on the NAA website were not sufficiently understood by the available staff at the NAA to be explored in depth for a method of sampling. Once again the need for small batch sampling was critical for practical purposes and as the records were in an approximate alphabetical order, methods of choosing an alphabetically sequenced batch were explored.[18] Each record was barcoded but not sequentially, and in 'number clusters' of unknown sequential ranges, such that the 376 012 records had start/finish barcodes over a range in excess of 800 000. Soldier serial numbers were duplicated in this series as well and therefore serial numbers were unusable. The boxes in which they were stored were barcoded, but similar problems arose as that encountered for the individual barcoded records.

Finally, a sampling method was proposed to the staff at the NAA (and approved as being a suitably random sample method by the Statistical Consulting Centre at the University of Melbourne) that was practically achievable. The B2455 series of soldier records was stored in 18 724 boxes. The NAA staff computer access system was capable of displaying 350 boxes, effectively unnumbered, on fifty-three screen pages (18 724 divided by 350). Within each box was anywhere between one and fifty records of roughly alphabetically ordered soldier files. The system of random selection that was devised required the generation of the first six numbers of a randomly generated number series of one to fifty-three, representing a computer screen page number, for which six sets of randomly generated numbers from one to 350 were produced, with the first four numbers representing four boxes to be selected on each page. The first soldier's name in each of the thus chosen boxes would be recorded (that is, six pages each supplying four names, with a total of twenty-four). Each of these twenty-four names would therefore constitute the *starting point* name from which to then count the following 400 records sequentially on the NAA RecordSearch database, producing a total of 9600 records, and resulting in a 95 per cent Confidence Interval +/– 1.0 per cent set of results. To address the rare event that a count of 400 records threatened to overlap with a previous count of 400, it was initially decided that the count would continue on sequentially excluding, or jumping, the previously counted records. However, in discussion with the Statistical

Consulting Centre, it was decided to refine the method further to ensure that this could not occur.

As the first box number on the page was random, by equally spacing the next three boxes in a loop over the field of 350 they would also be random and therefore overlap would be avoided. As this 'equally' spaced number was 87.5 (350 divided by 4), it was determined that the spaced numbers alternate between 87 and 88 to take us to the end of that page. Twenty-four names were thus generated, and by counting those and the records of the 399 soldiers' names of the alphabetical series NAA NameSearch, a sample size of 9600 records was captured for analysis with generated results at the 95 per cent Confidence Interval +/− 1.0%. A summary of the records to be assessed is shown in Table 7.

Table 7: Selected Sample Sizes

Official enlistments	416 809	AIF soldiers records to be counted	Confidence Interval of selected sample size
Less navy etc.	3 856		
Total military, 'mobilised, enlisted and trained'	412 953**		
NAA MT 1486/1 records	36 340 plus	1 600*	95% +/− 2.5%
NAA B2455 records	376 012	9 600	95% +/− 1.0%
Total enlistments from AIF records	412 352		

*The choice of a lower level of accuracy was considered adequate as the count of this series was to redefine 'Enlistments' only. Much interesting epidemiological data were collated from the count of these records.

** Great Britain, Statistics of the Military Effort of the British Empire during the Great War 1914–1920, The British War Office and London HM Stationery, London, 1922, p. 759.

Now that we have outlined the theoretical and methodological basis of the record review, we can resume this journey to find the truth about these men's experiences. It was necessary to provide a detailed explanation of the sampling method to highlight the inadequacies of the existing official records and to explain the basis of what will be startling results, which will no doubt be the subject of future scrutiny. It is also important to point out that the principles underpinning the sampling analysis presented here were well known in appropriate circles at the time of Butler's analysis of AIF casualty statistics. It was the failure of Butler and Bean to draw on these resources that has left the true extent of the AIF soldiers' pain and suffering in the First World War so woefully misunderstood to this day.

Notes

1. A Graham Butler, *Official Medical History of the Australian Army Medical Services, 1914–1918, Volume III*, Australian War Memorial, Canberra, 1942, p. 859, 894.
2. Leo van Bergen, *Before My Helpless Sight: Suffering, Dying and Military Medicine on the Western Front, 1914–1918* (trans. Liz Waters, 2009 ed), Ashgate Publishing Limited, 1999, p. 107.
3. Australian War Memorial, 'casualty', *Australian War Memorial Encyclopaedia*, Canberra, 24 July 2010, see: <www.awm.gov.au/encyclopedia/definitions/casualties.asp>.
4. T J Mitchell and G M Smith, *Medical Services History of the Great War: Casualties and Medical Statistics of the Great War*, Imperial War Museum, London, 1931, p. xvi, xvii.
5. Butler, *Official Medical History of the Australian Army Medical Services, 1914–1918, Volume III*, p. 881.
6. Bill Gammage, *The Broken Years: Australian Soldiers in the Great War*, Australian National University Press, Canberra, 1974, p. 283.
7. Patsy Adam-Smith, *The ANZACS*, Thomas Nelson, West Melbourne, 1978, p. 360.
8. Butler, *Official Medical History of the Australian Army Medical Services, 1914–1918, Volume III*, p. 897.
9. Jeffery Grey, *A Military History of Australia*, Cambridge University Press, Melbourne, 1990 (revised 2008), p. 118.
10. Mitchell and Smith, *Medical Services History of the Great War: Casualties and Medical Statistics of the Great War*, p. 275.
11. ibid., p. 12, Table 1.
12. Butler, *Official Medical History of the Australian Army Medical Services, 1914–1918, Volume III*, p. 927, Table 53.
13. Australian Government, 'Sources of information about military service', pamphlet, National Archives of Australia, 2010.
14. L Brunt, 'The Advent of the Sample Survey in the Social Sciences', *Journal of the Royal Statistical Society: Series D* (The Statistician), July 2001, vol. 50, no. 2, p. 179–189.
15. David Freedman, Robert Pisani, and Roger Purves, *Statistics*, WW Norton & Company, New York, 1980, p. 302.
16. ibid., p. 303.
17. Morris Hamburg, Peg Young, and Bryan Sayer, *Statistical analysis for decision making (Dryden Press Series in Management Science and Quantitative Methods)* (6th ed.), Dryden Press College Publishers &

Harcourt Brace, Fort Worth, 1994, p. 218.
18 These records were stored across four sites and were deemed 'less accessible' to researchers owing to the fact they were available in digitised form online. The size of a record is generally defined by the length of shelf space it takes up. In one of the four sites it is spread over, the B2455 series occupies a kilometre of shelf space.

CHAPTER 3

Counting the Diggers (1): Enlistments and Embarkations

The primary purpose of this and the next two chapters is to undertake the critically important task of detailing and defining the types of casualty data that were collected from the random sample of 9604 AIF soldier Attestation Papers. The data collected from this random sample are quantitatively analysed, most of it for the first time, and then extrapolated, to independently assess the accuracy of the official record, and highlight the extent of the omissions of injury and illness.

However, before defining the many interpretations that are required to process specific data from the soldiers' records, we must first define the entire field of the relevant soldier records that need to be assessed. In other words, what really was Australia's total soldier enlistment number for the First World War? Determining this number is the starting point. The official enlistment number cited today has been a resilient figure indeed.

This final enlistment total for the war survived the scrutiny of Australian official historians Bean, Scott and Butler in their post-war analysis. It has been cited by politicians in the spotlight of post-war treaty negotiations and post-war public displays of national pride. This figure has been cited by social and military historians in every prominent work published over the past ninety years that refers to enlistments in the First World War. The accuracy of this figure is now subjected to independent analysis, surprisingly, for the first time.

It will be recalled that Australia's enlistment figure in effect consists of the numbers of individual AIF soldier's Attestation Papers contained in the two NAA series, B2455 and MT1486/1. These two series can generally be defined as the files of those who embarked for overseas service (B2455), and those who did not (MT1486/1). Some individual records have been lost, but their number appears to be small—in the order of hundreds only. The individual records themselves are quite extensive, containing multiple copies, detailed corrections and the location and movement of each soldier on a day-by-day basis. These records were used to calculate payments and fines, summarised into pay books for every individual in the AIF. They had to be accurate and reliable, and they were.

While the official number of enlistments is 416 809, distinction is now made between *all* enlistments and Australia's *military* enlistments in the AIF. The total number of military enlistments, after deducting members of the navy and nurses, is 412 953. The total number of soldier records in the NAA records series is 412 352, remarkably close and indicating only a small loss of files.

In this analysis, *both* record series were sampled separately, using two different sampling techniques developed to suit their respective, quite different storage systems. The results of the analysis of the MT series are examined first.

The NAA, until 2010, defined the MT1486/1 series as enlistments of men who did not embark from Australia, and by implication, fulfilled some form of home duties. In 2010, the NAA changed the shorthand definition of this series to the quite different 'applications to enlist'. While this more accurately defines the contents of this series, it is still inadequate, as the following analysis will show. Furthermore, this simplistic redefining of the contents of the MT series appears to have led to the inclusion in an NAA website upgrade in September 2011 of a link to a presentation of enlistments 'Mapping our ANZACS' by location of enlistment in Australia using the contents of only the files in the B2455 series. This has been used as the basis on that link to state that Australia's enlistment number for the First World War was 'more than 375 000'. While this is the number of files in B2455, it is not Australia's enlistment figure.[1]

The MT1486/1 series was assessed using the methodology explained in the previous chapter by a physical examination of approximately 1600 of the 36 340 individual records held in the NAA storage facility in Melbourne. Not only is this examination revealing by accurately (95 per cent Confidence Interval +/− 2.5%) helping to assess part of Australia's true total enlistment figure, it also presents an epidemiological picture of the state of the health and, in some sense, mind of the male population at that time. These men, for a multitude of reasons, voluntarily presented themselves for medical and character examination in order to enlist to join the conflict overseas.

From the outset of the analysis of these records it was apparent that a considerable number of applicants did not pass the medical examination which required a certain level of 'fitness' for war. At the beginning of the war, the acceptance standards only allowed for the recruitment of the very best of the country's youth. But as the war dragged on many of the standards for physical attributes of height and chest expansion were lowered and the maximum age was raised. The upper age limit of forty-five years was later raised to fifty years, and was further increased to fifty-five years of age for the specific category of men who had experience in tunnelling, as the Western Front ground down and turned into static trench warfare.

Of the 36 340 men in the MT series who appeared to have officially applied to enlist, it is now estimated that 18 600, or just over half, failed the medical examination and their application for service was rejected outright. They effectively did not get past the gate, and certainly do not qualify to be counted as enlistments. They were applicants to enlist who failed, not enlistments. Specific medical diagnoses that gave cause for the rejection of these applicants included the common conditions of hearing and vision deficiencies, and the popularised condition of flat feet. Quantifying the occurrence of these conditions in this analysis was not considered a priority, but some other notable conditions were quantified from this data count.

For example, a remarkably high estimate of 1200 men presented with a hernia. They were rejected. A further estimated 1000 men had inadequate and/or irreparable dental problems. These dental acceptance criteria indicate aspects of the diet the volunteer soldier could expect in the service, and an appreciation by the authorities at the time of the many other potential health impacts, today more clearly understood, of poor dental hygiene. A few men with poor teeth were accepted, and subsequently given dental treatment; however, most were rejected outright. For a few, their file contained notations recommending that private dental treatment would possibly lead to a review of the applicant's rejection.

Additional categories of rejection on medical grounds raised more questions than they answered. Around 230 men presented with venereal disease (VD)—either gonorrhoea or syphilis—and were promptly rejected. This could be a useful measure of the incidence of this insidious disease among the general population, although given the stigma surrounding this condition at the time, it is probably more indicative of the numbers of men who did *not know* they were infected. Applicants displaying any symptoms of tuberculosis (TB) were also rejected although this culling did not prevent a widespread loss of manpower as a result of both VD and TB during the war.

A more intriguing condition that led to immediate rejection was the medical diagnosis of varicocele, a condition akin to varicose veins, but of the testes. This condition is rarely painful, its main impact being a possible lowering of the individual's sperm count.[2] A remarkably large number of men, estimated to be in excess of 1300, or nearly 7 per cent of the applicants rejected on medical grounds, were rejected for this condition. One is left to wonder what effect a lower sperm count was perceived to have on the fighting capabilities of the volunteer soldier.

Other, non-medical, reasons that are evident in the analysis for an applicant's rejection were that the applicant was too small, either in height or chest expansion (2550), too young (1000), or too important (around seventy). This last category included those applicants who had existing jobs in essential services such as munitions manufacture or administrative clerks within the naval service. Some applicants were rejected with no reason recorded on their file, or with the notation 'SNR' (soldier not required), seemingly applied to those men (400) whom the recruiting officer thought would not make good soldiers. Around fifty applicants were rejected because they stammered excessively and a similar number because of limited 'English' ethnicity, such as applicants with German backgrounds ('born in Germany') or those believed to have been born in China. Thomas Hong enlisted on 5 January 1916 at the age of twenty-two

Counting the Diggers (1): Enlistments and Embarkations 53

years. He was born in Australia and his father lived in Western Australia. He was discharged after five weeks with the following notation on his file: 'Not of substantial European descent.'

The next largest category of applications in this series that cannot be counted as enlistments are those that were *double counted*. Many men, in the range of 4000 to 5200, either had seen service in the AIF, then returned to Australia for rest or discharge, and then re-enrolled for home duty, for whom a second Attestation Paper was therefore created; or had a change of mind, and requested discharge from home duties in order to reapply for service overseas, and for whom a second Attestation Paper was also generated.

Then there is a group of Attestation Papers categorised under the heading 'Did Not Show'. In this case the papers are intact and complete in all respects except that the estimated 1750 successful applicants did not appear at the reporting depot to be formally inducted. Interestingly, a large proportion of these applications had been completed at country police stations for which the enlisting police constable received 10 shillings per application that was successfully completed. This scheme ran for a short time at the beginning of the war in an effort to boost enlistments but was abandoned due to concerns over its propriety.[3] Some 'Did Not Show' examples were like that of William Miller, who had a notation on his file that read 'will be back tomorrow'.[4]

Finally, there is a miscellaneous group categorised in the count as 'not applicable'. Examples of this classification were Attestation Papers for Rosalie Summer, Alice C McGregor and Lorna Simon who were nurses and should be categorised elsewhere. The raw data indicate a statistical range with 95% Confidence Interval of at least fifty and perhaps as many as 230 nurses incorrectly included in the MT1486/1 series. Another, more unusual example was that of one DS Kerr who, three weeks after his enlistment, was arrested and sent to jail to serve a long civil crime-related term after the execution of an outstanding arrest warrant. The police had been looking for him for some time. He obliged them by enlisting. Then there were duplicated files like those of RW Fawcett and PP Sullivan, whose papers were spread between two files, or HE Belbin who demanded to be enlisted into the artillery, but when told that it was not possible to guarantee that his request would be met, he refused to sign up. Still others refused to be vaccinated and were therefore rejected. Tables 8 and 9 summarise these preliminary findings.

Table 8: Analysis of Results—MT1486/1 Series©

Failure to enlist	Sample count	Extrapolated population	Rounded totals	95% Confidence Interval Range Min. Max.
Medically unfit	822	18 576	18 600	17 678–19 475
Unacceptable physique	113	2 553	2 550	2 117–3 048
Failed to show	78	1 769	1 750	1 400–2 187
Unknown rejection	56	1 265	1 250	960–1 635
Too young	45	1 016	1 000	744–1 354
SNR	18	408	400	242–641
Too important	3	67	70	14–198
Not applicable: double counted in/into AIF	204	4 610	4 600	4 033–5 238
Not applicable: nurse/navy etc.	19	429	450	259–668
Total failed enlistments	1 358*	30 690**	**30 700**	30 012–31 322

Source: Compiled by David Noonan from Attestation Papers, 2014.

Table 9: Examples of Rejection—Medically Unfit©

Examples of 'medically unfit'	Sample count	Extrapolated population	Rounded totals	95% Confidence Interval Range Min. Max.
Varicocele	58	1 310	1 300	999–1 685
Hernia	52	1 175	1 200	881–1 533
Bad teeth	44	994	1 000	725–1 329
VD	10	225	230	109–415

Source: Compiled by David Noonan from Attestation Papers, 2014.

Counting the Diggers (1): Enlistments and Embarkations

So who did successfully enlist? Of the remaining records, a surprisingly small number of men actually saw service around Australia in the depots or as guards in 'concentration' camps in this country. After the observed number is extrapolated, it appears that approximately ninety died from causes such as pneumonia, heart failure or accident. Approximately 500 were found, after the commencement of service and for a variety of reasons, to be medically unfit and discharged from duty. Their length of service ranged from a few weeks to many months. Around 1500 decided that service in the AIF was not for them and left, 'discharged at own request'. This generally occurred within weeks.

For reasons such as alcoholism and insubordination, a further estimated 1250 men were discharged SNR, and 1150 men were immediately transferred out of the AIF into a separate transport department, presumably deployed as drivers and railway workers, and were struck off the list. Out of the original number of 36 340, only the *remaining estimated 1150 men* in this series, plus or minus 300, *completed* home service duties until the cessation of hostilities, after which they were discharged. Table 10 summarises these findings.

Table 10: Actual Enlistments MT Series©

Deemed enlistments	Sample count	Extrapolated population	Rounded totals	95% Confidence Interval Range Min. Max.
Later discharged: own choice	67	1 514	1 500	1 179–1 912
Later discharged: SNR	55	1 242	1 250	940–1 609
Discharged: to transport	51	1 152	1 150	861–1 508
Completed service	50	1 129	1 150	842–1 482
Later discharged: medically unfit	23	519	500	330–777
Died	4	90	90	25–231
Total MT series enlistments	**250***	**5 649****	**5 650**	**5 018–6 328**

* Total sample size: 1358 + 250 = 1608
** Total files in MT1486/1 = **36 340**
Source: Compiled by David Noonan from Attestation Papers, 2014.

The net result of this cull of soldier Attestation Papers in the MT series only (from 36 340 to 5650) is a reduction of Australia's official enlistment figure (at this stage) by an estimated 30 700. This net result is stated in the 95% Confidence Interval of being within the range of 30 000 to 31 300.[5]

As a consequence, taking into account the random sample count of *only the MT series*, the accurate number of actual AIF enlistments in the First World War is reduced to 386 000 (+/–650).

As referred to earlier in this chapter, in 2011 the NAA introduced a page on its website entitled 'Mapping our Anzacs', on which it states that Australia's AIF enlistments were over 375 000 because that is the number of files in B2455 (but the number of actual enlistments in the MT series was unknown). However, in a visual display of a map of Australia with the origin by state of the numbers of enlistments, when plotted onto the web page graphic, the total only amounts to 367 500. Ironically, the NAA was very close to the mark but for the wrong reasons.

The number 386 000, as pointed out previously, was an enlistment *total* and included non-military personnel. When other 'not applicable' non-military personnel are accounted for, as identified in the main sample analysis of series B2455, it can now be determined, through detailed sampling of all Attestation Papers, that a further reduction provides a more accurate estimate of *379 000 men* (+/–650) enlisted in the AIF.[6] The balance of the official figure can be defined at best as an application to enlist, or misallocation over time, and should be seen more correctly as belonging to the non-military listings. The number 416 809 should be removed from the headline official figures as its original purpose of inflating Australia's contribution to this conflict is long out of date and the figure is incorrect. We can now examine Australia's embarkation number.

A large proportion of the men represented by this more accurate *enlistment* number of 379 000 did not set foot in an army base overseas. Following the 1933 Census, the embarkation figure of 331 781 was corrected down to 324 000 by the Commonwealth Statistician after he requested a recount by the War Records unit based at the Victoria Barracks in Melbourne. It determined that 7500 men had been double counted as they had been returned to Australia, in the main for medical recovery and then had embarked again when well. This resulted in a revised, though little publicised, rounded figure of 324 000 embarkations, remarkably identical to the NAA's and AWM's so-called Nominal Roll of 324 000 soldiers that, by those authorities' definition, was believed to have been likely compiled in preparation for arrangements to bring soldiers home. However, it is now claimed that this is doubtful and it appears more likely to be the consequence of the 1933 Census analysis. Nevertheless, it can be stated that the official figure of embarkations of AIF soldiers is *at most* 324 000, and not 331 781. While both Butler and Bean were aware of this new figure determined by the Commonwealth Statistician, *for reasons unknown, they did not correct the official record* when they both published their volumes four years later in 1942.

The majority of those enlisted men who *failed to embark* were discharged medically unfit. The Attestation Papers rarely recorded a medical condition for those cases that *occurred in Australia*, although when one was provided, it was usually the contraction of a VD—already a significant problem at home, but to become a disastrous problem overseas. The impact of sexually transmitted disease in the AIF was extensive and can now be accurately quantified for the first time among *all* of those who served. The files occasionally record that the affected soldier was transferred for treatment to a converted prison facility at Langwarrin in Victoria; and most of those cured were shipped off to war. Early in the war men infected in the Mediterranean campaign area were also sent back to Australia for treatment at Langwarrin. A facility established early on outside Sydney was considered not secure enough and was closed in 1915. Treatment until cured was not always provided and some records indicate that in cases where the disease was chronic, or the character of the soldier was such as to limit confidence that he would avoid reinfection, the soldier was discharged while still infected.

An estimate of the proportion of those soldiers *discharged in Australia* before embarkation on the grounds of being *medically unfit* was around 60 per cent. The next largest category of men who failed to embark were those who were simply too late and were discharged due to the cessation of hostilities. These amounted to approximately 20 per cent of all men who failed to embark. Enlistments prior to June 1918 were generally the last to embark before the war came to an end.

Desertion of enlisted men while still in Australia was not uncommon. There was an estimated 8750 men who failed to report for duty at some time prior to embarkation and simply disappeared. Some men disappeared shortly after their enlistment. Others disappeared after disciplinary punishment, or in a few cases while under treatment for VD, in which case their files noted the individual to be 'a venereal deserter'. Charlie Whiteside did not disappear. He was born in Ireland and his file recorded that, after serving for only twenty days, he was 'discharged using disloyal utterances in camp'. Stanley Williams (Serial number 5650) was a farmer when he enlisted in January 1915. He disembarked at Suez and contracted VD shortly thereafter in July, and was returned to Australia, arriving on 2 September for treatment at Langwarrin. He deserted two weeks later and was declared a 'venereal deserter'. He must have been located as he was formally discharged from the AIF in September 1917.

A further subcategory of desertion were those men who embarked at one port in Australia and failed to re-board before the troopship departed from another Australian port, usually Fremantle, as they headed for the battle fields. In a few instances, the soldier disembarked from the boat with a day's leave and disappeared in the port of Cape Town, deserting the army and sometimes a wife. In nearly all cases, the record shows that an inquiry took place, evidence was presented, missing items of the soldier's kit were recorded, and a finding was made that resulted in the issue of a warrant for their arrest. However, rarely did an arrest occur.

An exception to this was the experience of John Hall (2460), who was a farmer from Dubbo in New South Wales. He enlisted on 15 September 1916 at the age of twenty-four years, but seemed to have a change of mind and went missing in January 1917. His file indicated that 'information has been received' such that on the 20 November 1917 he was arrested on a remote cattle station 60 miles from Roma in outback Queensland masquerading as a returned soldier. A rollicking good yarn of escape and recapture is contained in the police report on page 31 of his records. Bolting horses, Aboriginal trackers and the arresting constable receiving a one pound bonus for his fine efforts in recapturing the escapee; the story belongs in a boy's own annual. The authorities decided to ship Hall out immediately and his records have him embarked from Sydney on 19 December 1917, headed off to war. However, John Hall had other ideas. He disembarked when the ship docked in Melbourne to pick up more men and supplies, and was not seen or heard of again. All warrants for the arrest of deserters were withdrawn early in 1920.

Another subcategory that was specifically recorded in the non-applicable category comprised the records of nursing sisters, most of who embarked to see service overseas. It is estimated that the total number of nurses in the B2455 series is approximately 2050 (1520, 2770).[7]

Other less important examples of non-applicability arising from the failure to embark included men who were discharged at their own request for which the most accepted circumstances being 'family reasons'. Wives' and mothers' objections also played a significant role in the early discharge of a husband or son. The notations 'soldier no longer required', 'unlikely to make a good soldier' or simply 'undesirable' were less frequent. Similarly infrequent was a failure to obtain the applicant's parents' consent. A small number of files treated as not applicable were for men who elected to fill administrative roles in Rabaul. Their task was to maintain the public service administration after the German garrison stationed there withdrew to Europe upon the declaration of war and the Australian Government undertook to fill the void. No shots were fired in this transition and service in Rabaul was declared not to be in a theatre of war on 21 September 1914. As a consequence, only one service medal was awarded for this tour of duty. It was entirely voluntary and many examples of requests for early discharge and subsequent return to Australia are evident in the records in this subcategory. This justified these servicemen not being counted as part of the fighting force; rather, their service was seen as equivalent to home service.

It is therefore the case that, as with enlistments, total embarkations from Australia are also overstated in the official figures. As previously discussed, the examination of this figure by the Commonwealth Statistician following the 1933 Census resulted in a determination that approximately 7500 soldiers had been double counted as they had embarked from Australia more than once. The record review indicated that this figure was higher, at 8140. This result has a range at the 95% Confidence Interval +/− 1%, of a low of 7080 and a high of 9300. The 1933 census finding falls within this possible range and so, in the interests of taking a conservative approach, will not be altered.

A particularly tragic example of this double embarkation is the case of Thomas Peter Williams (3488), who enlisted at the age of twenty-one years and contracted VD shortly after arriving overseas. He was returned to Australia and was hospitalised for nearly three months at Langwarrin as there were no facilities in Egypt at the outset of the war.[8] He then re-embarked to return overseas, was hospitalised briefly for tonsillitis, and then, in January 1918, he was again hospitalised suffering from myalgia, presumably as a result of shell shock. Sadly, Thomas was killed in action two months later. In 1923, his mother wrote a curt and numbing letter to the Department of Defence requesting his medals as they should have been received by that time; she knew that there had to be a delay because Thomas was her *fifth* son killed in this war.

Another case of a double embarkation is seen in the adventures of Reginald Sharples (3470), an 18-year-old railway worker. Reg enlisted on 30 July 1915 and found himself attached to the Mediterranean Expeditionary Force and taken on strength in the North African base near the Suez Canal on 8 January 1916. During his transfer from the disembarkation port at Alexandria to the base at Tel el Kebir the previous day, he thought it would be funny to decouple the last carriage of the troop train while it was in motion. The incident concluded without injury when the alarm was raised as laughter spread among the men along the length of the train, finally alerting the driver. But the authorities took a dim view of this incident. Reg was sentenced to a one-year hard labour jail term to be served *back in Australia* in the harsh Melbourne Pentridge Jail. Despite his father's protestations to politicians and authorities during the course of 1916 that he was just a boy who committed a practical joke, he served his full sentence, and embarked again early in 1917 to end up on the Western Front. He was hospitalised after sustaining an injury, then in September 1918 he was wounded in action, a few days before all Australian troops were withdrawn from the fighting. He returned safely to Australia, older and perhaps the wiser and discharged medically unfit.

The primary purpose of defining an embarkation figure of men who left Australia is to determine Australia's contribution of men to this conflict. In order to conform to this definition those men who were on the ships in transit at sea headed for Europe at the end of the war should not be included. They are rightly regarded as enlistments, just as those housed in depots undergoing training in Australia were regarded as enlistments only. As a result, the numbers of men on a troopship that was recalled at sea are treated as 'not applicable' for inclusion in the embarkation total. The record entitled 'Australian Imperial Force, Statistics of Casualties, etc.', compiled by the London AIF Headquarters Records Section, states that 3998 men were at sea, 'en route from Australia', on 11 November 1918. This appears to be borne out by the record review analysis. By adopting this definition and applying it to the embarkation figure determined by the Commonwealth Statistician, the effective number falls to something less than 320 000 men. Upon extrapolation, the analysis of 9604 actual soldier records very closely concurs with this estimate. The simple sample record review corrects the official figure of 331 781 and determines the correct number of effective embarkations for the First World War to be *318 100*, with a range of between 315 300 and 320 800 at the 95% Confidence Interval.[9]

This finding is critical as the total *318 100* will now be used in all further analysis presented in this book. It essentially defines the field against which all other categories can be measured. Its proximity to the finding of the Commonwealth Statistician provides a firm foundation for analysis when combined with the common sense assertion that troops recalled at sea were not part of Australia's fighting force and that nurses and those seeing service in Rabaul, New Guinea, belonged in other service categories. This revised figure provides us with an internationally accepted point of comparison of the strength of our men exposed to this conflict with that of soldiers from other nations. And it is upon this foundation that the most detailed and accurate analysis of Australian soldiers' commitment to this war can be built.

Notes

1 In addition to this misrepresentation of the B2455 series, confusion is compounded when the individual state figures are totalled as they only account for 356 350, and are still short of the mark when another 11 000 are added to the files the website claims have their enlistment location missing.

2   Oxford University Press, 'varicocele', in *Oxford Concise Medical Dictionary*, Elizabeth Martin (ed), Oxford University Press, Oxford, 1998, p. 692.
3   LL Robson, *The First AIF: A Study of its Recruitment 1914–1918*, p. 37.
4   National Archives of Australia, Melbourne store, Series MT1486/1, Box 723.
5   The statistical package used to establish the intervals was Minitab. For extreme (e.g. 10% or 90%) proportions, the distribution is more skewed away from the upper or lower 'edges' of the field than a standard bell distribution, which has its accuracy in the mid ranges of proportional values. This explains why the 'rounded totals' for extreme proportions will not be the mid-point of the stated range.
6   This is the net AIF enlistment figure after the following corrections: the number 386 000 contains approximately 4000 naval enlistments (A6700 Series) (A Graham Butler, *Official Medical History of the Australian Army Medical Services, 1914–1918, Volume III*, Australian War Memorial, Canberra, 1942, p. 882), and over 2050 nurses listed as AIF but who should be listed elsewhere, and members of 'the Tropical Force' sent to Rabaul which was not a theatre of war (a finding of approximately 1000).
7   This results from a Minitab 95% CI with a range of 1520 up to as many as 2770 nurses.
8   Claudia Thame, 'Health and the State: The Development of Collective Responsibilities for Health Care in Australia in the First Half of the Twentieth Century', thesis, Australian National University, 1974, p. 121.
9   As determined using Minitab: 1 Proportion Test and Confidence Interval.

CHAPTER 4

Counting the Diggers (2): Specific Medical Conditions

In the analysis of Australian research on the First World War, the appalling impacts of two types of casualty have been frequently discussed. They are the incidence of VD and shell shock. These two conditions had a devastating effect on the wellness of Australian servicemen and consequently on their military performance.

However, outside the work of Butler[1] and the records of the military establishment itself, the overall occurrence of VD among the soldiers has only been previously assessed broadly or in shallow terms. Exemplary here are observations such as Peter Stanley's in his 2010 book, *Bad Characters, Sex Crime Murder and Mutiny and the Australian Imperial Force*, in which he says, 'At least seven of Australia's sixty VC [Victoria Cross] recipients contracted VD—one in ten, just the proportion you would expect'.[2] The connection between a VC winner and VD is unclear.

Stanley cites Bernard Zwar (whom he describes as the senior AIF specialist on VD), whose figures show that overall about 10 per cent of the AIF contracted VD. Based on Stanley's own figures for the size of the AIF, this percentage equates to 40 000 men. But later in his book he appears to inflate the number without any explanation.

By the war's end at least 55,000 Australian soldiers had been treated for VD—the figure under states [sic] the actual total because in 1916 the medical system lost control of the statistics, and it omitted those who concealed the infection, or men who were killed before it was diagnosed. It is not clear whether the accepted total includes the number—around 10,000, it would seem—who contracted VD in Australia before embarkation.[3]

Stanley's assertions on the incidence of VD can, and will be, tested and discussed in Chapter 6. But for now it is noted that his reference to Zwar seems misplaced as Zwar appears to have interviewed only 300 men who were admitted to a barbed-wire compound established in the Egyptian desert at Mena in 1915.[4] Butler produced data that was extremely difficult to decipher, presenting separate databases covering data for Egypt, France and England over different timeframes. And the measure of the incidence of VD he used was *hospitalisations per 1000 men on strength at that time*, an approach he merely mentions in a footnote.[5] The potential for confusion caused by this measure matches that which surrounds the data on wounded and woundings and obstructs an assessment of the gross number of men impacted by VD. Butler's measure is *a rate* of occurrence, not a gross total. Similarly confusing is that in two places in his work Butler makes reference to time spent in hospital for treatment. At one point, in claiming that the stoppage of pay among men who contracted VD was unequal, as it differed depending on the type of VD, he says:

> Cases of gonorrhoea which, because of the local nature of the treatment, were retained in hospital till well—that is for a period of seldom less than six weeks—were heavily penalised as compared with cases of syphilis, which after a few days treatment in hospital, went to military convalescent camps where the stoppage ceased.[6]

In a second reference in *Volume III*, regarding treatment in hospital for VD, he presents the duration of stay in hospital in categories by month in percentage terms,[7] which once again does not demonstrate the gross impact. Finally, Butler produces two very different numbers for recorded admissions per 1000 men. On page 180 of *Volume III*, he claims that it was 158 per 1000, while on page 187 he notes the figure to be 84.79 per 1000 for the period '1915–1918, all theatres'. On that same page appears Butler's one and only statement of total hospital admissions for the war of 52 538, from which he deducts admissions for relapses of 8605 to arrive at a gross number of men admitted with VD of 43 933. Once again Butler is less than helpful.

In an excellent book, *Before My Helpless Sight: Suffering, Dying and Military Medicine on the Western Front, 1914–1918*, published in 1999 but only translated from the Dutch in 2009, Leo van Bergen, while pointing out that sheer physical fatigue reduced the soldiers' libido, stated:

> Nevertheless twice as many suffered from venereal disease as from any other complaint. Given the chances of infection in a single sexual act have been estimated at no more than about 3 percent, it is clear that many soldiers in the vicinity of the trenches and on short term leave must have shared their beds with prostitutes or local women.[8]

He goes on to conclude:

> The stress of combat and constant fear of death meant that many soldiers no longer felt bound by the sexual norms and the values prevailing in peacetime and in civilian surroundings. Above all, though, sex must have been a means of escape, a fleeting break from a dismal and cut-throat reality.

If this level of infection were brought back to Australia at the end of the war, it raises the question of what impact this had on the general population. Were the authorities prepared for this sudden injection of infected men back into post-war Australian society? What was the prevalence in the general community at that time? The potential harm of VD warranted its occurrence to be included in the record review.

Data collection for the admission to hospital in the AIF for VD presented very few problems owing to the detailed records of its incidence and treatment which were maintained for the purposes of pay suspensions while servicemen received treatment. The treatment methods used prior to the advent of antibiotics bear similarities to the treatment of chemotherapy in the case of cancer. Various heavy metals, such as mercury and arsenic-based compounds, were injected into the patient over a period of time, poisoning them to such an extent that the question was often raised of which would be killed off first, the infection or the patient. Lieutenant George Oliphant Duncan has hospital records that describe the administration of mercury via a series of injections. This example is unusual as rarely did officers' files detail treatment for these stigmatised conditions, just as there was a similar under-reporting of shell shock in officers' records, as will be discussed shortly.

Treatment was not the only difficulty in dealing with VD. The stigma associated with contracting these diseases invariably delayed medical attention being sought. Among servicemen, response to treatment and therefore the terms of hospitalisation were highly variable but durations of fewer than *four weeks* were rare and brief durations probably meant there had been a misdiagnosis. Its diagnosis was occasionally changed to scabies in which case a soldier's pay was reinstated; but *six months* in hospital was not uncommon. Reinfection was a compounding factor as was recurrence following premature release from hospital. Some examples of the extent of this problem are evident in the following records. Walter Sherman (3975) was admitted with VD on four occasions over the two and a half years of his service for periods of 21, 114, 80 and 36 days. Also in service for two and a half years, William Davidson (3112A) was admitted on three occasions for periods of 94, 87 and 92 days. Alex Depena (6944) was admitted once for a period of 157 days and Percy Sinclair (2521) was also admitted once but in his case he was hospitalised for a period of 196 days, or over six months. Charlie Duncan (605) was admitted on *five* occasions over the fewer than three years of his service, for periods of 96, 18, 80, 54 and 49 days. Indeed, Duncan had trouble staying *out* of hospital. A Queensland drover and horse breaker, he was admitted to hospital a total of *twelve* times, two due to wounding. Thus, much of Duncan's overseas service was spent in hospital.

The suspension of pay while under treatment did nothing to encourage the soldiers to report symptoms of VD, although the penalty was relaxed somewhat towards the end of the war, with a reduction in pay rather than a suspension. Furthermore, *unlike* every other case of hospitalisation, the soldier's next of kin *were not* notified that he had been admitted to hospital when the admission was for VD. Therefore, for the soldier's next of kin such as mother, wife or sister receiving a proportion of his pay, as many were, the cessation of payments was disastrous. Many a file contains the letters of panicked loved ones desperately enquiring into the wellbeing and circumstances of their soldier only for the upsetting truth to be revealed. This was a ham-fisted approach indicating a scale of desperation on the part of the military authorities in their attempts to control the spread of VD. And it was an approach that caused a great deal of resentment among the servicemen.

But it was not the war that brought VD to prominent public attention. Its impact on the general public in the decade *preceding* the war had already raised grave concerns. Milton James Lewis, in his 2003 book, *The People's Health: Public Health in Australia, 1788–1950* describes how in Britain at the time:

> The Royal Commission on Venereal Diseases, 1913–1916 saw the existing prevalence of VD as a 'terrible peril to our Imperial race' and the economic losses involved as 'a powerful argument for the initiation of general measures of prevention and treatment at the earliest possible date'. Poor Law patients and military and naval patients, the Congress recommended, were to be detained until cured and all prisons were to have treatment facilities.[9]

In Australia, the celebrated public health medical practitioner, JHL Cumpston, referred to the significance of this disease's social impact:

> Known as the 'Red plague', as distinct from the 'Black plague' (bubonic plague), the 'White plague' (tuberculosis) and the 'Yellow plague' (smallpox), venereal disease carried by Australian soldiers returning from the Middle East in 1915 caused much anxiety on the 'home-front'. The anxiety was heightened by the Federal Government's refusal to provide reliable information about the situation.[10]

Cumpston goes on to cite Coward, who claims that *The Worker*—a popular magazine of the time—drawing on statements made in the *Medical Journal of Australia*, asserted that 10 per cent of the whole expeditionary force had been infected since departure from Australia.[11] Lewis, in his 2003 medical review of public health at this time points out:

> VD was notoriously underreported, so official notification figures in themselves are not reliable indicators of incidence. In 1921, 17 per cent of just over 3000 hospital patients in Melbourne reacted positively to the Wassermann test for syphilis. In 1930, 10.5 per cent of almost 3000 men and 13.6 per cent of 1000 women in state hospitals in Sydney were carrying syphilis. Whilst these groups are not fully representative to general population, it would seem that around 10 per cent of lower class people had syphilis and probably more had gonorrhoea.[12]

However, these statistics, as Lewis highlights, were not representative of the general population because at that time hospital services were provided only for people of the lower socioeconomic strata of the Australian population. It was thought that the incidence in this strata was significantly higher than in the general population. For those who could afford it, treatment of all illnesses was provided in the home and the disease remained unreported.

A conference on VD was convened by the Commonwealth Department of Health in 1922 involving the Commonwealth and all state governments of Australia. Its purpose was to consider the effectiveness of the current system of legislation (which included mandatory reporting and provisions for the detention of people suffering from VD who refused to undertake or maintain treatment) and administrative measures in place at the time, enacted around Australia in order to control the spread of these diseases. The states had responded to this looming crisis in public health by introducing legislation to try to control VD along similar lines established earlier in England, albeit uncoordinated across the states: Victoria in December 1916; Queensland and Tasmania in February 1917; NSW in December 1918; and South Australia in December 1920.

The 1922 Conference on Venereal Diseases determined, among other matters, that the required *certificate of cure* would *not* be given unless certain conditions were met:

> In the case of secondary syphilis no certificate of cure shall be given unless three years had elapsed from the first appearance of the primary manifestation. In a case of primary syphilis no certificate of cure shall be given unless two years had elapsed from the first appearance [and] the patient shall have undergone treatment for a period of at least 12 months provided that during the first four months after appearance of the primary sore he shall have been efficiently treated with an approved arsenical compound, and with mercury, and the mercurial treatment shall have been continued for the remainder of the 12 months.[13]

What this tells us is that, even when a returned soldier was under treatment, he could not expect to be clear of the disease for two or, in some cases, three years after its contraction. A definitive estimate of its occurrence in the AIF cohort is therefore of significant value in measuring its potential impact on the general population in the immediate post-war period. The fact was that, once the soldier left the service, the AIF ceased to provide him with any further treatment services. This harsh approach was scrutinised during the investigation conducted by the Australian Royal Commission for the Assessment of War Disabilities into war pension entitlements in the years 1924 to 1925. And as a consequence, in a reversal of the previous position, the Repatriation Commission was made fully responsible for the treatment of men who contracted VD during their period of service. The results of the random sample analysis of the records will show that the authorities had good reason to be alarmed about the incidence of VD among the men of the AIF and the consequences for the general population after the war.

In contrast to the relative ease of assessing the incidence of VD, the recording of the occurrence of shell shock during the First World War was far more problematic than its diagnosis is today. The task for the record review first required the identification and definition of more than thirty different terms used in the individual soldier records to describe the symptoms of shell shock, or, as referred to today, post-traumatic stress syndrome (PTSS) or post-traumatic stress disorder (PTSD).

Previous anecdotal evidence has suggested that the high levels of traumatic stress suffered on the Western Front had never been seen in any conflict before, nor since. It is therefore important that some quite detailed background is provided here to better inform the first independent account of the incidence of this condition during the First World War via the sample analysis of the AIF soldier records presented in this book.

In the light of modern knowledge and understanding, one would think that a much clearer diagnosis of this condition is more achievable today. More than ninety years ago, significant prejudices, stigma and ignorance prevailed when these records were being compiled—either in the field, or in official post-war analyses. At the time, multiple terminologies existed, and medical practitioners' disagreement masked the extent and even the legitimacy of the diagnosis of this condition. The conflict among wartime medical practitioners is nowhere more evidenced than when one compares the goal of the regular military medical officer to get the soldier back into fighting fitness with the primary purpose of the *majority* of medical practitioners who *temporarily* served (enlisted from civilian practices), whose broader aim was to permanently cure the patient, rather than to merely *fix* them sufficiently to rejoin the battle.[14]

The problematic starting point of this examination is that the concept of this stress condition only evolved as the war developed into another year in 1915. Indeed, it is a widely held misconception that traumatic conditions caused by exposure to war were first recognised during *this* war. This is not the case, as will be discussed shortly. What was recognised early on as new in this war was the devastating increased exposure of the soldiers to modern shelling and machine gunfire. The term 'shell shock' was initially used to try to explain the cause of the death of soldiers who bore no physical signs of injury after having been in close proximity to an exploding shell. The definition was later broadened to explain changes in mental and physical performance that seemed to occur consistently after a soldier had been buried in debris, soil and mud thrown up by an exploding shell. The differentiation between the physical and mental effects meant that diagnoses were for 'shell shock (wounding)' or 'shell shock (sick)'. Opposing views were vehemently held over whether sufferers were malingerers, or mentally weak to begin with. Indeed, Butler belonged to the school that held the view that mental illness was already present in those who displayed symptoms of shell shock, and only needed an event to bring it out. He believed the cause to be 'constitutional'. Richard Lindstrom, in his 1997 thesis entitled 'The Australian Experience of Psychological Casualties in War 1915–1939',[15] points out that Butler's descriptions of the general arrangements for shell shock victims and his analysis of their shortcomings are very similar to those found in the British official medical history and contains little and selective detail regarding Australia's approach. Lindstrom states that:

> the most outstanding feature of Butler's work on this issue is its ambiguity. On the one hand it is able to present a value-free analysis of the environmental stresses that caused mental problems but in the next sentence—and elsewhere—asserts that breakdown was a matter of character—a moral problem. A soldier could either embrace the 'spirit of courage, faith and self-confidence' or choose 'defeat and dependence', a mentality that led to chronic neurosis. In other words he felt that most psychological casualties saw neurosis as a way of escaping duty and gaining a pension.[16]

Stephen Garton, in his 1996 publication *The Cost of War: Australians Return*, states that Butler argued that 'neurosis in the field' was of 'very minor importance' and that much so-called shell shock was merely fatigue.[17] Garton's excellent work in this area extensively examines the difficulties of diagnosis. He provides evidence to support his claim that Australian medical authorities consistently reported fewer cases of shell shock among the AIF compared with the British figures. At a Field Ambulance Station at Pozieres, France, an Australian medical officer estimated that a quarter of all the soldiers and fewer officers were suffering from shell shock when at that time the British figure was nearing 40 per cent.

Garton's inclusion of examples of shell shock based on the diagnosis of conditions such as the short-term loss of sight or epilepsy[18] highlights the contentious nature of its definition. It is arguable that these two conditions can be so defined. However, hospitalisations for defective vision for a few days have *not* been counted as shell shock in this record review, but rather as an injury, principally because arguments that shell shock can manifest in this way are weak. Indeed, exposure to low-density gas could explain many incidents of loss of eyesight. Epilepsy has been counted as an illness in this analysis but it could also be a consequence of injury. By definition, epilepsy requires multiple episodes of seizures, yet the records infrequently referred to multiple episodes. Single episodes could be the result of exposure to percussion or temporary cardiac syncope causing loss of consciousness and convulsion resulting from a high-stress experience. Mention of single episodes of seizure is quite common across the AIF records, and it almost invariably leads to discharge medically unfit. However, until further work is done in the analysis of its frequency during the war years, it is accepted as being no more frequent than epilepsy is today (0.5 per cent of the general population). In this record review epilepsy has been treated as an illness that is, by default, battle related. It is contended that the loss of sight and epilepsy are marginal to the analysis of the prevalence of shell shock, and that as the incidence of shell shock *is so great* their inclusion would detract from a definitive diagnosis or interpretation. One exception to this was identified in the records in a case in which hospital admission occurred, with the cause noted as 'prostrate convulsions'. This is categorised as shell shock.

Before we leave Garton's work in this area, it is worth noting that the record review is useful to address two further issues that he raises. He is indeed correct when he points to the significantly lower incidence of shell shock among the officers than among the other ranks. His reasoning on this issue reflects the other truism that Australia's officers were promoted from the ranks, but this does not support his claim that they were therefore made of sterner stuff.[19] Observations from the pilot count and early work on the main record review suggest that the reason for the apparent lower levels of shell shock among officers was purely and simply that such instances were regularly not recorded. This view is supported by the overall poor level of entries of any type for officers, and the almost complete absence of any references to officers being discharged medically unfit. The term used for the discharge of an officer is 'struck off strength', and masks a magnitude of causes. *It is to be noted* that a decision was made during the pilot count process that when an officer was recorded as being discharged (struck off strength) with an obvious wounding (including shell shock), illness or injury, an entry of 'discharge medically unfit' (or 'medically unfit shell shock') was made even if this was not directly stated in his record.

Another reflection Garton makes is that the incidence of shell shock began to level off from 1916 due to improvements in treatment immediately behind the front line [20], resulting in a faster return to fighting fitness which in turn led to non-diagnosis.[21] However, initial evidence captured from the count does not support this view. It could be that soldiers who were prone to shell shock had already left the field to be discharged medically unfit. This record review quantifies this proportion. Furthermore, contrary to Garton's assessment the treatment of shell shock did not improve as the war went on—it got worse.

Concern over shell shock continued to rise in the public domain and within medical circles after the war, resulting in a British Government inquiry into the condition in 1922, and the condition becoming a major focus of a 1924 Australian Royal Commission into pension entitlements. A 1922 report by the British War Office Committee presented to Parliament is the best representation of official attitudes to the administration of shell shock and the prevailing military medical policy on this condition at that time:

> The committee recognised from the outset of the inquiry that the term 'shell-shock' was wholly misleading but unfortunately its use had been established and the harm was already done. The alliteration and dramatic significance of the term had caught the public imagination and hence forward there was no escape from its use.[22]

The committee considered evidence from a variety of sources, including German and American medical authorities in this field, military officers and men with practical experience of observing various manifestations of shell shock under battle conditions and, although victims of the condition were called before the committee, of the fifty-nine witnesses only four were pensioners who had actually suffered from war neurosis.[23] The committee's findings were many, varied, inconclusive and confusing, as evidenced by the following observation:

Authorities are agreed that in the majority of cases of war neurosis, there already existed a congenital or acquired predisposition to pathological reaction in the individual concerned, and that this constitutional characteristic was of vast importance.

From the evidence given it appears equally certain that the neuroses of war may manifest themselves, provided stress is sufficiently severe and prolonged, even in those of sound nervous constitution, and it is generally accepted that under the conditions of modern warfare any individual may ultimately break down on the nervous side.[24]

It also appears *equally certain* that, as time went on, contrary to popular belief (and Garton's claims), the official administration of this condition *did not* seem to improve with growing awareness. The following extract from a note in the War Office Committee's report to the British Parliament is a grim description of the development of the treatment process for shell shock that occurred during the war and is worthy of quotation in full:

The following was the procedure adopted during the later stages of the war.

Early in 1917 all cases presenting symptoms of functional nervous disorder were sent to special hospitals as 'NYD' [Not Yet Diagnosed]. At these centres a differentiation was made by the Medical Officer-in-Charge as to whether the case was 'wounded' or 'sick'. The diagnosis was based on evidence supplied by the regimental Medical or other responsible officer. The diagnosis of 'shell shock (wound)' was made, if there had been direct contact with the effect of explosions even although there was no visible external wound. All other cases of nervousness were classed as neurasthenia, hysteria, etc.

After June 1917, when the special Neurological Centres had been established in each Army Area, all cases of functional nervous disorder were marked 'NYDN' [Not Yet Diagnosed Neurosis] and transferred to the centres. Army form W3436 was introduced; after admission of a case into a Neurological Centre this form was sent by the officer commanding the centre to the officer commanding the man's unit for evidence as to 'exceptional exposure to shell fire' or otherwise. On return of the form to the officer commanding the centre, the diagnosis was determined as to whether the man was 'wounded' or 'sick'.

It was found that this procedure did not clear up the difficulties; although the meaning was logical, it turned out to be unfair and unworkable in practice.

Eventually (September 1918) it was decided to abolish the classification of 'shell-shock wound' in France, and to determine a shell-shock wound only if the disability was of so serious a nature as to necessitate transfer to England and the decision for classification as a casualty should depend upon the recommendation of a Neurological Board at a special centre in the United Kingdom.[25]

The quotation speaks for itself.

Further confounding the quantification of the condition's diagnosis in the record review was the increasing number of expressions adopted by medical officers trying to diagnose the debility of soldiers after, and even before, their exposure to battle. We must bear in mind that the sounds of battle were constant reminders of what lay ahead for these men. When the 21 mines were simultaneously detonated under German trenches (two failed to explode and were lost) along the front at Messines at dawn on 6 June 1916, the explosion was heard in London as a muffled roar. The following list contains most but not all of the expressions found in the records of men of the AIF to denote the cause of *admission to hospital*. They demonstrate—sometimes tragically, sometimes euphemistically—a clear case of extreme trauma: Neuralgia, Myalgia, Rheumatism, Debility, Multiple neuritis, DAH (Disordered Action of the Heart), VDH (Valvular Disorder of the Heart), Irritable Heart, Tachycardia, Melancolitis, Neurosis, NYD (Not Yet Diagnosed), NYDN (Not Yet Diagnosed Neurosis), Neurasthenia, Hypochondrium neurosis, Stress, Hysteria, Concussion (leading to medical discharge some months later), Disorder of Accommodation, Effort Syndrome, Mental, Nervous Breakdown, Premature Senility, Senility, inability to stand noise of shell fire, Facial Paralysis, Nervous Prostrations, prostrate convulsions, Mental Instability, Facial

Neuralgia, insanity, stammering, weak-mindedness, Dementia Praecox, and Cardiac Insufficiency.

In order to support the inclusion of these terms in the record review under the broad umbrella of 'shell shock', they must be placed in context and legitimated via some independent authority. A 2005 publication from Psychology Press by the highly regarded Maudsley institution,[26] *Shell Shock to PTSD, Military Psychiatry from 1900 to the Gulf War* (Maudsley Monographs Series Number 47), comprehensively covers the history of diagnosis and treatment of *what it terms* 'so-called shell shock'. The opening paragraph is useful to simply and quickly legitimise some of the previous descriptors in the list as accurate nomenclature and thereby validate their inclusion in the count for the incidence of traumatic stress caused by war:

> Military psychiatry in the UK is generally regarded as having begun in World War I and, indeed, the recognition of psychiatric injury in general. Certainly, it then became an important service designed in the main to treat troops suffering from so-called shell shock, the acute effects of battle, so that they could be returned to their units as quickly as possible. However, a significant developmental phase predated this conflict when physicians attempted to explain and treat servicemen suffering from a range of unexplained, somatic disorders, including disordered action of the heart (DAH) and psychogenic rheumatism. These arose in the context of 'palpitation' seen during the Crimean war and irritable heart described by Da Costa in the American Civil war. In addition, military doctors encountered cases whose symptoms suggested a neurological cause. They were both acute (cases of exhaustion after combat), and chronic (veterans who remained debilitated for years after the discharge), mirroring neurasthenia in the civilian population.[27]

As mentioned earlier, this type of terminology slowly evolved over time. For example, 'irritable heart' became 'DAH' during the Boer War and an additional term of rheumatism came into use. Anthony Bowlby (1855–1929), a civil surgeon, described some of the symptoms associated with shell shock:

> Among the symptoms we find predominantly, in the foreground pain, in the form of headache, generally posterior, pains in the neck, pains in the back and limbs, so that these cases are generally sent back as cases of rheumatism; general feebleness of the muscular system amounting to paralysis, more or less pronounced.[28]

The Maudsley presents further evidence in the 2005 Monograph, that, in 1917, an authority recommended that terms such as 'irritable heart' and 'DAH' be replaced by the term 'effort syndrome' because they conveyed the 'meaning of a primary cardiac disorder' and were therefore potentially misleading.[29] This in turn saw the early recognition of 'non-ulcer dyspepsia' overtaking the diagnosis of 'effort syndrome' in the Second World War.[30] While the term is predominantly used in this later war, a number of the first AIF soldier records note 'non-ulcer dyspepsia' as the reason for hospitalisation, and were therefore included in the record review in the collective terms counted as shell shock.

The definition of the frequently used terms of 'senility' and 'premature senility' for admission to hospital, for discharge 'medically unfit', for men aged in their 30s and early 40s, and the classification of 'debility' after suffering from pyrexia (trench fever) or another serious illness are now discussed in more detail, for inclusion in the general classification of shell shock.

The medical dictionary *Encyclopaedia Medica* was first published in 1902, followed by a second edition in 1924. With the hindsight offered by experiences of war, the second edition did not change its definition or discussion of senile insanity. It presents the view that the decline of the nervous system that occurs with old age should not begin before the sixtieth year. On the other hand, the encyclopaedia states that various exciting factors will reduce this age such as excessive alcohol consumption, syphilis or influenza. It explains:

> Influenza has been increasingly *evident in recent years* as cause of abnormal senility. This is especially the case when there have been recurrences of the illness. When there is a combination of these toxic producing factors as in cases of syphilis with alcoholism, or where influenza follows one of them, the tendency to degeneration becomes very marked.

Rheumatism, gout, and chronic Bright's disease are by no means uncommon members in this group. Overexertion of the brain, mental stress and worry, malnutrition, and traumatism are also frequent exciting causes.[31] [Emphasis added]

Encyclopaedia Medica goes on to describe the psychosis of senility, in particular, 'melancholia':

This is the most common form of psychosis in senility ... those who are very depressed and miserable, with melancholic expression and attitude, who sit mute and not moving voluntarily for hours. They are generally sleepless and constipated, with feeble and irregular action of the heart, with coldness and lividity of the extremities.[32]

For the record review, the decision was taken to list a soldier who is 'discharged medically unfit' as 'a soldier discharged medically unfit as a consequence of shell shock' in cases where the record notes the cause of his discharge to be 'debility' (after a protracted period of illness, such as pyrexia or malaria). The basis for this interpretation is the cited *Encyclopaedia Medica* of the time. The argument is made here that, as in modern-day diagnostics, a protracted illness among First World War servicemen often precipitated the mental and physical breakdown that manifested in post-traumatic stress.

It is believed that, overall, causal allocation to shell shock in this analysis is a conservative underestimation of its occurrence as there is limited recorded evidence in the soldier files. A simple observation supports this contention. Officers' records rarely mention the incidence of traumatic stress, merely using the general euphemism of SOS, or 'struck off strength', with no cause given. As argued earlier, this treatment likely hides many instances of shell shock diagnoses, unless of course one believes that the officer was, indeed, made of sterner stuff.

At this point it is important to reiterate that the use of the term shell shock is a misnomer; but as the British War Office Committee stated in 1922, we are stuck with the term and it is too late to change it now. 'So-called shell shock' covers a wide range of traumatic stress diagnoses grouped together today under the descriptors PTSS or

PTSD. The term has been used as a broad umbrella in this analysis to cover a multitude of manifestations of traumatic stress suffered by soldiers in the First World War. Its use is a convenient substitute for 'severe traumatic stress', which still today is known by multiple terminologies.

The definition of shell shock, or PTSS/PTSD, is still debated today and strongly opposing views are held. By way of example, the following snapshots are presented below in order to conclude this discussion of a most chilling consequence of exposure to war.

Provided here are the abstracts of a number of recent articles published in the Australian Defence Force magazine *ADF Health Journal*. In October 2006, an article was published by Professor Alexander McFarlane, Head of the University of Adelaide Centre for Military and Veteran's Health and Professor Mark Creamer, Director of the Australian Centre for Post-traumatic Mental Health, entitled 'Current Knowledge about Psychological Trauma: A Response to Milton'.[33] It takes issue with an article published the year before by Group Captain (Retd) Rod Milton, entitled 'Psychological Trauma and the ADF'.[34] The abstract for the response states:

> We rebut a number of the assertions made by Milton in the October 2005 issue of *ADF Health*. A substantial body of epidemiological research informs about the prevalence, risks and burdens of disease associated with post-traumatic stress disorder (PTSD). To suggest that PTSD is created by treatment and the possibility of compensation denies the complexity of the issues at stake. There is effective treatment for PTSD and the Australian Defence Force has an important duty of care to ensure the early identification and treatment of ADF members adversely affected by their service. Equally, many service personnel benefit and are not damaged by the deployment experience, and the challenge is to build resilience and assist those who are injured. Early identification and treatment of psychological morbidity in the ADF is critical to operational effectiveness in an age of technological warfare. These disorders are known to have major detrimental effects on the information processing capacity of individuals, and this presents a major risk to the survival of the individual and group.

Another article in *ADF Health Journal*, published in December 2008, presents evidence that, far from a narrowing in definition, the field is expanding, as the paper describes the condition in the following terms: 'Traumatic brain injury (TBI) caused by a bomb blast has been described as the signature wound of the war on terror'.[35] Written by Major Nick Ford, a psychiatrist, and Brigadier Geoffrey Rosenfeld, Director of General Health Reserves and Director of Neurosurgery at the Alfred Hospital, the article's title is 'Mild Traumatic Brain Injury and Bomb Blast: Stress, Injury or Both?' It seems that the debate has not moved on very far since 1922. Two of the five points made in the December 2008 article's abstract are as follows:

> Concussion occurring in United States soldiers deployed in Iraq is strongly associated with post-traumatic stress disorder (PTSD) and physical health problems 3 to 4 months after they returned home. Multiple bomb blast exposures may be cumulative in the post-concussional effects. There are likely to be increasing numbers of Australian personnel returning from the Middle Eastern and Afghanistan who have had exposure to blast injury, and joint health professionals need to consider and document any TBI [traumatic bomb injury] component when assessing other aspects of their mental status.[36]

The concerns raised here about the potential effects of the exposure to multiple bomb blasts highlight the extent to which AIF soldiers were exposed to conditions in the field during the First World War that were conducive to shell shock. Multiple exposures to bomb blast, at times measured in hundreds of thousands, would have been a frequent occurrence in the trenches along the Western Front as barrages lasted for days on end prior to an advance. And the fact that periods of deployment were measured in years would have exacerbated this impact. The suggestion that exposure to blasts may be cumulative in their effect further underscores the chilling, likely prevalence of mental health problems for the men of the first AIF.

It is contended that this detailed discussion on shell shock provides sufficient substance to allow for the practical interpretation and classification of an extremely complex medical condition, as proposed for in the main random sample count of the record review.

The extent of the impact of shell shock demands, at the very least, an attempt at its quantification, and in a manner that will produce a conservative outcome.

Moving on, there are several causes of death, in particular non-battle causes, which also warrant assessment in the record review owing simply to their devastating impact. Accidental death among the soldiers of the First World War often involved horses, but also incidents of drowning and even electrocution. Other causes of non-battle death included suicide and murder. The examination of soldier records also highlighted the causes of death due to illness, three of which were present at significant levels. The pandemic of Spanish Flu, now known to be the H1N1 virus, swept through Australia's military forces as it did through all belligerent armies. By quantifying its impact, a comparison can be made in particular with the devastating impact of the disease on the American forces. The other deadly disease to be quantified is cerebro-spinal meningitis (CSM). While largely overshadowed by the worldwide devastation caused by Spanish Flu, CSM had a serious impact on the AIF, particularly soldiers gathered together for training in camps in Victoria and South Australia in 1916. Its impact was similar to the well documented, but to date generally underestimated death toll from tuberculosis (TB) during the war. All three causes of non-battle death can be quantified and date-of-occurrence plots produced for each. The first two of these causes require further discussion, because they provide a measure of the efficacy of Australian civil and medical authorities in addressing these problems, which has not been previously quantified.

Prior to the general epidemic of 1915, the head of the Australian Department of Community Services and Health, the celebrated JH Cumpston, pointed to sporadic and small outbreaks of CSM occurring mainly in NSW.[37] Its occurrence increased and became notifiable first in South Australia in 1902 and then later in all states by 1915. By then a very serious and extensive outbreak had commenced in Victoria and South Australia, and it became acute in all states in 1916, subsiding slightly during 1917 and at the end of 1918, finally ceasing to be an epidemic. Its occurrence in Australia coincided with the epidemic's sweep through Europe and, according to Cumpston, 'the disease rampaged through the military camps of all combatant nations in World War I'.[38] The civilian population was not immune. Cumpston reported that, in the four months from August to

November 1915, the incidence of reported cases in Victoria was over 600, of which 200 were military cases and the other two-thirds were civilian, and many resulted in death. At its height, efforts to control the spread of CSM included the closure of theatres in Melbourne. Deaths from the disease in the AIF can be quantified and a date plot of its occurrence produced. This will provide an enlightening measure of its impact for comparison with the incidence of Spanish Flu. But more importantly, it reveals how Australian public health standards and responses, in particular by utilising isolation, were leading the world, and significantly reduced the impact on both the civilian and military populations.

It is argued here that the impact of Spanish Flu on Australia's forces was mild in comparison to that facing other military forces such as the United States Army. While this assertion is not new, the reasons behind the limited impact on Australians deserve discussion. Recent research in 2010 into this limited impact on the AIF was funded by the US Department of Defence and carried out by Dennis Shanks and a large multi-disciplinary team. Their study concluded that Australian soldiers were less impacted because of multiple prior exposures to influenza viruses during their longer war service compared to the exposure of US servicemen. Shanks et al. state that: 'The protective effect of increased service likely reflected increased acquired immunity to influenza viruses and endemic bacterial strains that caused secondary pneumonia and most of the deaths during the 1918–1919 influenza pandemic.'[39] And subsequently, 'in the fall of 1918, soldiers who were new to military service were at the highest risk of dying after influenza virus infection'.[40] The record review provides evidence that disputes these conclusions and raises the question of why Australia's *civilian population* was also lightly impacted, and why there were over 50 000 American soldier deaths in camps and depots across America *before* embarkation.[41] This death toll, predominantly from Spanish Flu, represents 40 per cent of the USA's claimed war-related deaths from this conflict. More will be said about this in Chapter 7, but an important observation in relation to Australia's medical responses of the time is worth noting here.

It is generally accepted that Australia's *non-indigenous* population suffered 12 000 deaths from Spanish Flu. But when compared to other nations this is still a relatively small death toll. Again referencing Milton Lewis, in his 2003 work:

15 to 50% of the populations of countries in Europe, the Americas, India, Africa, East Asia and Pacific were affected, and 21 to 30 million people, depending on estimates, died worldwide. Australia maintained strict maritime quarantine, particularly against ships from South Africa and New Zealand. New Zealand instituted no maritime quarantine, and its European population suffered more than double the death rate of Australia's. Cumpston's quarantine measures probably kept at bay for a while the more virulent strain from the northern hemisphere, perhaps mitigating the virulence and so producing the lower mortality rate in comparison to New Zealand. Commonwealth control of interstate quarantine had been accepted in November 1918, but the states broke ranks when outbreaks began in Melbourne and Sydney in January. New South Wales interdicted sea and land traffic with Victoria where the first cases had appeared. Queensland indicated an intention to close its border with New South Wales, which suffered about half the country's deaths. Western Australia seized the Commonwealth transcontinental train, suspending traffic on the line. The governmental crisis continued until June 1919 when it was clear that the States' unilateral actions had not protected them and the Commonwealth took over quarantine again. The Federal Quarantine Act was amended in 1920 to incorporate a provision that in emergencies the Commonwealth would override any state measure.[42]

These clumsy but nevertheless effective efforts at control and containment in Australia reflected the previous efforts of the Commonwealth's first Director-General of Public Health, JHL Cumpston, in 1913, by initiating public protection through quarantine. It is contended that this approach to disease control owes much to the AIF's extensively developed isolation camps in its overseas and Australian bases which were strictly used for the containment of other infectious diseases like mumps and measles, and outbreaks of CSM in bases in Australia and France in 1916. The soldier records show frequent references to soldiers being sent to isolation camps following mumps or CSM exposure. Just as Cumpston was a world leader in public health control, it is argued that Australia's military maintained world-leading health control systems, developed over the course of the war, so were readily and therefore quickly made available in the ensuing panic upon the arrival of the devastating Spanish Flu pandemic in Australia. Stephen Garton sets the scene:

> Australians feared that returning soldiers would bring the flu home, and deaths on troopships prompted swift action. Australian authorities introduced stringent quarantine measures involving detentions of more than a week if cases of infection were discovered. Such measures were condemned as a 'flu muddle' by soldier organisations who blamed authorities for allowing the troopships to dock in infected ports.[43]

It was a widely held view that large numbers of deaths occurred as a consequence of the close contact among soldiers on the troopships on the way home. While this was possibly the case among American troops, both going to the war and when returning home (although this will be disproved in Chapter 7), it is contended that this was not the case for Australian soldiers returning at the end of the First World War. The record review supports this contention, based on the Australian Attestation Papers which include death, injury and illness aboard troopships going to and from the war zone. Nor is it the case that AIF soldiers were exposed to the flu when they docked at ports on the way home. An accurate count and location of this disease's impact will add substance to the claim that Australia's civil and military medical services used quarantining and isolation to great effect.

Notes

1. Butler, *Official Medical History of the Australian Army Medical Services, 1914–1918, Volume III*, Australian War Memorial, Canberra, 1942, p. 148–189.
2. Peter Stanley, *Bad Characters, Sex, Crime, Mutiny, Murder and the Australian Imperial Force*, Murdoch Books, Sydney, 2010, p. 242.
3. ibid., p. 36, 228.
4. Zwar, in Butler, *Official Medical History of the Australian Army Medical Services, 1914–1918, Volume III*, p. 173.
5. ibid., p. 152.
6. ibid., p. 154.

7   Butler, *Official Medical History of the Australian Army Medical Services, 1914–1918, Volume III*, p. 189.
8   Leo van Bergen, *Before My Helpless Sight: Suffering, Dying and Military Medicine on the Western Front, 1914–1918* (trans. Liz Waters, 2009 ed.), Ashgate Publishing Limited, 1999 (reprint, 2009), p. 149.
9   Milton James Lewis, *The People's Health: Public Health in Australia, 1788–1950 (Contributions in Medical Studies Series), Volume I*, Praeger, Westport, CT, 2003, p. 231.
10 JHL Cumpston, Milton James Lewis, and Australian Department of Community Services and Health, *Health and Disease in Australia: A History*, Australian Government Publishing Service, Canberra, 1989, p. 273.
11 D Coward, 'The Impact of War on NSW, Some Aspects of Social and Political History, 1914–1917', thesis, Australian National University, 1974, p. 159.
12 Lewis, *The People's Health: Public Health in Australia, 1788–1950 (Contributions in Medical Studies Series)*, p. 230.
13 Cumpston, Lewis, and Australian Department of Community Services and Health, *Health and Disease in Australia: A History*, p. 266, 267.
14 Peter Leese, *Shell Shock: Traumatic Neurosis and the British Soldiers of the First World War*, Palgrave Macmillan, 2002, p. 34, 41.
15 Richard Lindstrom, 'The Australian Experience of Psychological Casualties in War 1915–1939', PhD thesis, Victoria University of Technology, 1997, p. 12.
16 ibid., p. 13.
17 Stephen Garton, *The Cost of War: Australians Return*, Oxford University Press, Melbourne, 1996, p. 153.
18 ibid., p. 145, 146.
19 ibid., p. 155.
20 ibid., p. 152.
21 Documenting diagnosis for hospital stays of less than seven days was not prioritised.
22 British War Office Committee, 'Report of the War Office Enquiry into "Shell Shock"', British War Office, 1922, p. 4.
23 Fiona Reid, *Broken Men, Shell Shock, Treatment and Recovery in Brtain 1914–1930*, Continuum, UK, 2010, p. 85.
24 British War Office Committee, 'Report of the War Office Enquiry into "Shell Shock"', p. 97.
25 ibid., p. 119.
26 Henry Maudsley, from whom the series of monographs takes its name, was the founder of The Maudsley Hospital and the most prominent English psychiatrist of his generation. The hospital treated shell shock victims from WW1 and is now a school of Kings College London, entrusted with the duty of advancing psychiatry through teaching and research. The monograph series reports high-quality empirical work on a single topic of relevance to mental health, carried out at the Maudsley.
27 Edgar Jones and Simon Wessley (eds), *Shell Shock to PTSD, Military Psychiatry from 1900 to the Gulf War (Maudsley Monographs Series)*,

Psychology Press on behalf of The Maudsley, Hove and New York, Number 47, 2005, p. 1.
28 Bowlby, in ibid., p. 11.
29 ibid., p. 194.
30 ibid., p. 196.
31 Alexander Goodall and Chalmers Watson, 'Potassii Bromidum to Singultus', in *Encyclopaedia Medica*, William Green and Sons, Edinburgh, 1924, p. 569, 571. [Italics have been added for emphasis.]
32 ibid., p. 574.
33 Alexander McFarlane and Mark Creamer, 'Current knowledge about psychological trauma: a response to Milton', *ADF Health Journal*, vol. 7, no. 2, October, 2006.
34 Rod Milton, 'Psychological trauma and the ADF', *ADF Health Journal*, vol. 6, no. 2, October 2005.
35 Nick Ford and Jeffrey Rosenfeld, 'Mild traumatic brain injury and bomb blast: stress injury or both?', *ADF Health Journal*, vol. 9, no. 2, December 2008.
36 ibid.
37 Cumpston, Lewis, and Australian Department of Community Services and Health, *Health and Disease in Australia: A History*, vol. 201, no. 15, 12 June 2010, p. 321.
38 ibid., p. 323.
39 G Dennis Shanks and et al, 'Mortality Risk Factors During the 1918–1919 Influenza Pandemic in the Australian Army', *The Journal of Infectious Diseases*, vol. 201, no. 15, June 2010, p. 1880.
40 ibid., p. 1888.
41 United States Army Medical Department, *The Medical Department of the United States Army in the World War, Vol XV, Part 2, Medical and Casualty Statistics*, US Army Surgeon General's Office, US, 1925, Table 96, p. 954.
42 Lewis, *The People's Health: Public Health in Australia, 1788–1950 (Contributions In Medical Studies Series)*, p. 181.
43 Garton, *The Cost of War: Australians Return*, p. 15.

CHAPTER 5
Counting the Diggers (3): Multiple Examples of Harm

AIF individual soldier records provide specific information about the extensive array of casualties suffered by these civilian soldiers. A very important point needs to be made here. As the record review in this book moves towards producing an aggregated result representing the true extent of the pain and suffering of these men, we must not lose sight of the individual experiences that comprise the terrible numbers of total casualties. This chapter aims to remind us of the many varied, mostly tragic consequences of exposure to the conflict of the First World War, for men who were essentially civilians with only a few months of preparation. It should be noted that in selecting the following service records, a conscious effort was made not to choose sensationalist or extreme examples and therefore it is believed that the selection that follows represents a balanced cross-section of soldier experiences. Certainly more mundane records exist, but the examples presented in this chapter do raise the ominous spectre of a tragically extensive casualty toll. A second purpose in providing these examples is to demonstrate the many judgements and interpretations that were required to be made regarding this array of experiences so that the end results can be supported by the claim that they are comprehensive, accurate and conservative.

Most soldiers' records start with the striking feature of a 2.5-centimetre letter stamped on the first page: 'A' for alive on discharge, 'B' for prisoner of war, 'D' for soldier deceased, 'W' for an officer and 'Z' for an officer deceased. Before examining the records, a category was required to account for 'non-applicable' soldier records, essentially eliminating those men who did not go to war. This category of 'not applicable' is broad and was discussed in the previous chapter. It *generally* accounts for all those enlisted personnel *who did not embark* overseas to a theatre of war. Some examples of the potential reasons for not embarking are as follows: W Burton was discharged medically unfit shortly after enlisting, S Burton at his own request and WA Burton at his parents' request (these three Burton men were not related). Charles William Webber enlisted on 13 July 1915. His file contains a letter from his wife to a senior politician stating that her husband had enlisted without her knowledge; she was in financial difficulty and suffered from poor health. Charles was discharged 'for family reasons owing to wife's poor health' in November 1915. The authorities appeared relatively lenient in granting a requested discharge prior to embarkation. However, this attitude changed dramatically once the soldier had left Australia. LT Whitehead's (1029) mother wrote a tragic letter of request in August 1918 that her son be sent home as she had already lost two sons in the war. Her request was refused. Her son survived. Medical Officer Captain AK Gault requested to be returned to Australia for 'family reasons' in January 1918; the request was granted.

Other examples of the 'not applicable' category include that of David Webber, who enlisted on 4 January 1917, yet four weeks later was discharged 'services no longer required'. Still others were discovered to be under- or over-age. Frank Ward enlisted on 18 September 1916 and was sent to a garrison at Rabaul. The volunteers stationed at Rabaul could effectively come and go as they pleased and the region was declared by the Australian Government to not be a 'theatre of war' on 21 September 1914. As a result of this declaration, their service was seen as administrative only and they received the British Medal awarded to all servicemen who embarked but did not receive the Victory Medal awarded for service in a theatre of war. This was advised to Captain GE Simcock, who saw service in Rabaul, following his enquiry regarding his eligibility for another medal after the war, and his complaint that he had only received one, the British Medal.

Others were simply too late, like Norman Graham, who was an eighteen-and-a-half-year-old drover who enlisted on 30 July 1918. He 'passed his riding test' a week later but was demobilised on 18 November 1918, still not having left Australia. At this late stage of the war the army was still sending cavalrymen. The time taken to prepare soldiers for embarkation varied widely but enlistments from about May 1918 were increasingly unlikely to embark and were instead likely to be discharged due to the cessation of hostilities. Others, we have previously mentioned, were in transit at sea when the war ended. In such cases, nearly all troopships were recalled at sea and these men were discharged back in Australia 'due to cessation of hostilities'. Consequently they were awarded one medal only as they were considered not to have served in a theatre of war. An example of this was the case of William Sievers, who enlisted on 23 July 1918, underwent preparation at the Broadmeadows recruitment depot outside Melbourne and embarked on 22 October on troopship *Boonah*, which was recalled at sea and returned to Australia where he was discharged on 1 February 1919. All men in these circumstances are *not* included in the record review in order to arrive at a number of Australia's *actual fighting force* commitment. This treatment will lower Australia's participation rate as currently represented by official embarkation figures but it accurately represents the intention of this statistic and aligns with the similar practice adopted by other belligerents in producing their official histories of the conflict, such as Britain, Canada and the USA.

In another inclusion to the *did-not-embark* category, there are a *very small* number of cases where a count under the category of 'non-applicability' is made for the soldier who effectively spent his time of service overseas in jail so that there was no contribution to war service. This treatment is supported by the refusal of the Army Medal Board to award any medals in these cases. Exemplary here is the case of Reg Williams (5432), who arrived in England in late 1916, was admitted to hospital on 21 January 1917 with VD, was discharged from hospital, and thereafter was dispatched to France in early February, where he went absent without leave (AWL) for seventeen hours and was fined thirty days pay. Reg did it properly the next time and went AWL on 19 April until he was apprehended three weeks later. He was sentenced to life imprisonment on 14 May 1917. Four weeks later, as was common, his sentence was reduced to two years. He was released from jail on 18 May 1918 with the unserved portion (a year) of his sentence suspended. Seven days later he again went AWL, presumably while the authorities were preparing to dispatch him back to his unit on the Western Front. He walked into camp three months later and was again sentenced to a two-year jail term. He was discharged and released from prison on 6 September 1919. He did not receive any medals and received very little pay.

The recording of a death in the soldier's record is straightforward; however, *when* it occurred is not. The death of a soldier is recorded if it occurs prior to embarkation, or after return to Australia but prior to discharge, in addition to death during service overseas. Returned servicemen who died shortly after discharge will be the subject of later scrutiny when post-war impacts are examined in Chapter 8. However, examples exist of death after the disbandment of the AIF that were attributed to service and formally acknowledged as such, but the soldier's name is not included in the Roll of Honour. Such an example is that of RC Williams (10010), who enlisted on 21 January 1916 at the age of twenty-four years. Later that year he was admitted to hospital on two occasions, once for tonsillitis and then a protracted period of ninety days while being treated for VD. In July 1920, during his return to Australia, he was admitted to the ship's hospital suffering from pleurisy. He was discharged medically unfit upon his arrival home, then contracted TB, and after a long battle he died in July 1922. A note on his file from the Repatriation Commission to War Records states that his death was due to war service, after a representation from his next of kin claiming that he had contracted TB on board the troopship. His family received a Memorial Plaque and Scroll, but his name was not included on the Roll of Honour. Data entries in the record review for this soldier include two hospitalisations for battle-related illness and one for non-battle-related illness, as well as an entry for his medically unfit discharge and his war-related death. Arguments will be made in Chapter 8, as previously mentioned, about the criteria for entry on the Roll of Honour, particularly in relation to its cut-off date of 31 March 1921. Suffice to say, at this stage, that the counting in this analysis of this soldier as a war-related death (after the cut-off date), as it clearly was, was *rarely done* in the record review count. This example has been chosen deliberately to highlight its exceptional treatment in this way and to expose the arbitrary nature of the Roll of Honour cut-off date criteria.

Some cases were not as clear. Walter Shephard (15054) was thirty-one years of age when he enlisted on 26 October 1915. He was admitted to hospital in September 1917 with pleurisy and evacuated to England five weeks later. And then on 16 December 1917 it was determined to return him to Australia as discharged medically unfit, with a diagnosis of TB. He was bedridden for some six months upon his return until his death at the State Sanatorium, Perth. It is not known why the authorities deemed it necessary to discharge him from the AIF medically unfit on 6 August 1918, eight days before he died with his wife by his side. His medical board report concludes that he had contracted the disease while on active service but, most unusually, nothing on his file indicates that he was included on the Roll of Honour or that the associated Memorial Plaque and Scroll were issued to his wife. There is merely a handwritten note entered on the record that reads 'died after discharge'. The data entry in the record review count for this soldier will therefore be for one battle-related hospitalisation, one discharged medically unfit, and his death will be counted as related to war service. Yet Walter's name *is* included on the AWM Roll of Honour. One is left to speculate on how this failed to be recorded on his file, but an observation in relation to many other cases appears to support the following assertion. If a deceased soldier had active next of kin who pressured the authorities persistently, a soldier's death after the war or discharge resulted in a review, and occasionally led to his name being recorded on the Roll of Honour. Yet Walter's widow does not appear to have received a Memorial Plaque or Scroll either. Perhaps she did not want them.

The efforts of the next of kin of Ottawa Sharrock (6123) were rewarded. This soldier enlisted just prior to his twenty-first birthday and ten months later was hospitalised suffering from influenza at the end of 1916. He was then diagnosed with TB early in 1917 and was discharged medically unfit with condition 'improved'. However, he subsequently died on 17 December 1919 and his father made an application for the inclusion of his son's name on the Roll of Honour. His death certificate states that the cause of death was 'gas poisoning'. It is unclear whether this was suicide or whether it was shorthand for ruined lungs linked to TB, which in turn was linked to being gassed on the battlefield. Yet in his records there is *no mention* of such a wounding occurring. In the absence of any other evidence, this soldier's death was not counted as self-inflicted. And his name is on the Roll of Honour.

Other occurrences of death *after* discharge also presented problems. Two records, coincidentally one following the other alphabetically of soldiers with identical names of John Webster, are cases in point. The John Webster with the serial number 11 had documentation in his file that he had died well before 10 April 1922, by which time he would have been twenty-six years of age. His record showed that he was discharged from the AIF during the war, as he was given a commission in the British Army. He is not on the Roll of Honour. Yet the circumstantial evidence on his file suggests that he was killed while serving as an officer in the British Army, hence *during* the war. The second John Webster, serial number 2206, tells the story of a soldier hospitalised four times, three for VD. The other hospitalisation was for shrapnel wounds which resulted in the amputation of his arm, leading to discharge, medically unfit, with a pension for his mother and himself. He died from cardiac arrest in 1924 aged forty-six. His mother wrote to the army convinced that his death was due to his war service. But his record remains unaltered, with the notation 'died after discharge'. *Neither example* was counted in the record review as war related. However, in Chapter 8, the case will be put for these soldiers, and those with similar outcomes, to be included in Australian death casualties of the First World War. The likes of these two John Websters should, and will be counted, in the analysis of post-war impacts examined in Chapter 8.

A case of a death after discharge that *is* on the Roll of Honour is that of Herbert Sievwright, who contracted TB in July 1917. He was discharged medically unfit in May 1918, and died from the disease in December 1920. His death is counted as war related in this analysis. Then there is the case of Edward Gawley, appointed Captain upon enlistment as he was a dentist. After service overseas he returned to Australia after the war, left the service in August 1919 but died in October 1920 from 'chronic nephritis' (kidney failure). He is not on the Roll of Honour and was *not* counted as a war-related death in this record review, although nephritis was rife among the men of the AIF and he may well have contracted the disease during his period of service.

The recording of the date taken on strength (that is, when the soldier was placed on active service) was deemed necessary for the purposes of analysis of the correlation between the time from enlistment to battle exposure and then subsequent death. Often it is quite clear, so that the date on which the individual arrived at his first appointment, say, in France, is noted. However, if a soldier took part in the Gallipoli campaign, frequently the date of his arrival in this theatre is not recorded; for such cases it has been conservatively decided that the Gallipoli landing date of 25 April 1915 will be adopted for this record review. This has the effect of increasing a soldier's time spent in the field. Occasionally, it was observed that a stamp appeared on the record stating that the soldier embarked from Alexandria on 3 or 4 April when sailing time to the Gallipoli Peninsula was one or two days. According to Professor Robin Prior, the troops were sent to the island of Lemnos to practise landings before facing the real thing on 25 April 1915.

A similar absence of date occurs in some records for soldiers who arrived on the Western Front via Marseilles, when soldiers were moved there from staging bases in North Africa in 1916. With respect to these bases, unless the soldiers were assigned to the Light Horse, Serapeum, Suez, Alexandria, Zeitoun, Mudros, Tel-el-Kebir or Chezireh, they are not treated as theatres of war for the purposes of this statistical assessment. For servicemen who arrived in France from these staging bases in 1916, the only record is the date of disembarkation at the Port of Marseille. For unknown reasons (it is suspected that circumstances were somewhat disorganised at that time), the majority of these records do not list the subsequent date of assignment to a fighting unit. Normally, among soldiers being moved from England to Etaples, for example, the next recorded date is for other events, such as transfers or casualties; but for the men who landed in France via Marseille a clear-cut TOS is rarely noted in their records. In these cases, the date TOS is recorded in the count analysis conducted after the record review, as the disembarkation date in Marseille. This is again conservative because clearly the time spent in Marseille being allocated and transferred to a unit would have been days or even weeks. Transfers to training battalions from these French landing bases are not considered to be 'in the field' and therefore do not trigger TOS.

Once the date of TOS is recorded then the records can be explored to determine the number of days for which men were exposed to battle before their demise, if that was their fate. This data collection informs the analysis presented in Chapter 6 of the possible correlation with other factors such as length of time spent in training, length of time of survival and whether this changed during the course of the war, or with age or rank. The calculation of the time spent in the field is difficult and dependent on record details, but it can be carried out to a level that can be regarded as accurate to arrive at a good estimate for the intended purpose.

The time 'out of the field' includes time spent away on leave or at a specific training school; time spent in hospital and convalescence depots; time spent AWL, of which there was a great deal, followed by often substantial time spent in jail as a consequence; and the considerable amount of time taken to move men into and out of the Western Front. Simple triggers for date selection might be the date of wounding followed by a note in the record such as 'March out England via …' to return to the soldier's unit, 'March in France' or simply 'rejoin unit ex hospital'.

The following example represents one of the more onerous for the calculation of time spent in the field. William Alfred Hone (893) enlisted on 18 March 1916, aged twenty-one years. He was admitted to hospital in August 1916 'not yet diagnosed', or NYD, a term we have shown was commonly used to refer to traumatic stress around that time (as well as NYDN). He was discharged on 5 September only to be readmitted the following day. He had still not left England at that stage. He finally rejoined his unit in the field in France on 5 January 1917, but was admitted to hospital the next day with rheumatism and later diagnosed with VDH. Hone was discharged from hospital on 21 January but readmitted on 13 February 1917 with scabies. He did not rejoin his battalion until 12 July 1917, six months later. However, on the *same* day he returned to his unit, he was admitted to hospital suffering from 'nervous prostrations'. He was *sent back* to the front on 12 September 1917 only to be readmitted to hospital on 17 October with facial paralysis. He was sent back to England towards the end of November, committed various minor crimes, and *was returned* to the front on 23 June 1918. He was killed in action on 22 August 1918. The data collected for the record review of William's file recorded four woundings from shell shock and two battle-related illnesses (scabies and 'agina tactories'[1]). From the time when he had been TOS until he was killed—a total of 630 days or twenty-one months—he had only spent 112 days or fewer than four months in the field. Much of the balance of seventeen months since he was TOS had been spent in hospital.

Injury and illness were not the only cause of excessive time spent away from 'the field'. Francis Charles Wilkin (1357) was twenty-two years of age when he enlisted on 7 July 1915 and was assigned to the Light Horse Reserve Regiment in March of the following year. It would have been better if Frank had stayed at home, as this volunteer was to spend a large part of 1916, most of 1917 and over half of 1918 in jail, escaped from jail or AWL. In total, he was to forfeit 548 days' pay. He was hospitalised twice; in March 1916 for diarrhoea and in September 1916 for sixteen days after contracting VD. He was finally marched out of the Light Horse Regiment on 5 August 1918; they had had enough of him, and he was TOS with the 29th Brigade nine days later. He was killed in action shortly afterwards on 30 September 1918, tragically only four days before all Australian troops were withdrawn from the Western Front. This soldier's data entry will consist of two entries for illnesses, battle related, and his death after effectively just forty-seven days in the field over three years of service.

Recording the date of a man's enlistment will allow an assessment of age at enlistment, distribution of age and changes in the rates of enlistment during the course of the war. Some comment is required on the method adopted for the collection of data on soldiers' ages. Only officers' records consistently recorded a birthdate to the day. In the main, for other ranks, age at enlistment by month and year only was recorded, and some age by year only. This required a calculation to determine the month and year of birth. Age as utilised in this analysis is therefore primarily accurate to the month only. However, this lack of precision is inconsequential for the purposes for which this data will be used.

The category of injury covers the multitude of mainly accidental incidents resulting in a physical injury that required hospitalisation, whether in the field or in general service. Examples are frequent cases of synovitis, a potentially serious condition also known as 'washer-woman knee' as it results from kneeling for long periods of time. There is also the equally frequent incidence of hernias. It was not unusual for either condition to lead to discharge, medically unfit.

Any injury that may have been caused by self-harm was closely scrutinised by the authorities; and if self-harm was found to be the cause, the soldier would be sentenced to jail terms, to be served on discharge from hospital.

Hospitalisation for septic sores, or abscesses on hands, feet and the like, is entered as an injury, if not specifically referred to as a wounding. *Readmission* to hospital as a result of a previous admission for wounding is also categorised as an *injury admission*. It cannot be treated as another wounding. Any accidental shooting that occurred in a non-battle circumstance is treated as an injury. Broken limbs are another common example in this injury category.

Where a wounding is recorded in a soldier's record but notated with 'remained on duty' or similar, this occurrence is *not* counted in the record review, as the criterion of hospitalisation has not been met. For example, Percy Phillip Shepley (4185) enrolled on 31 August 1915 at the age of twenty years. He was admitted to hospital for heat exhaustion three weeks after his disembarkation at Tel-el-Kebir. Later in France he was reported to be wounded in action on 6 August 1916. This entry was subsequently altered two months later to 'wounded at duty'. He suffered from shrapnel wounds to his thigh on 22 April 1918, rejoining his unit on 13 June 1918. He then received a bullet wound to his shoulder and was admitted once again on 20 August 1918 for three months and then returned to Australia. He appears to have applied for pension benefits in 1954 (possibly as an age entitlement on turning 60, and is treated as such in the analysis). Data entry for this soldier only consisted of two woundings and one injury for the heat exhaustion. The wounding on 6 August 1916 is not counted owing to the notation in his record that suggests that he remained on duty. Also, it appears from his records that he was to be returned to Australia for discharge on medical grounds due to the gunshot wound. However, by the time he was processed and discharged on 14 April 1919, he had recovered sufficiently to be discharged owing to 'cessation of hostilities'.

The distinction between 'battle' and 'non-battle' in the definition of illness was initiated in the British official medical history, as previously discussed. The categorisation of 'battle'-related illness is self-explanatory and examples are given shortly. The definition of non-battle is not as clear. The approach was to draw some distinction between illnesses that commonly occur among the general public in Australia and those illnesses that result from exposure in general service to battle in the field. This distinction was merely following the convention at the time and the numbers in both categories are totalled to calculate the total number of hospitalisations at the end in this record review. The limited list of illnesses commonly occurring in the general public at the time included in this category are appendicitis, mumps, measles and tonsillitis. Examples of battle-related illness include trench foot, trench fever and pyrexia, malaria, diarrhoea (often revised to a diagnosis of dysentery), scabies and many other skin-related conditions. In terms of skin-related conditions, there was a devastating array of bacterial skin infections at the time which could not be treated but simply had to run their course, as antibiotics had not been developed. Included in the battle category is the incidence of VD, although this is also counted separately. As the numbers in the categories are added to produce total hospitalisation numbers, this treatment as battle related is merely administrative. *Where hospitalisation occurs without the cause being recorded, the event is counted as 'battle related'.* A rough estimate of the occurrence of this default treatment was at less than 5 per cent.

Often an illness or wounding resulted in a soldier first being admitted to a field hospital; and then being transferred to a base hospital, specifically a transfer to 'Blighty' (the term used to describe England); admission in England to one, two or even three hospitals before a transfer to a convalescence depot, before leave is granted; and then followed by a transfer overseas to rejoin his unit. However, in such cases only *one* hospitalisation is counted. The record must show that the soldier has been discharged for at least a day, not for the purpose of transfer, before any subsequent hospitalisation is counted as a separate event. (The only exception to this continuous hospitalisation rule is in the case of admission for VD, which will be discussed further below.) In the event of a transfer from one hospital to another where the record shows that the admitting diagnosis has changed, the rule remains that only one hospitalisation is counted.

A change in diagnosis occurs most often in the event of an illness that presents as a fever which may be described as trench fever on admission, pyrexia on one transfer, then PUO (pyrexia of unknown origin) on another. Similarly interchangeable diagnoses are evident in relation to the conditions on admission described as diarrhoea, gastritis, enteritis and dysentery. Still another variation occurs when an admission is for PUO but upon transfer the diagnosis is changed to rheumatism, and then subsequently myalgia, prior to the soldier's discharge. This has been extensively discussed previously and will generally be recorded as a 'shell shock' discharge.

A good example of such is the case of Harold Gordon Carpenter (3717). He had just turned twenty-three years of age when he enlisted on 19 July 1915. He was TOS early in March 1916 but was admitted to hospital within four weeks, diagnosed with lumbago, a diagnosis subsequently changed to PUO, then influenza, and finally 'influenza and irritable heart'. He did not leave hospital. He was invalided to Australia on 10 June 1916 and discharged medically unfit, the cause recorded as irritable heart. He applied for pension benefits in 1927. The data entered for this soldier is a *single* hospitalisation under illness, battle related, and medical discharge due to shell shock.

It was evident that the incidence of mumps among the soldiers was common, and debilitating, with the average time spent in hospital in the order of two to three weeks. It could be argued that rates of infection were significantly heightened due to the close contact of army life. The records show that the strict adoption of isolation camps in the AIF played a role in the control of the spread of infectious disease. However, it is still likely that the incidence of mumps or measles was higher in the army compared to the rates in the general public. Nevertheless, these illnesses are incorporated into the category 'non-battle'. Hospitalisation for dental treatment is not counted. It was generally short-term or day admission only.

If the misplaced belief still exists that, once a soldier was hospitalised, seriously wounded or seriously ill, they were then returned to Australia for discharge, the following common experiences should dispel it. James Francis Whitehead (1938) enlisted on 30 June 1916 at the age of nineteen years. He was TOS unusually quickly at the end of October of that year, but was admitted to hospital one month later in France, a day after he arrived there diagnosed with influenza. He was transferred back to England to be admitted there on 7 December, with 'debility after influenza'. He was returned to France five weeks later. On 8 June 1917, he was wounded in action and evacuated to England. He again returned to France and rejoined his unit on 8

October 1917. Then in May 1918, there begins a series of short hospital admissions: admitted 18 May, then discharged 21 May (flu); admitted 23 May, then discharged 27 May (fever); and admitted 19 June, then discharged 12 July (myalgia). He was again admitted on 27 August 1918 with a very common injury to the knee, synovitis. This resulted in his evacuation to England for treatment which lasted some months. He was returned to Australia discharged medically unfit and was hospitalised for influenza on the ship on the way home, followed by ten days in the Shore Hospital at Portsea. He applied for pension benefits in 1927 and again in 1945. He died in 1951. This soldier's data entry is for two woundings (gunshot wound [GSW] and myalgia), one of which is for shell shock; four hospitalisations for battle-related illness (mainly influenza); one hospitalisation for injury (knee); and a discharge, medically unfit (assumed to be a result of his knee injury). While the debility following influenza could be counted as a case of shell shock, the hospitalisation was continuous, albeit back in England, and of much shorter duration under the debility diagnosis. It was treated as simply a case of illness.

There is a widespread understanding that some soldiers suffered from a casualty more than once but it is not generally appreciated that multiple hospitalisations were the norm. Benjamin Clifford Davies (2240) enlisted on 24 April 1915 at the age of twenty-one years. He landed on the beach at Gallipoli on 14 August and three weeks later was evacuated suffering from acute enteric fever. He spent two further periods in hospital for rheumatism and influenza in North African depots before being dispatched to the Western Front, disembarking at Marseilles on 8 June 1916. Eight weeks later he was wounded in action and evacuated to England where he spent sixteen months, during which time he recuperated from his wounds, got married to nineteen-year-old Florence Davenport, and had a further three hospitalisations for tonsillitis, mumps and suspected influenza. He was returned to France on 18 December 1917, one week before his first wedding anniversary and served a further two months before he was again hospitalised with PUO. He rejoined his unit and three weeks later was wounded again and evacuated to England. He was again hospitalised during his convalescence for influenza, finally returning to his unit on 20 August 1918. Sadly, he was killed in action one month later on 19 September 1918, only two weeks before all Australian troops were withdrawn from the Western

Front. In all, Benjamin Davies was hospitalised ten times, three times for wounding or shell shock, five times for battle, and twice for non-battle-related illness. Of the 1131 days of his service, he spent 911 days away from his unit, recovering from either his illness or wounds. Florence was to remarry within four years and received his Memorial Plaque. His father received the official photo of his son's grave in France. Benjamin's story is not exceptional.

A separate category of hospitalisation was compiled in the record review for shell shock, to quantify the enormity of the traumatic stress suffered by soldiers during, and long after, the First World War. Although this condition has already been discussed at length in the previous chapter, the interpretations of some examples are included below, and later in the discussion of the 'medically unfit' category. When stress-related symptoms were recorded in the soldiers' records as shell shock, it was categorised as a wounding and next of kin were advised as such. It is treated as a wounding in this count. Two records are discussed below, one of which presents a clear case of such classification and the other not so. Fred Furness Whitehead (3434) enlisted on 27 March 1917 at the age of twenty-seven years. Six months after disembarking at Moascar he was admitted to hospital on 15 June 1918 with malaria, but rejoined his unit two months later. He was admitted to hospital on 25 October, diagnosis 'debility'. His records show that he remained in hospital until he left for Australia *six months later* to be discharged medically unfit. He applied for pension benefits in 1935. His data entry is for one of illness, battle related (malaria); one wounding (debility from shell shock); and discharge caused by shell shock (owing to the length of time he spent in hospital). Ernest Albert West (10187) was aged twenty-four years when he enlisted on 14 January 1916. He was TOS in August 1916 but was admitted to hospital with 'shellshock' on 7 April 1917. He was discharged to duty three weeks later, but although he was qualified as a veterinary surgeon he was transferred in August to be a driver ('in excess', an expression used regularly which seems to imply part-time employment) at base headquarters, which was often the task assigned to those who had been wounded. He was admitted to hospital again on 4 November 1917 diagnosed with DAH, and discharged to a convalescence depot. Again he was readmitted on 23 November and then transferred to England, and finally returned to Australia two months later for discharge, cause 'shellshock. DAH'. He applied for pension benefits in 1928. His data entry is for three woundings (all for shell shock), and a medical discharge due to shell shock.

An attempt was made to quantify the impact of the Spanish Flu pandemic on the AIF. This was practically constrained owing to the lack of diagnosis noted in the records of this highly infectious, deadly and fast-acting influenza. Butler identified some statistics of the condition in the official medical services history but the incidence in the AIF appears to be quite low. A conservative approach is adopted here in accounting for a death resulting from the contraction of Spanish Flu. It is counted as such if the soldier's papers record a diagnosis of bronchitis or pleurisy, rapidly developing into pneumonia, followed by death in a matter of days. The outbreaks occurred in the French base at Etaples in 1916 and in England and France in mid to late 1918 and early 1919. A case in point is that of Captain Clerke Colquhoun Burton, who enlisted on 8 February 1915. He was thirty-one years of age and his previous military experience only consisted of a period of time spent in the school cadets. In his civilian career he was a fire loss adjuster and he did not survive the war. He was appointed Second Lieutenant and joined his battalion on the Gallipoli Peninsula on 3 September 1915. Nine weeks later he was evacuated with enteric fever, and then discharged in early January 1916 only to be readmitted one month later with dysentery. He was promoted to captain and transferred first to England, then to France, and then back to England for service in the canteens and catering for the AIF Headquarters for two and a quarter years. On 2 December 1918, he was attached to the Repatriation and Demobilisation Department in London. The specific date of his admission to hospital was not recorded but he suddenly died of illness in less than two weeks. His death certificate listed influenza followed by septic pneumonia, which quickly led to his death on 14 December 1918. As was common, he was unceremoniously struck off strength that day but he was accorded full military honours at his funeral. The data entry for this soldier is for two illnesses, battle related; and death from Spanish Flu.

Another example that also raises issues of interpretation is that of Clement West (809). He enlisted on 22 August 1914 and, despite his age of forty-nine years, was accepted, probably owing to his twelve years of service in the Royal Irish Rifles. He was wounded upon landing at Gallipoli on 25 April, evacuated only to be returned to the Gallipoli Peninsula on 18 November, but not before a hospitalisation for pneumonia that he contracted while recovering from his wound. Five days after his return to Gallipoli he was again admitted to hospital, suffering from neurasthenia. This diagnosis was changed to enteric, then VDH and he was discharged medically unfit. His medical record shows that he 'strained his heart on the Peninsula carrying water' which left him with pain over the heart and shortness of breath, and the reason noted for his discharge in July 1916 was 'strain and exposure'. He enlisted for home service only to suddenly die of pneumonia in April 1919. As only eight days passed between the date of his admission and the date of his death, it appears that Clement West died of Spanish Flu. He was included in Australia's Roll of Honour. His data entry is for two woundings: one for shell shock and one for illness, battle related (for the hospitalisation for pneumonia). He was entered as being discharged medically unfit from shell shock and was also included as a death from Spanish Flu.

No distinction is made in the count among the causes that lead to discharged medically unfit (that is, from wounding, injury or illness), with the exception of those cases where the record clearly shows that stress-related symptoms have led to that discharge, which are counted separately.

An example of such a case is that of James Albert Hart (2362). He was thirty-three years of age when he enlisted on 30 April 1915. He was admitted to hospital in September of that year with 'heart and bladder trouble'. Discharged and dispatched to service overseas, he disembarked at Marseilles towards the end of June 1916 only to be wounded three weeks later. He contracted dysentery while in hospital, recovered, convalesced, and rejoined his unit *ten* months after his wounding. Five weeks later he was admitted to hospital with rheumatism, which was subsequently rediagnosed as myalgia. He rejoined his unit after receiving three months of treatment on 30 August 1917. On 14 December 1917, he was admitted to hospital with a fever and diagnosed as having contracted PUO. He was transferred to England and eventually discharged to a convalescence depot at the end of March 1917. Within a month he was readmitted with gastritis, then rediagnosed with 'debility' and returned to Australia to be finally discharged medically unfit some ten months later, having undergone lengthy treatment at Caulfield Hospital in Melbourne, presumably for this condition. In this case the incidence of myalgia is treated as shell shock and counted as a wounding. The data therefore recorded for James Hart is two woundings (one for wounding, one for shell shock) and four admissions for illness. The discharged medically unfit is counted as due to shell shock. He applied for pension benefits in 1922 and again in 1930. He died in 1955 at the age of seventy-three years.

Herbert Hart (7065) was a 33-year-old librarian whose case represents another example of the apparent difficulty of diagnosing shell shock, even quite late in the war. He enlisted on 27 March 1917 and was TOS in France on 12 February 1918. He was listed as wounded in action on 30 March and his next of kin, his wife, was so advised on 24 April. His records were then altered to delete 'wounded in action' which was replaced with 'sick' and later 'NYDN'. This was further altered to 'sick (stammering)'. His wife was advised of the revised diagnosis of 'sick' on 24 June 1918. He rejoined his unit on 27 September of that year and was transferred to canteen duties. Subsequently he returned to Australia on 27 April 1919 and was discharged medically unfit with no cause recorded. The records reveal that these shell shock cases always seem to carry some ominous circumstantial evidence—in this case, for example, that Herbert was seriously damaged. He appears to have applied for pension benefits in 1927 and again in 1933. The evidence that he applied twice does not augur well and the sense of foreboding created by his record is not relieved with the recording of his death in 1939 at the age of only fifty-five years. The fact that his death appears on his record suggests a connection with his war service, possibly that he was in receipt of a pension. His data entry is for one hospitalisation for shell shock and discharged medically unfit due to shell shock, as no other evidence exists for the cause of his unfitness, other than his assignment to canteen duties.

Geoffrey John Hart's (964) experience was not uncommon in that as a young man he was diagnosed with rheumatism. He was nearly twenty-one years of age when he enlisted on 15 March 1915. On 1 November 1915, he was admitted to hospital suffering from dysentery and PUO contracted at Gallipoli and was moved to Malta. He was discharged on 16 January 1916, only to be readmitted five days later, this time for rheumatism. He returned to duty on 6 March and was transferred to France, where he was admitted to hospital suffering from mumps on 27 May for two weeks, returning to his unit in June. He sustained a minor gunshot wound to the head on 5 August 1916, once again rejoining his unit within a fortnight. He was then hospitalised on 5 November 1916 after sustaining abrasions to his feet and was transferred to England. 'Abrasions to his feet' seems an odd injury and it may have been a trench foot diagnosis. Inexplicably he did not rejoin his unit until the following year, in September 1917, after a ten month absence. The next entry on his record notes that he returned to Australia in February 1919 and was discharged, recorded as 'termination of period of enlistment' (TPE). He applied for pension benefits in 1924 and again in 1932. He died in 1956 at the age of sixty-two years. Data entry for this soldier is for two woundings, as the hospitalisation for rheumatism is treated as shell shock, one illness for battle-related causes and one for a non-battle-related cause (mumps), with one entry for the injury he sustained.

Many fine, fit young men succumbed to the indiscriminate condition of shell shock. Archibald Joseph Carter (26213) was a blacksmith when, at the age of twenty-three years, he enlisted on 27 March 1916. Not long after he was TOS in France on 10 January 1917, he was admitted to hospital with diarrhoea. He returned to his unit four months later but only lasted two months when he was again admitted and spent a further five weeks in hospital in June and July, diagnosed with DAH. He had been buried by earth thrown up by a shell blast. The medical board determined that he was unfit for service, and his record notes that he was 'buried by Shell—strain of service'. He was discharged in June 1918, his file reading 'medically unfit-disability-DAH'. It appears that he applied for pension benefits in 1925. Nothing further is known of this young blacksmith, but his record conveys a sense that he faced a difficult future. Data entry for this soldier is for one wounding for the hospitalisation with shell shock and one hospitalisation for illness, battle related. His medical discharge is counted as unfit due to shell shock.

James Joseph Graham (3429) listed his employment as a cook when at the age of thirty-seven years he enlisted, on 28 February 1916, only to be discharged medically unfit after eight days. He would live to regret his decision to re-enlist the next year on 14 August 1917. James was rushed through the system and was thrown into the deep end when he arrived in Moascar only eight weeks later on 19 October. He was admitted to hospital on four occasions for various durations of between two and six weeks, diagnosed with asthenia (weakness or loss of strength), in February, March, August and finally for four weeks in November 1918, after which he was returned to Australia and discharged medically unfit. He appeared to apply for pension benefits in 1930 and again in 1951. He died in 1955 aged seventy-three years. It is to be noted that the second application in 1951 was more likely to have been for an age-based pension benefit, so this will not be counted in the post-war impact analysis discussed in the final chapter. The data entry for this soldier is for four woundings and medical discharge, all due to shell shock.

Shell shock came in many guises, affecting young and old. Les Da Pinna (3271) enlisted on 22 March 1915 and was placed with the 6th Field Ambulance. He was nineteen years of age when they shipped him to Gallipoli. Young recruits were often assigned field ambulance duties, presumably because this was considered less dangerous, but no less horrendous. He was admitted to hospital and diagnosed first with debility, a diagnosis changed to diarrhoea, then dysentery, and finally nervous breakdown, all sustained at Gallipoli. He was invalided to England and then to Australia and on 13 July 1916 he was discharged medically unfit due to 'dysentery'. He applied for pension benefits in 1933 and may have been successful, as his file notes that he died in 1956. The data entry is for one hospitalisation for wounding (nervous breakdown) and one hospitalisation for illness, battle related (dysentery), as the final papers in his records clearly show two hospitalisations. The entry for the cause of the medically unfit discharge is shell shock, overriding—in light of the circumstances—the file notation of the cause of dysentery.

Relatively older recruits were often treated poorly, often with disdain. Henry Mackie Hall (3790) was a carpenter when he enlisted at the age of forty-four years and seven months on 19 July 1915. His age was just under the acceptable limit at that time. He received a gunshot wound to his face on 11 August 1916 and was admitted to the Canadian General Hospital in France at Etaples. He was returned to England for treatment, and subsequently rejoined his unit on 15 December 1916. He was initially reported missing in action on 11 April 1917, but then POW (and wounded at the time of capture). Hall 'had fairly harsh treatment in Germany', suffering from fever and other illness, and was hospitalised on at least one occasion, although his records are contradictory on this point. He was repatriated back to Australia and discharged medically unfit, cause 'premature senility', which according to the reason provided on his medical report was 'constitutional' and not as a consequence of 'active service', although notated as 'due (to) service'. And in response to the question on the same medical report 'Is the present degree of [premature senility] disability permanent?' the answer recorded is 'no' (on the last of several medical reports dated 17 August 1919). Henry's is a case that underscores the use of the term 'senility' in soldiers' medical records of the time, which is interpreted in this analysis as referring to what is now termed PTSS or PTSD. The data entry for this soldier is for two woundings; POW; and one illness, battle related. He is also counted as being discharged medically unfit due to shell shock. There is no evidence that he applied for a pension benefit; but he was certainly discharged without one.

Similarly badly treated was one Herbert Joshua Hall (1917), no relation to the previous example, who enlisted on 8 February 1916, aged forty-three years; he was married and a wool classer by trade. He was first admitted to hospital in France on 8 May 1917 suffering from trench fever. He was then discharged to the company clearing station with the same diagnosis. A record of him sustaining a shrapnel wound to his hand on the same day is inconsistent, and as no further reference was made to it, it was not counted. The next day, 9 May, he was transferred to yet another hospital, still in France, and admitted diagnosed with myalgia. Shortly after, he was transferred to England, again hospitalised and at the end of September classified as suffering from debility and old age and was returned to Australia discharged medically unfit. His medical board records, of which there are many, described disabilities that are noted as pre-existing and that he was 'over age', and state that he was suffering from senility, that his condition on discharge was 'tremulous shell shock', and that he suffered from 'nervousness and osteosclerosis'. He was awarded a small pension on 20 March 1918, and committed suicide on 14 December 1920. In response to an application from his next of kin to the Department of Repatriation, an investigation was undertaken to determine whether Herbert Hall had seen service that may have resulted in shell shock. The outcome of that enquiry is unclear other than that he was deemed to be not eligible for inclusion on the Roll of Honour. In other words his death was not considered to be war related. In light of this record and the appeal made by his next of kin, this soldier's data entry is for one wounding caused by shell shock for the diagnosis of myalgia; one battle-related illness, as the two admissions were sequential; death as a consequence of his war-related experience; and a discharge, medically unfit due to shell shock rather than age. It is contended, given the circumstances, that an injustice was done to Herbert Hall.

In another example, age was definitely not a factor in relation to the diagnosis of senility. William Shephard (7321) was thirty-six when he enlisted on 14 October 1916. He was eventually TOS in France on 11 August 1917. On 7 March 1918, he was wounded in action, having been gassed, and was evacuated to England, with the notation upon his admission reading 'gassed slight'. Shortly thereafter, on 21 April 1918, it was decided to return him to Australia for a discharge, medically unfit due to 'premature senility'. He was thirty-seven years of age. He applied for pension benefits in 1933 and died in 1951 at the age of seventy-one. Data entry for this soldier is for one hospitalisation (wounding), and one medical discharge (unfit due to shell shock).

Some men were lucky. The category now considered accounts for those soldiers who were not recorded as being hospitalised at any time during their service. General observations can be made about their duties in order to identify the least risky occupations of the war. For example, SW Durston (685) enlisted on 20 June 1917 and was assigned administrative duties assisting military staff in England. As he did not leave the UK during the war, he was only awarded the British Medal and was not hospitalised during his war service. GH Dussell (3295) enlisted on 10 December 1917 and similarly did not leave the UK, serving as a cook at a veterinarian hospital. The case of one Captain James Edgar Hall is somewhat unclear other than the fact that, in his brief service, he was not hospitalised. He was appointed to the AIF as captain on 28 July 1916 with his file marked 'for voyage only'. Three weeks later he embarked for England on the troopship *Boorara*, disembarked in England on 13 October and then returned to Australia, departing on 26 December 1916, and had his appointment terminated on 9 March 1917. That is it—one trip and one medal.

Others arrived as the war was in its final phases. CE McCarry (50918) enlisted on 8 October 1917, but for reasons unknown was not TOS in the field until a year later on 1 October 1918 and was not hospitalised. Others included in this category were GE Wilkins (21139), whose records show that he was not hospitalised but was discharged medically unfit; and J Hood (19258), who, while he was wounded, was recorded as remaining on duty. This soldier and his record also reflect the most commonly assigned duty that limited the likelihood of hospitalisation during the war regardless of posting: the role of driver. Allocation to veterinarian services and the Australian Flying Corps (AFC) are some other types of service duty in which the men were fortunate to have largely avoided hospitalisation. This will be discussed in detail in Chapter 6.

There are also records in the files for those soldiers who were taken prisoner of war. Death in captivity and wounding, illness and injury prior to capture have also been counted in the record review. In most cases, these men were repatriated back to England remarkably quickly; arriving there before the end of 1918, and nearly all were discharged medically unfit. However, some were not. Hugh West (2464), a labourer aged twenty-four years, enlisted on 8 July 1915 and was TOS on 3 March 1916. Exactly six months later he was taken prisoner in France. In June of the following year he was recaptured at the border trying to escape. Undeterred, he tried again on 3 September 1917, the anniversary of his capture, and successfully made his way via Belgium to England where he arrived on 4 October. He was rewarded with a Military Medal and early discharge home to Australia on 10 April 1918, having married in England in the meantime.

Instances of hospitalisation for the treatment of VD have been recorded including the number of days the soldier spent in hospital. These records are quite accurate as it was the practice to suspend the soldier's pay during this period of hospitalisation. This, however, provided a significant incentive, apart from the horrific treatment methods used at the time, for the soldier to seek to be discharged prematurely, often to result in readmission a few days later. In the relatively frequent event that a soldier was readmitted with this disease within seven days of being discharged, only the original hospitalisation is counted and the number of days of treatment during the second admission period is added to the first to give one admission and one total number of days.

The following example requires a degree of interpretation. Percy Raymond Sinclair (2521) was twenty-two years of age when he enlisted on 12 February 1916 and he disembarked at Plymouth on 2 November of that year. Six weeks later he was in France. On 15 May

1917, he was admitted to hospital for three weeks diagnosed with rheumatism. Following his discharge from hospital, he served for only two weeks before he was again admitted suffering from rheumatism. This kept him away from his unit for over two months. A further admission to hospital was recorded on 8 November 1917 that resulted in him being invalided back to England with the file notation reading 'PUO and VD'. He was discharged from hospital on 7 March 1918 only to be readmitted while still in England on 9 April with myalgia. He rejoined his unit at Le Havre on 20 June 1918 until he was admitted to hospital on 6 February 1919 suffering from VD. He was to remain in hospital for an extraordinary 196 days, after which he was returned to Australia to be discharged TPE. The data entry for Percy Sinclair is for three woundings (counting all as shell shock—two for rheumatism and one for myalgia), and two illnesses, battle related (PUO and VD). His admission in 1917 for PUO *and* VD unusually did not result in his pay being docked; he was saved by the primary illness being recorded as PUO and therefore this incidence of VD is not recorded in the data entry for this record review.

A record of soldiers holding officer rank was collated with the view to conducting an analysis of casualty rates, survival rates and age relative to other ranks. The last held rank of officer is the level recorded in the count. Generally, these records were far less clear on the subject of movement and casualties than the records for 'other ranks'. And very few officers' records are notated with 'discharged, medically unfit'. *Contrary* to this trend is the case of Major Vernon J Whitehead, a solicitor and barrister in the army before joining the AIF on 16 February 1915. He was evacuated from Gallipoli on 30 August of that year, his record indicating that he was suffering from dysentery. He was readmitted to hospital on 5 January 1917 after seeing action in Belgium. He was diagnosed with 'delusional insanity' and his wife was so advised. A subsequent medical report records that he was buried by earth thrown up by a shell burst prior to his previous evacuation from Gallipoli. He was 'struck off strength', the cause noted as 'unsuitable' on one form, 'insanity' on another. He was then returned to Australia and his 'Appointment Terminated—unsuitable' on 26 May 1917. However, his record does not show withdrawal of his commission. He continued to serve, ultimately as the legal officer of the Fourth Division, until his retirement in 1934 with the rank of Honorary Colonel. The entry for the count in this case is for one wounding for shell shock, one battle-related illness for dysentery and medical discharge for shell shock; in all probability, he was shell shocked.

Time and again, the treatment of officers was quite different from that of other ranks, particularly with regard to traumatic stress. In general it can be concluded from the examination of a number of officer files that not only did they contain less information on medical matters, but also that the details of stress-related wounding were scant or absent altogether. Gilbert Menzies Burton, Lieutenant, aged twenty-one years, enlisted on 25 September 1916 and joined the AFC. He had previously served two years in the citizen forces and was immediately promoted to Second Lieutenant, although acceptance into pilot training included a commission. He arrived in England at the end of 1916 and, as is the case with most members of the AFC, he spent most of his time in training in either England or Scotland. He graduated as a pilot on 29 November 1917. On 12 February 1918, he was admitted to hospital 'NYD' (as mentioned previously, this was a term commonly used for shell shock at the time). On 10 March 1918, he embarked for return to Australia with the notation on his file reading 'for Change concussion' and his appointment was finally terminated on 19 June 1918, indicating that he was receiving treatment over these months back in Australia.[2] Burton's file shows that he was *recommended for leave* to Australia on 4 February 1918, before his admission to hospital, and again on 22 February after his admission to hospital. Only the one word 'concussion' is used to support a recommendation that he be returned to Australia on 10 March, but provides an indication that he was seriously unwell. In this case, the data entry is for one wounding (assuming 'concussion' is referring to traumatic stress), and discharged medically unfit as a result of shell shock.

The case of Captain Samuel Edward Sinclair also poses some difficulties for interpretation. He enlisted on 16 September 1914 at the age of thirty-one years, and was mentioned in dispatches and awarded the Military Cross for his services at Gallipoli. He was admitted to hospital at the end of July 1915 with enteritis, rejoining his unit four weeks later. As previously mentioned, the medical records of officers are generally scant, and Sinclair's was no exception. He spent one week in hospital in April 1916 but the cause was not recorded. He was then transferred to France where, on 14 August

1916, he was admitted to hospital with a broken leg and was evacuated to England. He was readmitted to hospital on 29 October 1916 and appears to have been transferred to a further two hospitals, with his file notations reading 'enlarged glands' and 'VD'. On 13 February 1917, it is noted on his file that he was to be returned to Australia for discharge and that he had left Plymouth that same day. However, he was not discharged from hospital until 20 June 1917 and finally had his appointment terminated in Australia on 17 October 1917, presumably having undergone treatment in the officer barracks. The reasons cited for his 'discharge' were trachoma (chronic conjunctivitis), fractured leg, organic valvular diseased heart and enlarged glands. In this case it could be argued that the officer was suffering from post-traumatic stress owing to the diagnosis of VDH. However, due to the existence of the other conditions, his discharge is not recorded as stress-related. The data entry for this officer is for one hospitalisation due to injury; two hospitalisations due to illness, battle related (one being the default option where no cause is shown); and a medically unfit discharge. He applied for pension benefits in 1933 and died two years later at the age of fifty-three.

Many soldier records include a pro forma document, or its carbon copy, of a request from the Repatriation Commission to Army Records for a copy of the Form B103, being the chief medical record kept during a soldier's service period. It is believed that these requests for medical information were triggered by an application for pension benefits; however, this did not indicate that such an application was successful. Indeed, initially many applications were harshly viewed, which eventually led to a Royal Commission in 1924 into the pension system. Exemplary here is the case of Francis Gibbs (5569), who was thirty-nine when he enlisted on 6 March 1916. Twelve months later he was admitted to hospital with a septic foot where he remained for three weeks. He was admitted again on 30 July 1917, diagnosed with PUO then dyspepsia, finally rejoining his battalion on 4 October only to be readmitted to hospital on 29 October suffering from rheumatism. He was evacuated to England on 11 November when diagnosed with myalgia. Approximately three months after his admission he was returned to Australia on 1 February 1918 to be discharged medically unfit, owing to myalgia. An application dated 25 April 1918 for a pension for himself, his wife and his four daughters was 'rejected, [as the] claimant is suffering no incapacity due to service'. Nine days later he was handed his discharged medically unfit certificate. His records indicate that he applied again for a pension in 1922 and pension benefits in 1954 (the outcomes of which are unknown, but the second application may have been for funeral expenses support available to the family). The data entry for this soldier is for one wounding for shell shock (myalgia); one injury; one illness, battle related; and a medical discharge due to shell shock.

When discussing the conflict between the Repatriation Commission and returned soldiers' organisations in *The Cost of War: Australians Return*, Garton highlights that one of the most significant controversies was over the phenomenon of the 'burnt out' soldier. By the early 1930s, the Returned and Services League (RSL) welfare officers were becoming concerned about the number of cases of ageing and unemployed men seeking assistance. This problem undoubtedly reflected the ageing of the returned soldier population in the community and also the increasing difficulties many faced from the effects of the Great Depression. Garton continues:

> In 1930 Canada had introduced a special pension for the 'burnt out' veteran, and New Zealand followed suit in 1935. They [the RSL] campaigned for a pension for men who were 'prematurely aged' and 'permanently unemployable' by virtue of their war experience. Of course the relationship between war and premature ageing was not really amenable to proof. This did not deter the League, who argued that the problem was a serious one and had already been recognised overseas.[3]

In 1936 the Lyons government passed legislation to introduce a 'Service Pension' for returned men aged over sixty and women over fifty-five years of age in the impoverished circumstances (determined by a means test), those deemed permanently unemployable, and those suffering tuberculosis whether war caused or not.

A plot of the recorded years of the soldiers' pension applications as evidenced in their Attestation Papers will demonstrate the rise in these application numbers in response to those public inquiries and the dates of changing pension entitlements. This will challenge the strength of the hypothesis that it was the economic hardship of the depression that precipitated an increase in the number of returned soldiers seeking some form of supplementary income.

The many soldiers' records cited and examined in this chapter, which represent a small number of the total, have been presented to facilitate the examination of the finer details contained in the records that required interpretation necessary to carry out this analysis. Disagreement with these interpretations may arise for some but the overall impact of any disagreement on the end result will be minor when compared to the enormity of the extent of total AIF casualties of the First World War. The interpretations may end up in different boxes but the totals will remain the same. The examples cited here are an ominous sign of what these total casualties will prove to be.

Notes

1   Unknown condition but possibly more appropriately categorised as shell shock. Due to this uncertainty it is left as the default option of 'battle-related illnesses'.
2   If he had been well, standard procedure would have seen him discharged days after disembarkation.
3   Stephen Garton, *The Cost of War: Australians Return*, Oxford University Press, Melbourne, p. 95.

CHAPTER 6

Those We Forget: Total Australian Casualties of the First World War

Much has been written about this war—so much so, that '*positivity*' (specific information) finished decades ago. Generalised impressions or individual experiences are now all that remains to be explored and analysed. But maybe the vagaries of impressions or details of diaries of the history of this war have swung too far and a return to focus on the specifics of statistics will bring the pendulum back to the centre of discussions on the impact of the First World War. The statistical results presented below, however, are *estimates*. Each has a range that is based upon the extrapolation of specific occurrences in the 9604 soldiers' Attestation Papers examined in this record review. For each result the range is initially provided, but in order to avoid an overload of information for the reader it is not continually repeated throughout the chapter. Where possible, the results are represented in visual form in order to convey an overall picture and display the relative impact for each result. Limited as they are as *estimates*, some of these findings have until now only been guessed at, and often incorrectly at that, such as the incidence of shell shock and VD. Other estimates have not been considered at all, like the time of lost soldier availability due to their absence while undergoing treatment for VD or the tragic loss of men due to suicide. However, it should not be overlooked that the official medical casualty statistics were estimates too, subject to poor sampling and limited definition. With the limitations of any estimate in mind, what follows is an accurate assessment of Australia's true casualties from the First World War.

Enlistments and Embarkations

As was demonstrated in Chapter 3, the official figure of 416 809 enlistments was overstated by nearly 10 per cent, despite a Royal Commission examining, verifying and reporting upon a large proportion of this number. Through detailed sampling from across all of the Attestation Papers, a more accurate estimate has been arrived at: *379 000* men +/– 650 enlisted in the AIF.[1] The balance of the official figure can be defined at best as an application to enlist, or a misallocation over time and more correctly belonging in non-conflict military listings. The number 416 809 should be removed from the headline official figures not only because it is incorrect, but also because its original purpose of inflating Australia's contribution to this conflict is long out of date and was inappropriate to begin with.

In addition, a large proportion of the men represented by this more accurate enlistment number did not set foot in an army base in a theatre of war overseas. The simple sample analysis of the record review corrects the official figure of 331 781 embarkations and determines that the correct number of effective embarkations for war is *318 100* with a range of 315 300–320 800 at the 95% Confidence Interval.[2] This finding is critical, as this total of 318 100 will be used in all further analysis in this book. It essentially defines the field against which all other categories will be measured and its calculation is consistent with the international practice of other belligerent countries. Its proximity to the finding of the Commonwealth Statistician in 1938 provides a firm foundation for this analysis when combined with the logical assertion that troops recalled at sea were not part of Australia's 'fighting' force and that nurses and those who saw service in New Guinea belonged in other service categories.[3] It is upon this foundation that the most detailed and accurate analysis of Australian soldiers' commitment to this war can now be built.

War Deaths

A visual representation of the death toll of the AIF by campaign in the First World War is now possible,[4] basing this toll on the date of a soldier's death,[5] and can be seen in Figure 2 below. This data also

Figure 2

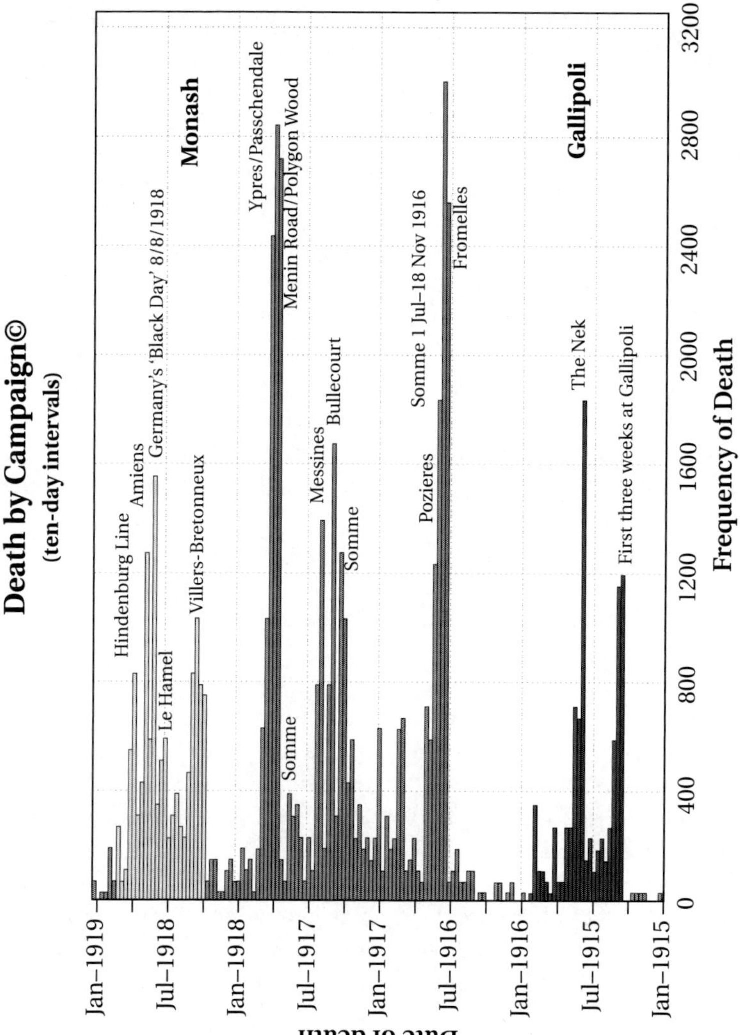

Death by Campaign©
(ten-day intervals)

Source: Compiled by David Noonan from Attestation Papers, 2014.

represent death from *all* causes, as some occurred sometime after the initial incident or contraction of an illness that eventually caused the death. However, for the general visual effect being conveyed here, extraction of non-battle deaths was not deemed necessary although further research in this area is warranted. In this graphic shown in Figure 2, we have for the first time a depiction of the relative occurrence of death in the campaigns involving AIF personnel in the First World War. The war period is split into ten-day intervals and the plots represent the number of deaths in each of the major campaigns of the war. Certainly deaths were occurring along the Western Front *and* the Northern Africa region at the same time, but this does not distort the overall picture conveyed and importantly the relative significance of the AIF experience.

This graphic puts the Gallipoli campaign (the darkest section in the lowest part of the graph) in its place in relation to the disaster of Fromelles. The second spike at Gallipoli represents the attempt to take The Nek and the wider August offensive (including losses at Lone Pine) which cost as many men as the fierce fighting required for the landing of the forces on the peninsula. Figure 2 also shows the period of relative calm in the first six months of 1916, when the AIF was evacuated from Gallipoli to Alexandria and held there for a few months, for fear of a counter-attack from Turkey, which, when it did not eventuate, allowed these men of the AIF to be shipped off for service on the Western Front.

After another few months of reorganisation and little action following the landing at Marseilles (a period that is typified by the limited recording of soldier movements in the Attestation Papers), they were presented to the front at Fromelles on 18 July 1916. Figure 2 reveals the relative losses at Pozières (23 July–3 September 1916), where Australian artillery killed many Australian soldiers through lost communication and confusion; and the Germans counter-attack using artillery to obliterate Pozières, which was by then occupied by Australian soldiers.[6] It places the often-called victory at Messines (7–14 June 1917) in the context of the costly campaign that it actually was. It also puts into perspective the tragedy of the decision of General Sir Douglas Haig, as Commander-in-Chief, to fight on into the winter and through the mud of 1917, endeavouring to take the *higher* ground around Passchendaele and break through as part of an equally delusional aim to get to the coast, only to hand it back within weeks when it was realised that the ground taken was strategically indefensible. 'What had taken four months to win was evacuated in three days' in January 1918.[7]

Finally, in this thumbnail sketch of the large amount of information that is contained in the graphic of Figure 2, it puts into perspective the losses suffered under the command of Sir John Monash (the lightest section in the top section of the graph), and by their magnitude, raises the question of this engineer General's reputation for looking after his troops, primarily through the use of all the mechanical means at his disposal, prior to exposing them to battle. Monash's authorised biographer, Geoffery Serle, records this reputed prioritisation:

> Monash had his first conference with his four divisional commanders (1st Division still being absent) on 6 June [1918]. Hobbs made a little demonstration, drawing attention to the fact that for the first time in the history of the AIF all the commanders and their senior staff officers present were Australian. The agenda was wide ranging ... Monash put on the agenda: 'Safeguarding troops against casualties' and 'Cumulative small gas losses'. He began by announcing that he planned regular possibly fortnightly interchanges of views.[8]

From March 1918 until the Australians were finally withdrawn in the first week of October, *no longer a fighting force*, Monash had combined command of the entire AIF with the final division, the Fourth, coming under his control in July 1918. During this period, from the time the AIF retook Villers-Bretonneux, the AIF under Monash was in attack mode. And for the first time, troops were moving forward. Why did Monash push his men so relentlessly and with losses so great? Were these losses a reflection on the quite different form of warfare being waged now, in the open and out of the trenches? Germany's high command believed that losses inflicted by Australian and Canadian soldiers on 8 August 1918 were a tremendous blow, some claiming that it broke Germany's war effort.[9] This would have been self-evident to the allied military as thousands of German soldiers started to surrender.[10]

Monash's offensive was ruthless. In his own words, on a page headed 'The value of the offensive' in his 1920 book, with the rather self-serving title of *The Australian Victories in France in 1918*, Monash says:

> 'Feed your troops on victory', is a maxim that does not appear in any textbook, but it is nevertheless true. The aim and end of all the efforts of all the heavy sacrifices of the Australian nation was victory in the field. Nothing that could be done could lead more swiftly and more directly to its fulfilment than an energetic offensive policy.[11]

Monash's maxim came at a very high cost for our fledgling nation's civilian soldiers. Comparative to other belligerents, it was devastating, as will be seen.

The analysis of this record review found that the total death toll of members of the AIF over the duration of its existence was *62 300* (ranging from 61 900 to 62 700 or +/− 400), of which 53 600 were attributable to battle causes and 8700 to non-battle causes. This death toll is in excess of the official figure of 60 000 and is higher than the current number on the Roll of Honour which stands at 61 512. As a consequence of this death toll, we can now say 255 800 men survived this war, a statistic to be used in due course. Further analysis of deaths resulting from this conflict is presented in Chapter 8 on the post-war impact, as the death toll does not finish with the disbandment of the AIF on 31 March 1921.

Non-Battle Deaths

Non-battle deaths amounted to an estimated *8700* (ranging from 8530 to 8870 or +/− 170). The causes of such deaths were varied and some of the significant ones were analysed in the counting process. Sadly, the sensitive issue of soldier death from suicide arises here. As the count progressed, it became apparent that the number of recorded suicides was such as to warrant a separate classification. Where a suicide had occurred, medals were awarded and the soldier's name appears on the Roll of Honour. However, some exceptions do exist, as in the case of George Gay. George took a commission with the British Army in March 1918 and, as a result, was formally discharged from the AIF. While returning home to Australia he disembarked prematurely when the ship docked in Fremantle (he was returning to Sydney) and committed suicide a few days later on 16 January 1921. His records are quite clear on the circumstances of his death but he is not on the Roll of Honour. He is not counted as a death from suicide in this analysis, as technically he was no longer a member of the AIF.

A debatable decision arose as to whether to count the following example as suicide. Harry Gavans was thirty-two years of age, a journalist and a Methodist, who died of acute alcohol poisoning on 4 January 1919 in his barracks. An inquiry heard evidence from several sources but did not determine the death to be suicide. There was little doubt that he was melancholy when last seen in his room. Evidence was presented that he took a bottle of scotch from a roommate's locker and drank it. He was found unconscious and was put into bed. He died later that night. Harry's death was not counted as a suicide in the present analysis, as it was assumed to be a sad accident.

The reluctance of the authorities to accept responsibility for—let alone acknowledge—self-harm among the servicemen was far greater than it is today. This was regularly in evidence in the numerous inquiries conducted into circumstances surrounding wounding in the field when it was believed to be self-inflicted. However, it was extremely rare for a soldier who had shot his toe off or shot himself through the hand to be found guilty of self-harm, or 'conduct unbecoming'. He was charged for self-inflicted wounding, but rarely found guilty, to then serve a prison term after his release from hospital. The review of the records estimates the number of suicides to be approximately 550. The 95% Confidence Interval range is between the minimum of 300 and a possible maximum of nearly 920. The recording of a death as self-inflicted is extremely sensitive to the extrapolated outcome as a small number can make a significant difference, emphasising that a cautious approach is important here. For example, if the contrary view were to be taken regarding the circumstances of the deaths of Gay and Gavans and they were recorded as suicides, the previous estimate of 550 would climb to over 630 with a range, at the 95% Confidence Interval, from a low of 330 to a high of nearly 1200. To try to give this toll of 550 deaths some context, it is approximately six to eight times higher than the rate of suicide in this male cohort in Australia from 2001 to 2011 as reported by the Australian Bureau of Statistics.[12]

Another sad finding arose in this area. It became apparent that many suicides seemed to occur as the soldier was returning home from the war. Philip Hall (3342) was twenty-six years of age when he enlisted shortly after Australia declared its involvement in the war. Not long after his landing at Gallipoli his lung was punctured by shrapnel. As he lay wounded he was run over by a water tank carriage, crushing both his legs. He survived and returned to Australia in a hospital ship, and was admitted to hospital in Brisbane. A few weeks later he requested one week's leave to go home. He shot himself a few days before his scheduled return to hospital and was found by his mother on 21 October 1915. Regulations in place at that time disallowed a refund of funeral expenses to the mother for soldiers who died after returning to Australia. Eventually this was corrected. A further problem arose five years later when Phillip Hall's mother applied for a war gratuity. She was refused on the basis that the injury he suffered in the path of the cart at Gallipoli was self-inflicted. The correspondence on this file is quite tragic, but eventually the error was acknowledged and Mrs Hall received her due allowance.

Richard Williams (2029) was hospitalised in April 1918 with a severe case of trench feet. His file notes that he began to 'crack up' in February 1918—it would seem the trench feet hospitalisation was too much. He was again hospitalised in June with shell shock and discharged medically unfit. On 11 November 1918, he threw himself overboard as the ship arrived in Fremantle, leaving behind a suicide note. This particularly tragic nature of the timing of suicide warranted the creation of a time plot of the instance of suicide in the analysis. The concentration of suicides seen in the *three* years from 1919 to 1921 can be seen in Figure 3 below and was well in excess of earlier comparative numbers of six to eight times, perhaps rising to ten times the average annual non-war benchmark. It would seem that many men left to go to war unprepared and untrained for what they were about to experience; and they were also unprepared and unsupported for what they had to face when they were sent home.

Other causes of death of a non-battle nature were analysed as well. The memory of the deadly impact on the AIF of the outbreak of CSM was somewhat overwhelmed by the pandemic of Spanish Flu. The CSM outbreak predominantly affected troops based in the rural camps in Victoria in 1915 and in all Australian states in 1916 and 1917. The analysis of the records is presented in the form of the time plot shown in Figure 3, which indicates that it cost the lives of 860 men (with a range from 540 to 1300) enlisted in the AIF. (Note that each of the extrapolated results has a range of 95% Confidence Interval. This range appears in brackets after the result.)

Figure 3: Death from Suicide and Cerebro-Spinal Meningitis

Source: Compiled by David Noonan from Attestation Papers, 2014.

The analysis indicates that the number of deaths from Spanish Flu was nearly 1600 (1150, 2175) and, when combined with CSM, a total of nearly 2500 men were to die from these two diseases. As tragic as these numbers appear, they mask what was perhaps a superior effort by the Australian Medical Corps to contain the influenza outbreak which is now known to be the H1N1 virus. In Chapter 7, comparisons are made with the medical performance of other countries, in particular the USA, which will throw new light on this disease's relative impact and the efforts to contain it. Suffice to say at this point that the USA lost a staggering 58 100 men to disease, including 34 858 in their own camps at home, nearly half of which were due to Spanish Flu.[13] The idea that American troops contracted influenza in the confines of troopships is largely a myth. They contracted it in camps across America and died in the thousands before they had even embarked for war. The American responsible for the USA medical and casualty statistics, the Surgeon General Major General MW Ireland, in discussing some of the difficulties inherent to their compilation, thanklessly noted:

> The greatest difficulty encountered was in obtaining accurate records from troops travelling on transports. This was

due to the fact that the medical officers were not generally in medical charge on transports, and no arrangements were made with the Navy, or with civilian transport surgeons, for medical reports for sick army personnel en route. As a result the reports of the sick and wounded from transports were practically worthless. The inadequacy of these transport reports during the influenza epidemic in September and October 1918 probably accounts in great part for the discrepancy (amounting to 1649) in the number of deaths from disease reported by the Adjutant General and by the Surgeon General as having occurred in the American Expeditionary Forces and on transports. It is only fair to say, however, that a part of the discrepancy is probably attributable to the inability of our medical authorities to obtain records of all deaths which occurred among our men in the hospitals of our allies.[14]

The date plot displayed in Figure 4 below represents the timing of the impact of both Spanish Flu and pneumonia on the men of the AIF. The occurrence of respiratory disease was widespread among all the belligerents, and affected the vast majority of men in the AIF on multiple occasions. Bronchitis, pleurisy and pneumonia, which were accompanied by the simple notation on the soldier's file for an admission to hospital with 'flu', were more prevalent over the winters of 1917 and 1918, and particularly 1916 and 1917. Even exposure at Gallipoli, where the campaign was fought mainly in the summer months, resulted in many men being admitted for frostbite, exposure and related respiratory illnesses. All respiratory conditions were counted in the category 'illness, battle related'. The findings for this category and the 'non-battle related illness' category will be discussed shortly. However, the particular occurrence of a death from pneumonia (quite apart from deaths from Spanish Flu) was assessed to conclude that around 1330 (920, 1860) soldiers died from this cause, often progressing from bronchitis and pleurisy. There were also many records of soldiers who survived pneumonia, but were subsequently discharged medically unfit suffering from chronic bronchitis.

Figure 4: Death from Spanish Flu and Pneumonia

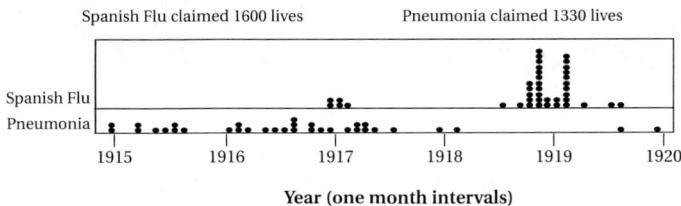

Source: Compiled by David Noonan from Attestation Papers, 2014.

Another illness that was also particularly costly was TB. Around 900 (570, 1350) men lost their lives from this illness despite the precaution of screening every soldier for the disease upon enlistment.

Illness was not the only cause of non-battle death. Accidents accounted for approximately 850 (500, 1370) deaths. The causes were quite varied. Dennis Patrick Sheridan (5189) died from electrocution. Robert Wilkins (611) was running for a troop train when he slipped and fell under it. Arthur George Bosanquet (3394A) was knocked off his bicycle. Doug Sharp (6902) died from a fractured skull sustained when he hit his head on the deck of the ship on its way to England after he was punched by a fellow soldier. Many were horse related, like the death of Henry Bradley Sheridan (3379), who fell from his horse. Some men drowned and consequent inquiries concluded that the death was accidental, as was the unfortunate case for Captain Benjamin Digby Gibson. These records were closely scrutinised in the analysis and the circumstances surrounding the incident examined carefully. It was found that the incidence of murder was surprisingly low. Examples ranged from a soldier being beaten to death by civilians while on leave in Paris, to a private who shot his Non Commissioned Officer (NCO) in his room and claimed that the NCO had committed suicide in front of him. This was the case when Corporal Joseph Durkin (5372) was murdered on 27 November 1917. Private V Asser was initially acquitted of wrongdoing as the coroner declared the death to be a suicide, but a subsequent inquiry came to the conclusion that it was indeed murder, as the NCO's arm would have had to have been very much longer than it was in order to reach the rifle's trigger in the manner described by the private. As for the murderer, notated on his file is the advice that he 'suffered extreme punishment of the law'. It is estimated that 120 soldiers lost their lives as a result of murder.

Prisoners of War

The dates of when AIF soldiers were taken as POWs were also recorded. These are shown in graphical form in Figure 5, along with the identification of the corresponding battles. The official figure, and there are three figures for the total number of AIF POWs,[15] is relatively close to London's War Records Office number of 4084 men (see Chapter 1, Table 5). The record review and count produced a result of 3993 (3260, 4840). Figure 5 highlights not only when the AIF lost their soldiers as POWs but also when most losses took place. The battle of Bullecourt was particularly costly in this regard.

Figure 5: Prisoners of War©

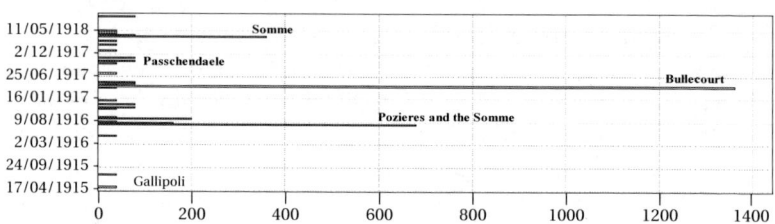

Approximate time plot of the loss of men taken Prisoners of War©

Australia had 4000 men taken captive, approximately 600 did not return

Source: Compiled by David Noonan from Attestation Papers, 2014.

Quite a number of men taken prisoner were repatriated back to England, often via Holland, *before* the end of the war as part of an apparent prisoner exchange program. Stephan Hall (1546) became a POW on 20 July 1916. He was handed over in Holland in January 1918 and arrived in London a week later. Wisbey Sinclair (1781) was not quite so fortunate. He was taken prisoner shortly after Hall on 29 July 1916 but was not processed through Holland until June 1918, and it was then two months before he arrived in England on 18 August 1918. Captain Joseph Honeysett's timing was unfortunate. After his capture on 16 May 1917 he waited until 17 October 1918 to attempt to escape. He 'only got 100 yards' when he was shot in the leg. He was repatriated to England on 19 December 1918 and admitted to hospital. He was awarded the Military Cross for his endeavours.

At the end of the war most prisoners returned to England remarkably quickly, before Christmas 1918. The analysis of the record review revealed that approximately 600 AIF men died in captivity, mainly due to the wounds (400 men) that resulted in their capture. Officers represented about 150 of the AIF servicemen captured during the war. Their proportional representation of POW numbers was slightly lower (about 4 per cent) than that of the other ranks, but this is not surprising given the number of officers who were not exposed to the front. This factor will be discussed shortly. There was no record encountered in the count process of an officer dying while a POW, suggesting that few did. In the main the AIF prisoners appeared to be treated well and were able to get a postcard or letter sent to their next of kin via the Red Cross not long after their internment, and the brief text in such letters often mentioned their satisfactory treatment. William Henry Carr (1642) is a sad case in point. He was wounded and captured in April 1917. He was interned and wrote to his family describing how he was being treated well and asking that they send parcels to him via the Red Cross. He was released and returned to Britain in July 1918 and declared medically unfit due to a severely fractured leg. He died from meningitis the next month at sea on the way home.

War Wounding and Shell Shock

Australia's official war statistics state that hospitalisations for wounding totalled 155 000 during this war. It is claimed here that this figure significantly underestimates the actual number of wounding hospitalisations by a third (34 per cent).

During the existence of the AIF the number of hospitalisations for wounding was estimated to be *208 600* (208 100, 209 100) of which *63 400*, or 30 per cent, was due to an admission for shell shock. While shell shock was counted as a wounding in the official classifications, substantial evidence was obtained during the count process which indicated significant levels of misdiagnosis for shell shock and the resultant treatment of these hospitalisations in the records as due to an illness (such as rheumatism), leading to these not being counted by the War Records Office at all.

In order to avoid common confusion with this wounding statistic, it must be stated again that this statistic of 208 600 represents a hospitalisation or admission, and they were suffered or incurred by *147 000* men or nearly half (46 per cent of 318 100) of the total number of men who embarked to serve in a theatre of war, or those that actually did (48 per cent of 308 100).

Just over 100 000 of these men were wounded once, a further 35 000 were wounded twice and over 2500 men were wounded a staggering four or more times, mainly being admitted to hospital with shell shock. Of the total number of hospitalisations for wounding of 208 600, over 17 600 were admissions of 14 000 men who did not survive the war. This raises another facet of these figures. Men who were killed were removed from the conflict earlier and permanently. So we might ask: what was the impact on those who survived? This is easy to assess,[16] and it transpires that of those men who did survive this war over *half* (52 per cent of 255 800) were wounded, many (47 000) multiple times (a factor of 1.44), or approximately 133 000 men with 191 000 admissions for wounding. The numbers are difficult to absorb because of their overwhelming size but they must be comprehended. Perhaps a better appreciation is achieved when one considers that each one of these 147 000 soldiers wounded represents a man being hit by a bullet or shrapnel, burnt or gassed, shocked speechless, or made deaf or blind; and nearly half of them (of those wounded and subsequently who could), had to return to the conflict for it to happen again. In the interim such men had spent time in hospital on at least one occasion, suffering from *serious illness*, as will be discussed below. The incidence of shell shock has been estimated, as mentioned, to be the cause of 30 per cent of the hospitalisations in this wounding category. It can now be said that this was borne by an estimated 41 800 men, or one in seven men (13.5 per cent) who served in a theatre of war. For nearly a quarter of them (9600), they would be hospitalised two, three, four or even five times, suffering from this condition. Obviously some men recovered, but, as will be seen shortly, just over one in ten of those men who survived would be discharged medically unfit due to shell shock.

One of the worst examples of multiple hospitalisations was that of Thomas Arthur Williams (2227), who enlisted a year after the war was declared, in August 1915. He was twenty-two years of age. He was hospitalised a total of sixteen times, six of which were classified as wounding. He was gassed once and on five other occasions was admitted to hospital with shell shock. During his service he was returned to Australia to recover and then *sent back* overseas. He eventually suffered a nervous breakdown at the end of November 1918 while recovering from an operation for appendicitis, and was discharged medically unfit. The circumstances of his life after that time are unknown, but it is likely that life was not good for Thomas thereafter. There is no record of him asking for a pension.

The officer rank is covered in detail shortly, but the case of Lieutenant Henry Wilkinson is relevant to note here. He enlisted shortly after the declaration of war in September 1914 at twenty-seven years of age. He was hospitalised a total of ten times during his war service, seven of them for physical wounding by bullets or shrapnel, including one occasion when he was gassed. The other three hospitalisations involved two for injury and one admission for dysentery. Monash accepted his premature resignation on 11 December 1918 as a consequence of him being 'war worn'. He was not declared medically unfit because he was an officer; he was struck off strength effective on the day he resigned in England. It is presumed that his officer's pay level also ceased on that date. Across the ranks of officer, no other record of termination exists on their record; they were simply struck off strength. Also relevant when discussing cases of multiple admissions is the service of Lieutenant Robert Louis Graham. He was thirty-seven years of age when he enlisted a couple of weeks after the declaration of war, and was hospitalised on ten occasions. Seven admissions were a consequence of wounding, and in three of these the cause was acute rheumatism, which was treated as shell shock in this analysis. Each time he recovered. He was hospitalised on two further occasions suffering from different injuries, and had a further admission in May 1919 suffering from epilepsy, which in this count was classified as battle illness by default. He was discharged fit at the termination of his service and his records show that he applied for pension benefits in 1921 and again in 1926. He died in 1958 at the age of eighty-one years.

War Injury

It can now be said, for the first time, that there were *98 700* (98 200, 99 200) hospitalisations for injury alone, or nearly one in three of the men who embarked. Many of these men were eventually discharged medically unfit as a consequence, a topic that will be discussed further shortly. The injuries suffered had a variety of causes, although interaction with animals such as dogs, camels and horses played a large part. Sydney Williams (306) was particularly unfortunate. He sustained a serious break of his right ankle while 'riding over rough and stony country when his horse stumbled and fell'. The next day, while he was being evacuated to hospital, the horse in front of him lashed out and fractured the same leg. He was subsequently discharged medically unfit due to these injuries. Albert Gibson (1007) and (another) Sydney Williams (2462) suffered ruptured testes after being kicked by a horse; Albert was sent home. William Hook (6811) contracted rabies after being bitten by a dog while on leave in Alexandria. He survived. John Silva (2780) was hospitalised for nearly a month after suffering from a severe camel bite. Still other injuries were just bad luck. The war was over on 29 November 1918 when Claude Hooper (54438) was skylarking using a broom handle to block the door to his hut, preventing two others from entering. They used force, the broom handle broke and Claude lost the sight in one eye.

War Illness

Respiratory disease was rife and pneumonia, pleurisy and TB took their toll as the data for deaths testify. Sanitation was non-existent at Gallipoli where dysentery and diarrhoea cut a swathe through fit men. Infection in the trenches did the same on the Western Front and in Flanders, where men were forced to wade knee and thigh deep in a cesspool of filthy water that filled the trenches. The smallest scratch could become septic, with one of the very real consequences of trench feet being gangrene. Septicaemia killed men in the absence of antibiotics. Nephritis was regularly diagnosed. Ear and eye infections sent men home deaf and blind. Fevers raged through the ranks, leaving medical officers overwhelmed and not even sure of the origins of these fevers. The notation PUO appears regularly in the records, referring to pyrexia of unknown origin, and was often used interchangeably with trench fever. Skin diseases were almost universal and required admission to hospital. Boils, abscesses, infected eczema, septic sores and scabies infected nearly every soldier on the front line as did influenza, which was mostly annotated as 'flu'. Malaria was particularly debilitating in North Africa, Palestine and the Dardanelle. Gastroenteritis was common. Laryngitis appears regularly in the soldiers' records with the cause noted as infection, gas or shock. And then there was VD.

Venereal Disease

The only specific medical illness to be counted separately in the record review was the incidence of VD. Butler's treatment of the subject has been discussed, and he recorded approximately 52 500 admissions overseas for VD contracted by approximately 44 000 men.[17] On this subject it appears from the results of the analysis of soldier records that Butler got it about right; but it is necessary to unravel his data to confirm this is the case. He represents these gross numbers in a table as 84.79 under the column 'Admission rate per 1,000 per annum'. One is left to question what he means by 'per annum'. It was established that the force overseas was 318 000 men so the number of admissions of 52 500 translates to an incidence of 164 per 1000. Even if the official numbers of those who embarked are used, which were 331 000, the rate still reaches 158 per 1000. So how did he arrive at a figure of 84.79 (leaving aside the question of what amounts to 0.79 of a man)? Butler has used an unfathomable measure of men potentially liable to contract this disease as not the total force of men sent overseas, but as a number he describes as 'per *1000 per annum of mean average strength*' (emphasis added). He then states that the '*average mean average daily strength*' (emphasis added, and this is not a typographical error) of the AIF overseas from 1915 to 1918 was 154 960 men, resulting in an admission rate per 1000 per annum of 84.79. Seven pages previously, buried in the text, Butler states: 'The total incidence on 330 714 embarkations works out at 158 per thousand, exactly the same figure given by MacPhail for the Canadian forces.'[18] As discussed earlier, Butler and his presentation of data is the source of much frustration and his tables should be explored with caution. MacPhail was responsible for compiling Canada's official medical history for this war and he shall be referred to shortly.

The AIF took a great many steps in its attempt to control this disease, including extensive prophylactic and early treatment measures that Butler describes as abortive.[19]

Leo van Bergen claims the following comparative statistics:

> According to official statistics the most sexually active were troops from Dominion countries. The British Army—in which an estimated 400 000 cases of sexually transmitted disease occurred during the war as a whole—had an official rate of venereal disease of 3.7 percent in 1916 [37 per 1000] whereas more than 20 percent of Canadian soldiers [200 per 1000] had some form of venereal disease (...) the number of soldiers who contracted venereal disease—as said, 400 000 in total of whom 150 000 required hospital treatment.[20]

So great care is required in the identification of the incidence of VD and in the determination of the distinction between diagnosis and hospitalisation.[21] In the first section of the quotation above van Bergen uses the word 'cases', while in the second he refers to 'number of soldiers'. This parallels the same problem with the misinterpretation of the classification of wounding. Some comparative data will follow shortly.

The AIF Attestation Papers only recorded hospitalisations for VD and not diagnosis only, with the exception of a small amount of data which cover cases of soldiers being discharged after initially being hospitalised to a convalescence depot for day-care treatment. It was rare for a reference to be made to hospitalisation when it occurred while the soldier was still in Australia awaiting embarkation. It is therefore useful that Butler has specified admissions to Langwarrin, a secure hospital in Victoria,[22] as these can be treated as additional to the numbers identified in the records review.

The analysis of the count of 9604 Attestation Papers revealed that approximately *42 200* Australian soldiers were admitted for VD *56 600* times overseas during the existence of the AIF. These numbers are not that dissimilar from Butler's findings. If it is assumed that Butler's admissions data in Australia of 12 689[23] for VD represent one man admitted on one occasion, and excludes those sent home for treatment, this brings the total to nearly *55 000* men admitted on *69 300* occasions. What can now be said is that at least one in seven men (or more than 13.3 per cent) were hospitalised from contracting VD overseas, exceeding all earlier 'guesstimates' (see Chapter 4) of 10 per cent by over a third, which results in an admission rate overseas of 178 per 1000 men. Yet once again interpretation of these data must be treated with caution, as this is an admission rate and does not represent the number of patients; but it is a useful measure that can be used to make comparisons with other armies. This general comparative work is carried out in Chapter 7 but some of this work is presented here with respect to VD.

The incidence of VD in the US Army in Europe was approximately 74 per 1000 and about the same back in America, according to Canadian medical sources.[24] The US medical history indicates higher *admissions* of 91 per 1000 for VD.[25] It is contended that the comparatively low US figure, almost half that of the AIF, was simply due to US troops' limited exposure to prostitutes because of their shorter period of service in the war, which resulted in a limited amount of leave—they went straight from training depots into the front line. Indeed, it will be seen in the next chapter that US troop exposure to the war was only 200 days. There is no doubt that they were well on the way to levels in excess of those experienced by the AIF with an equivalent time of service. The incidence of VD admissions in the British Expeditionary Force during the war was remarkably similar in France and Flanders (24.7 per 1000 men) when compared to the incidence at home in the United Kingdom (25.1 per 1000 men).[26] German figures, which are discussed in Chapter 7, indicate an admission rate of 27 per 1000. Canadian forces had a rate of 158 per 1000 men for VD, peaking in the winter of 1914–1915, in England, at 222 per 1000.[27] These rates are in the order of magnitude of the infection rates seen among the men of the AIF, some of whom faced the notorious additional exposure to the disease in the Egypt, Sinai and Palestine theatres of war that contributed significantly to the incidence of VD. Butler's *relative* figures suggest rates that were 50 per cent higher in these theatres than those recorded across all theatres of war for the AIF.

It is contended that this *does not* reflect badly on the medical performance of the AIF but does reflect an element of social history that is worthy of further consideration. The Canadian official medical historian, MacPhail, observed that the incidence of VD was higher for American and all Dominion forces than among the British Army:

This bad eminence does not of itself testify to a higher degree of chastity in the English soldiers, as it is probable that living in accustomed surroundings they had their own arrangements.[28]

In other words, the Dominion forces were away, far from home, when leave was granted so if they desired the company of a woman they had little option but to seek out professional services. Medical services did what they could, but social pressures delayed the issuance of condoms to British troops until later in the war, and not at all to American troops. The German military had long before the war promoted the use of condoms, and Germany exported nearly all of the condoms supplied to Europe, Australia and Canada in the fifteen years up until the start of the war. During the war, the American companies Scmid and Youngs became the main supplier to the allies.[29]

Butler claimed that the AIF medical services actively promoted preventative measures, although only 200 000 condoms were issued in all of the AIF treatment centres in the United Kingdom in the two years up until June 1919.[30] The existence of this statistic for this particularly limited timeframe in Butler's medical history suggests that the Australian authorities may also have been slow in promoting the use of condoms.

However, a *far more important* issue needs to be raised here. It has previously been pointed out that the count of VD cases undertaken for the present analysis was conservative in two areas. First, where a discharge was followed by a readmission within *seven* days, the decision was made that it not be counted as a separate hospitalisation, since effectively the soldier had not been cured at the first hospitalisation. Second, with the advent of a proportion of soldiers in England being treated on a day-care basis, the number of days of hospitalisation was dramatically reduced for those fortunate enough to be at the right time and the right place to be treated in this way. Nevertheless, they were not able to rejoin their unit in the field until cured; so effectively they were unavailable for active service.

Bearing in mind this conservative approach taken in the records analysis, the calculation of the number of days spent by these men in hospital remains staggering and highlights the cost of VD in terms of the availability of men during the war. The amount of time for which hospital beds were occupied overseas by men suffering from VD was calculated at *2.839 million* days. Is it any wonder that the authorities were deeply concerned about the drain this condition had on their resources? The average length of stay in hospital was over fifty days. If this is applied to the admissions in Australia (and it can be, as they are admissions), then the impact in terms of hospital bed days rises to *3.475 million* days, far in excess of any other illness cause for hospitalisation. Thus, Butler had failed to quantify the true and most important impact of VD on the AIF.

But time spent in hospital is not all there is to this issue. While a specific count of the time it took to return the soldier to active duty was not made, the observation can be made that some men took weeks, a small number (in excess of 6000 men) even had to return to the field from Australia where they had been sent for treatment, and many were returned to their units from Britain. It is entirely conservative to suggest that it took an average of two to three weeks for soldiers to return to the field, which pushes the non-availability of AIF servicemen with VD out to over *4 million* days (including lost time spent in hospital in Australia). To put this into some perspective, the number of days for which all Australian POWs were lost due to captivity from the date of capture until 11 November 1918 was *2.4 million* days. After the losses of death and losses of men from wounding, VD was the next major factor limiting Australia's war effort.

Sad as the impact of VD is, this finding *must not* detract or distract from the main purpose of this record review which is to assess the *total* impact of wounding, injury and illness of this war, of which VD was only one part. There were flu, infection, fevers, horrible skin conditions, respiratory diseases, diarrhoea and dysentery. There were illness, injury and wounding.

Total Number of Hospitalisations

For the first time, this scrupulous examination of AIF Attestation Papers has revealed that those men who made it to a theatre of war were admitted to hospital suffering from wounds, injuries and illnesses on over *737 000* occasions. Including admissions for VD in Australia, the number of hospitalisations exceeds *three-quarters of a million*. This estimate exceeds the partial and inaccurate wounding statistic in the official casualty records of 155 000 by a *factor of five* (see Chapter 1, Table 5).

When taken as a whole the analysis of the Attestation Papers results in an estimate of *430 000* admissions of AIF soldiers to hospital for illness alone, of which nearly 90 per cent (384 000) were for battle-related illnesses. When this appalling toll is combined with the number of hospitalisations for injury (98 700), the number of admissions climbs to nearly 530 000. The sheer size of the number is startling enough, but that it has taken so long for this figure to be determined underscores the concerns expressed by some post-war historians of an overreliance on Bean's and Butler's official histories. It is now claimed that the military war records, whether in Britain or Australia, did not assess the level of wounding correctly, understating them by a third (155 000 versus 208 000) mainly due to the under-diagnosis of shell shock, and that the official medical assessment of the total injury and illness impacts was also incorrect or omitted. It is argued here that when the three-quarters of a million hospitalisations are adjusted to account for those who did not survive the war by deducting their hospitalisations, *those who did survive* this war were admitted to hospital an average of *nearly three times each.*

Not Hospitalised

Nearly three-quarters of a million hospitalisations raises the question: were there *any* soldiers not hospitalised? The answer is yes. The analysis indicates that just over 21 000 soldiers were not hospitalised during their period of service. And it is worth examining this category in some detail.

It is widely understood that Britain provided most *but not all* of the heavy lifting for the supply and administration required by the Dominion countries involved in the war. Based on an examination of the records and the occupations of soldiers, Australia provided largely for its own transport and the administrative duties required to manage soldiers' pay, sustenance, medical services, record-keeping and postal services. As such most of the men employed in these services were not exposed directly to the fighting. It follows that the great proportion of those men who were not hospitalised were classed as behind the scenes, engaged in roles such as driver, light rail operator, postal clerk, batman, pay clerk, vet hospital cook, and member of the AFC, whether as a pilot or an aircraft mechanic, who in most instances spent the entire war training in England or Scotland. The officer ranks will be discussed further shortly, but for now it is worth highlighting a wonderful example from this category: the records of Captain George Hubert Wilkins, who stated upon his enlistment on 1 May 1917 that his occupation was 'explorer'. He immediately joined the AFC and, when found to be colour blind, was put in charge of the photographic section of the War Records Office in London. He was then appointed as an official photographer based at the AIF headquarters in Boulogne in June 1918. He was awarded the Military Cross shortly thereafter, but unusually and unfortunately, for reasons unknown, his records do not disclose the circumstances. However, his records do disclose that later, in November 1919, he attempted to return to Australia as a competitor in an air race from Great Britain to Australia. Yet he failed to complete the flight, getting only as far as Malta. He then returned to Great Britain, where he was required to pay his own passage of 55 pounds to return to Australia. He was not hospitalised during his service and his was certainly not a typical example of service.

More common were the scenarios exemplified by the following cases. Many carry the characteristic of no hospitalisation but the soldier was discharged medically unfit. This was the case for Alfred Wilkinson (3475), who was caught close to a bursting shell, causing him to be rendered deaf. However, he remained on duty and was only discharged medically unfit the following year. Walter Hood (1053) was a farmer who served most of his time in the Australian Veterinary Hospital contingent. He was never admitted to hospital but was discharged medically unfit in April 1919 diagnosed with colitis. Reg Williams (3167) enlisted as a cook in September 1914 and was appointed as a gunner. His medical record is brief, with one reference to an infected thumb that did not require hospitalisation. However, he was discharged on 1 January 1920 as medically unfit with his record noting that he suffered from shell shock in 1917, was never in hospital, but developed headaches and frequent 'dizziness'. Of the 21000 men who were not hospitalised, there were approximately 1200 men discharged medically unfit. Further reference to these non-hospitalised men will be made in Chapter 8, as over one-third of them (7100) felt the need to apply for a pension after the war, and some applied twice.

Other examples of *non-hospitalised* cases follow. John Richard Hall (66) was a butcher who joined the Postal Corps in September 1914. He served in this capacity in Egypt, France and England, where he married and subsequently returned to Australia to be discharged fit and well, and was awarded all three possible medals—the British Medal for service overseas, the Victory Medal for service in a theatre of war, and the 1914–1915 Star for enlisting in those years provided they saw service. John Hood (19285) was appointed as a driver in England in September 1916, before proceeding to France two months later. He was wounded in action in May 1918 but he remained on duty and was not hospitalised. The rest of his war service was uneventful. Robert Hood (403) enlisted and joined the tunnelling section at the end of 1916. His service was also uneventful; and he was discharged fit on 12 May 1919. He is listed in the analysis as not being hospitalised. However, sadly, he appears on the Roll of Honour as a result of his suicide a year later. This soldier will be further discussed in Chapter 8.

The *safest* occupation by weight of numbers during the First World War was that of driver. Robert Graham (184) was a thirty-five years of age and a shearer when he enlisted in January 1916. He was appointed as a driver upon arrival in England, served in France in that role and was awarded a Meritorious Service Medal. He was discharged in 1919 upon the TPE, having spent no time in hospital. But such cases of non-hospitalisation were rare.

From general observations it can be said that approximately half of all cases of soldiers who were not hospitalised in this war were characterised by them receiving only one medal, the British Medal, indicating that they were never in a theatre of war. Such cases amounted to about 10 000 out of the 318 100 men who embarked from Australia[31] representing the nation's fighting force. The following two examples lifted from the B2455 series are provided to demonstrate how this scenario may have occurred. Cyril Charles Hook (61872) enlisted on 2 May 1918, embarked on 5 October and arrived in England after 11 November by which time the war had ceased; consequently he received only one medal. And he was not hospitalised during his service. William Bede Hook enlisted in April 1918. He was an accountant and was immediately appointed to the rank of lieutenant (hence no serial number). He managed to get to England in September 1918, but did not arrive in France until December of that year, by which time the war was over. As a result, he received one medal, and was not hospitalised during his service.

Discharged Medically Unfit

The category of servicemen who were discharged medically unfit also produced some startling results. From the record review, it is now estimated that during the existence of the AIF, *130 500* soldiers were discharged medically unfit. This is over *half* of all men who survived (255 800).[32] Of those discharged medically unfit, it is conservatively estimated that *27 700*, or over one in five, were declared medically unfit as a result of some form of traumatic stress or shell shock. This proportion of medically unfit discharges is probably an underestimate. Why? First, the cause for *hospitalisation* was nearly always noted somewhere in the soldier's record; yet the reason for a *medical discharge* was infrequently given. Often it was evident on the basis of the soldier's record of hospitalisation; but where this was not the case, and the soldier was suddenly medically discharged, the record was treated conservatively and not assigned to the category of those who had suffered from shell shock. This was the practice even where the soldier had a history of hospitalisation for traumatic stress. Second, there were undoubtedly under-diagnoses of shell shock, particularly in declaring a soldier medically unfit for further service, citing observed illness as the cause. And third, the onset of shell shock may have manifested itself after the soldier's discharge, becoming evident in unrecorded pension-related data. The few examples provided below highlight these points.

John James Gibbs (2441) was buried by a shell burst in September 1917 on *three* occasions. He was admitted to hospital for a month (no cause given) before being hospitalised again in December, this time specifically being diagnosed as suffering from shell shock. By April 1918, it had been decided that he should return to Australia. On the way home he was treated for VD and discharged medically unfit, diagnosed with shell shock. Sadly, according to his records, John Gibbs was still stuttering at his last medical examination upon discharge, a condition that had emerged twelve months previously. Charles Earnest Gibbs (2371) received a gunshot wound to the chest in April 1917, causing him to be discharged medically unfit in March 1918, with his file marked 'disability—GSW Thorax'. Some time shortly after this date, he was admitted to Parkside Mental Hospital in Adelaide where, according to a file note dated 3 October 1920, he was suffering from a 'chronic mental disorder and is not likely to recover or be discharged'. He died in that institution in 1939 at the age of fifty-three years. When analysing this case it was decided to account for Charles Gibson as being only discharged medically unfit and not medically unfit as a result of shell shock, as it was not clear whether his condition was in fact war related.

Another judgement was required in the case of Reginald Samuel Williams (98), who held the rank of Regimental Quarter Master Sergeant. He landed at Gallipoli with the first wave of men and was subsequently admitted to hospital on 26 July 1915 suffering from 'debility'. He was returned to Gallipoli on 1 December only to be evacuated three days later with a diagnosis of 'dilated heart'. He received his first reprimand for drunkenness on 16 January 1916. What followed were a succession of arrests and detentions for drunkenness until, in June 1916, his file was marked 'services no longer required (owing to excessive drinking habits)' and he was returned to Australia for 'discharge SNLR' (soldier no longer required), somewhat in disgrace. From his records it would appear that he then joined the Australian Air Force in Australia and was considered for a meritorious service award in 1925. In considering his suitability for this award the Air Force requested the details of his service in the AIF. It is unclear whether Reg received the award but it appears that he died aged in his early fifties, still a member of the Air Force; his post-war service did not indicate a man suffering from alcoholism. He received all three medals. A judgement was made that Reg was suffering from shell shock when he was discharged in 1916 and that the appropriate accounting of this case in the analysis was that he was discharged medically unfit, as a result of shell shock.

A remarkable example exists in the records of a not uncommon practice of returning some men to Australia who were mentally and physically exhausted, but for whom no specific symptom could be identified with which to discharge them medically unfit. Instead, such men were returned to Australia for 'submarine guard duties'. This meant that they quietly served out their term in the army staring out to sea until discharged TPE. These cases could arguably be treated as soldiers medically unfit for service, but in line with the cautious approach taken in the current analysis they were treated as a normal discharge. Exemplary here is the case of William Edward Sing (355A), twenty-eights years of age and a horseman from Queensland, who enlisted in October 1914. He was to be awarded the Distinguished Service Medal and the Belgian Croix de Guerre. He was hospitalised nine times, three for wounding, of which one admission was for shell shock suffered at Gallipoli in October 1915; he had gained a reputation as a sniper and was mentioned in dispatches. His last hospitalisation was for a gunshot wound to his back in February 1918. He rejoined his unit in May and served in the field until early July 1918 when he was ordered to return to Australia for submarine guard duty until his discharge (TPE) in December 1918. It is not known how many enemy casualties sniper William Sing was ultimately credited with by the time he left France, but at Gallipoli, just before his hospitalisation for shell shock, it stood at 201 Turkish soldiers. A book has been written about William Sing. He was counted as being discharged medically unfit, suffering from shell shock, in this review.

Officers

Until now it has been impossible to examine the impact of this war on the category of men who served as officers, separated from the other ranks, as the records were not segregated. Strong views are held on the comparative performance of an officer and a sapper. The sample analysis and its data can now be used to explore the multiple facets of these data at levels that have not previously been possible, including the performance of, and the impact upon, the officers of the AIF, for comparison with the other ranks.

As with all the previous categories this examination is not straightforward. An observation made during the course of reading the 9604 records was that a clear distinction became increasingly evident between those officers who gave their all, many their lives, and those who appeared adept at doing not much at all. This distinction required careful analysis.

Before continuing this discussion, a few caveats are necessary. The AIF sent hundreds of chaplains to this war with the appointed rank of captains. They were removed for the purposes of the following analysis as they could not be regarded as men who actively took part in conflict. Also removed were the officers who were appointed after 11 November 1918.[33] These were men who had spent the war in the 'other ranks' category. It is true that the AIF appointed many men from the ranks to officer status—these men were initially promoted to second lieutenant and then to first lieutenant. Yet it was observed to be very rare for such men to receive any further promotion. The level of captain was generally an appointment made at the outset due to the individual's previous experience or membership of the reserves or a particular profession.

For example, the following was identified in relation to the policy governing officer appointments, highlighting the Australian Army's need for the services of doctors and more importantly, dentists. Upon enlistment a doctor would be appointed captain, a surgeon would be appointed major, a dental mechanic became a lieutenant, a dentist became a captain or major and a dental surgeon was appointed to the rank of lieutenant colonel.[34] Other professions rose out of the ranks on the basis of their performance although accountants were often appointed to the rank of lieutenant when they joined up. The other role that automatically carried the rank of lieutenant was the entry into training to be a pilot in the new AFC.

It should be borne in mind, when considering the devastation wrought by the technological advances seen in this war with equipment such as machine guns, flame throwers, tanks and artillery, that there was another advance in technology that was utilised to some effect in warfare for the first time. It was the telephone, available to assist in the conduct of this war with the potential for remote and mass communication by wire or signals. Having said this, instances still appear in the records of men being sent to pigeon training school as late as 1917. The use of signal technology allowed many of the officers conducting the battle to remain behind the worst of it, bunkered in relative safety. Certainly lines of communication were continuously disrupted as wires were cut, but it was not the officers who repaired the breaks. The effect of this development in modern warfare management will be explored further below.

The first obvious step in the assessment of the officer ranks was to compare the death rate of AIF officers with that of other ranks. Despite the distinctions in level of commitment or exposure previously mentioned, the surprising result initially revealed was that these rates were virtually *identical*. Approximately 3400 officers lost their lives, or 19.7 per cent of those who served. This compares to 19.6 per cent for the other ranks. Something else appeared to be at play here.

With the exclusions of chaplains and late-appointed officers, the AIF included the services of approximately 17 250 officers, made up of 700 colonels or lieutenant colonels, 1700 majors, 3650 captains, and approximately 11 200 lieutenants. These ranks were the highest held by these individuals until the end of the war. The capabilities provided by Excel software (including 400 000 cells of recorded data captured in this record review in each spread sheet) allowed for and facilitated the analysis of the death rate of each officer ranking. And this analysis in large part reflects the influence of the telephone in the management of battle warfare, as is now demonstrated. The death rate of the rank of colonel or lieutenant colonel was 5.8 per cent, while for majors the death rate rose to 16.9 per cent. Interestingly the officer level of lieutenant reflected the other ranks identically, at 19.6 per cent. The officers who carried the greatest weight were the captains, among whom more than one in four (26.4 per cent) lost their lives in the First World War. As the most senior officer in the field they led from the front and died on the front, communicating information and taking directions by telephone from more senior ranks in the rear. Compounding this death toll of captains-in-the-field is the fact that many men holding the rank of captain had little involvement in fighting because they were the doctors and surgeons and to a much lesser extent the administrators, occupied behind the lines or back in England. This appears to have had quite a significant effect in increasing the death rate of captains-in-the-field, and supports the contention that the only way the members of this class of officer in the First World War managed to survive was if they were lucky enough to be seriously wounded and struck off strength. What can be observed at this point, presented in a slightly different manner, is that 13 per 100 captains were *not* hospitalised compared to 1 per 100 for officers as a whole. A further 38 per 100 of the captains who survived were *not* wounded compared to 24 per 100 of officers as a whole. If it is assumed that these men were medical or administrative staff, the captain-in-the-field paid dearly. The appalling death and wounding rates born by this officer class fell on the shoulders of fewer than half of them. It is therefore estimated that every second captain in the field was killed, but this area warrants further research, as it is only an observation at this stage.

It can now also be claimed that officers were more likely to be wounded than other ranks (0.76 to 0.65)[35] but less likely to be injured (0.25 to 0.31). Officers were far less likely to be hospitalised with illness (1.02 to 1.37) and significantly less likely to contract VD (0.08 to 0.18);[36] indeed, officers were twice as likely to avoid hospitalisation as other ranks (0.12 to 0.06 *not* hospitalised). Interestingly, the incidence of hospitalisation due to shell shock was similar for officers and other ranks (officers 0.22 to other ranks 0.20). The assertion that officers tended to be struck off strength rather than discharged medically unfit is borne out by the figures for the incidence of being discharged medically unfit (officers 0.18 to other ranks 0.33)[37] or to be discharged medically unfit—shell shock (officers 0.06 to other ranks 0.09), despite being hospitalised for the condition at a similar or slightly higher rate.

Survivability and Risk

It was stated earlier that deaths in battle amounted to *53 600* men. The analysis of this death toll made possible by this record review reveals a chilling confirmation of previously speculated outcomes to underscore the extent of the bloodbath created by the killing technology used in the First World War. It can now be estimated that around *1600* men did not last *two* days, *5000* were dead within *two weeks* from being TOS and *10 000* did not last *a month*. The average length of time from being TOS to the recorded date of death, after deducting time spent away from the front due to hospitalisation, a specific training course or granted leave,[38] was *six months*.

When Leo van Bergen discusses the bloodshed of this war he makes a very powerful point:

> Neither the generals nor ordinary soldiers, nor 'the circumstances' were primarily responsible for the debacle. The blame lies with the war, a more or less autonomous process that never submits to human decision-making but forces decisions upon us. War does not allow those engaged in it to change its nature or direction as they see fit, let alone to make it stop. In the First World War this meant that the circumstances of the time—massive firepower on both sides and the huge armies, impossible to protect during an advance—inevitably lead to butchery. The mass slaughter would have taken place no matter which generals were in charge and no matter what decisions they made.[39]

One could take issue with van Bergen and argue that some protection for advancing troops developed when the operations of war learnt to provide these advancing troops with the cover of a creeping barrage during the course of 1916. However, there is a way to statistically prove van Bergen's assertion that death in this war was entirely indiscriminate. The platform upon which the argument will be built is the age of servicemen at the time of their death.

Modern-day statistical analysis opens up the processing of the data collected in the 9604-strong sample count to unique, never-before-attempted questioning. Correlation using regression analysis was enabled through the push of a button, or two. Even the analysis of the ages of the men when they enlisted could be explored in depth.

Figure 6: Age at enlistment by year: officers and other ranks

Age at Enlistment by Year: Officers and Other Ranks ©

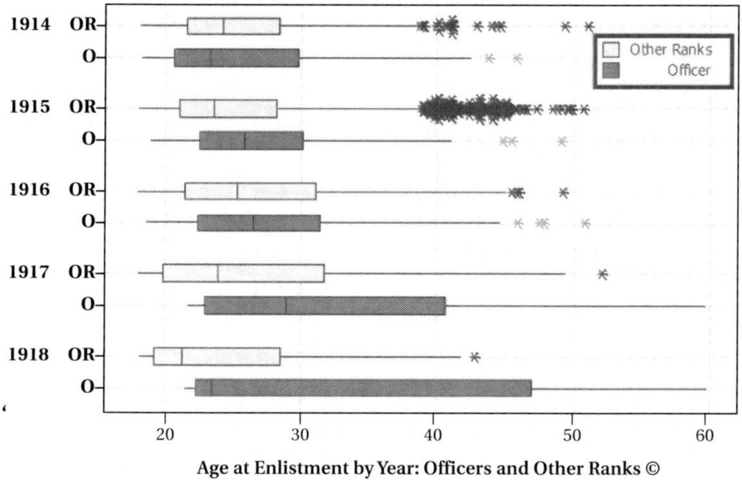

Source: Compiled by David Noonan from Attestation Papers, 2014.

The graphic shown in Figure 6 depicts soldiers' age at the time of enlistment at a level of detail never before presented. The boxes represent the middle two quartiles of the range of ages for each year, for officers and other ranks. The line within each box represents the median of the age range for that year. The median age for other ranks fell from its high of about twenty-five years in 1916 to around twenty-one years in 1918 as Australia began to run out of men interested in enlistment and the ominous signs of the war's tragic cost were becoming increasingly evident. Only the young and perhaps naïve were attracted to participate. The median age for officers fell from its peak in 1917 of about twenty-nine years to approximately twenty-three years in 1918. The third quartile stretched out to forty-seven years in 1918 as the pool of eligible officers shrunk and greater reliance was placed on graduates from military college. The lines protruding from either side of each box track the upper and lower limits of the vast majority of men enlisting in that year. It can be seen that the cut-off for other ranks shifted from forty-five years in 1916 to fifty in 1917, and for officers from forty-five years in 1916 to sixty in 1917 as enlistment quotas were not satisfied. The small crosses, or outliers, represent men who were statistically unusually older. These are in particular evidence in 1915. They represent the outcome of a particular call by the authorities in that year for miners to enlist, for whom an exception was made by lifting their eligibility age from forty-five to fifty years. This was a result of the realisation that the Western Front had become a static line and the tactic of tunnelling under the enemy line came into play.

The role played by the age of enlistment led to the analysis of whether there was a correlation between a soldier's age and his survivability. It would be reasonable to expect that the young man, as fit as he will ever be in his lifetime, naïve to the risks, full of testosterone and energy and a belief that he was bullet-proof, *would die sooner* than a soldier aged in his late thirties or early forties, who would likely be wiser, more risk averse, and perhaps have a wife and children at home. However, the outcome of this analysis was not as expected.

There appeared to be *no correlation* between the ages of a soldier at the time of their death and the time they spent in the field. As previously mentioned, the latter measure was arrived at by calculating the time between when the soldier was TOS and the day he died, and subtracting the time he had spent away from the fighting due to wounding, injury, illness, training in specific depots or specific skills or on leave, which left the actual number of days for which he was exposed to the war. Sometimes this was exposure in the trenches, sometimes in depots in support. In the latter case soldiers were not exposed to fighting but were nevertheless *on duty in the field*.

This finding of no correlation means that a soldier's age at death had absolutely *nothing* to do with his survivability. Australian servicemen lasted on average six months but the distribution of time around this average was the same for each year of age. In other words these men faced unadulterated slaughter. The artillery obliterated any chance of improved prospects of survival for any soldiers who may have been risk averse.

However, the death, pain and suffering did not end here. The post-war impact is discussed in Chapter 8, which will bring together in its entirety the true cost paid by these men and those around them for Australia's involvement in this war. It will thereby seek to include the incidence of injury and illness, the omissions of those we forget, together with an accurate measure of death and woundings, and war-related post-war death and suffering. This is the least we can do to honour their memory.

Notes

1. This is the net AIF enlistment figure after the following corrections were made: the number 386 000 contains approximately 4000 naval enlistments (A6700 Series) (A Graham Butler, *Official Medical History of the Australian Army Medical Services, 1914–1918, Volume III*, Australian War Memorial, Canberra, 1942, p. 882), and over 2050 nurses listed as AIF but who should be listed elsewhere, and members of 'the Tropical Force' sent to Rabaul which was not a theatre of war (a finding of approximately 1000).
2. As determined using Minitab: 1 Proportion Test and Confidence Interval.
3. Commonwealth of Australia, *Census of The Commonwealth of Australia, 30th June 1933: Volume III—Statistician's Report*, Commonwealth Government Printer, Canberra, 1933.
4. Achieved using Excel and Minitab statistical and graphical software.
5. Joan Beaumont et al., *Australian Defence: Sources and Statistics (The Australian Centenary History of Defence Series)*, vol. VI, Oxford University Press, South Melbourne, Australia, 2001. This publication contains a table of all 'AIF casualties' (the context suggests killed, wounded and POW) on page 276 on a monthly basis sourcing *Medical Services Official History of the Great War* (Great Britain, *Statistics of the Military Effort of the British Empire during the Great War 1914–1920*, The British War Office and London HM Stationary, London, 1922, pp. 257–71, 284–7). Because of the monthly interval it distorts the relative effect between campaigns—for example, showing Ypres to be more damaging than Fromelles. It is contended that the following presentation is a more accurate reflection of the impact of specific campaigns rather than the months of war and is specifically related to the occurrence of death.

6   Robin Prior and Trevor Wilson, *The Somme*, Yale University Press, New Haven, 2005, p. 177.
7   Robin Prior and Trevor Wilson, *Passchendaele: The Untold Story*, Scribe, Melbourne, 2003, p. 200.
8   Geoffrey Serle, *John Monash: A Biography*, Melbourne University Press, Melbourne, 1982, p. 331.
9   David Steveson, *1914–1918: The History of the First World War*, Allen Lane, United States of America, 2004, p. 141.
10 Sir John Monash, *The Australian Victories in France in 1918*, Lothian, Melbourne, 1923, p. 140.
11 ibid., p. 313.
12 The Australian Bureau of Statistics data show male suicide rates on average of 18 males per 100 000 per annum over the last ten years. The gross amount of 550 deaths picked up in the AIF records can be viewed as having occurred over four or five years, leading to an annualised equivalent of over 110 men, six to eight times higher. This somewhat imprecise comparative measure is considered acceptable due to its overwhelming indication of war-related stress. See: <www.abs.gov.au>.
13 United States Army Medical Department, *The Medical Department of the United States Army in the World War, Vol XV, Part 2, Medical and Casualty Statistics*, US Army Surgeon General's Office, US, Table 48, p. 135, p. 147.
14 ibid., p. 7.
15 See Table 5, Chapter 1: the various numbers were 4044, 4057, 4084, and 4098.
16 The 17 600 wounding admissions were suffered by 14 000 men who would subsequently be killed. By removing these figures from the total of men wounded and the total number of woundings, we are left with the net impact on those that *survived a wounding*: 191 000 admissions suffered by 133 000 men.
17 Butler, *Official Medical History of the Australian Army Medical Services, 1914–1918, Volume III*, p. 187.
18 Canada's official medical history puts the figure at around 160 per 1000. Sir Andrew MacPhail, *Official History of the Canadian Forces in the Great War 1914–1918, The Medical Services*, Minister of National Defense, under Direction of the General Staff, Ottawa, Canada, 1925, p. 179.
19 Butler states that admissions for VD made to hospitals, compounds, etc. in Australia stood at 12 689. The only treating hospital in Australia was at Langwarrin, where he states the total admissions of men returned to Australia for treatment was 6649. At the same time Butler cites detection rates in the 'Call Up' in October 1916 in Australia of nearly 20 per thousand. Yet this level was not supported by the evidence obtained from the analysis of the MT series presented in Chapter 2, which found that of the applicants for enlistment to the AIF somewhere between seven and at most twelve per 1000 were infected. However, the 'Call Up' survey was compulsory, thereby capturing a true population sample, whereas the enlistment survey is of volunteers who would be unlikely to present themselves if they thought they had VD. The lower level might therefore be an indicator of the level of those infected who did not know they were

infected. Less than 200 000 condoms were issued in AIF treatment depots in England in the two years to June 1919. ibid., p. 178, 189.
20 Leo van Bergen, *Before My Helpless Sight:Suffering, Dying and Military Medicine on the Western Front, 1914–1918* (trans. Liz Waters, 2009 ed.), Ashgate Publishing Limited, 1999 (reprint, 2009), p. 150, 151.
21 Canada's official medical history puts the figure at around 160 per 1000. Sir Andrew MacPhail, *Official History of the Canadian Forces in the Great War 1914–1918, The Medical Services*, p. 287.
22 Butler, *Official Medical History of the Australian Army Medical Services, 1914–1918, Volume III*, p. 178.
23 ibid., p. 189.
24 MacPhail, *Official History of the Canadian Forces in the Great War 1914–1918, The Medical Services*, p. 287.
25 United States Army Medical Department, *The Medical Department of the United States Army in the World War, Vol XV, Part 2, Medical and Casualty Statistics*, p. 576.
26 Mitchell and Smith, *Medical Services Official History of the Great War: Casualties and Medical Statistics of the Great War*, p. 73.
27 Butler, *Official Medical History of the Australian Army Medical Services, 1914–1918, Volume III*, p. 179.
28 MacPhail, *Official History of the Canadian Forces in the Great War 1914–1918, The Medical Services*, p. 287.
29 Aine Collier, *The Humble Little Condom: A History*, Prometheus Books, Amherst, NY, 2007, pp. 169–191.
30 Butler, *Official Medical History of the Australian Army Medical Services, 1914–1918, Volume III*, p. 189.
31 This is important because we need to understand the proportion of AIF soldiers exposed to this war. Of the total force sent to this conflict, the proportion actually exposed in the field to a theatre of war was higher than that of the forces of Britain, the USA, Canada, Germany and France. These comparative proportions will be raised again in Chapter 7 when examining national comparative statistics.
32 This is the result of 318 100 embarkations less 62 300 deaths.
33 Ivan Webley enlisted in the Australian Flying Corps in January 1918, was appointed second lieutenant and embarked the following month. He was qualified as a pilot and lieutenant on 11 November 1918 and returned to Australia twelve months later having been hospitalised once with gastritis. He is included as an officer in the count.
34 Thomas Conwell Williams was a Sydney dental surgeon who held the rank of major in the Citizen Military Force. He enlisted in September 1915 and quickly attained the rank of lieutenant-colonel. After some training he was put in command of the 10th Artillery Brigade and saw service in the field in North Africa and France. He did not act in a dentistry capacity and was highly decorated. Thomas Waitsen Williams was thirty-one years of age and a Bendigo dentist who lived with his mother. He also had Citizen Force experience. He was appointed to the rank of adjutant at Gallipoli, fought in the field with the Light Horse Brigade, was appointed captain in France and joined the anti-aircraft

section in the middle of 1917. He finished the war with the rank of major and was mentioned in dispatches. He was ill and injured at Gallipoli and was discharged medically unfit in 1919. He did not act in a dentistry capacity.

35   Another way of looking at these comparative numbers using this example is to say that, for every 100 officers, 76 hospitalisations for wounding occurred compared to 65 hospitalisations suffered among 100 soldiers of other ranks.

36   Officers were often treated in their rooms for any illness but given the seriousness of this disease it is contended that the officers were hospitalised. It is more likely that the diagnosis of this disease was not recorded on some occasions as its presence reflected badly on the officer rank.

37   A decision was made to list an officer as discharged medically unfit when it was clear that he was seriously ill or wounded even though his record showed that he was merely struck off strength; therefore, this proportion significantly masks the assertion on the face of it.

38   The length of time on average spent away from the front was around three months, the vast majority of which was due to hospitalisation.

39   van Bergen, *Before My Helpless Sight: Suffering, Dying and Military Medicine on the Western Front, 1914–1918*, p. 7.

CHAPTER 7
Some Comparisons in this Global War

A comparative analysis of casualty statistics among selected nations in the First World War is of value. The primary aim is not to present a macabre picture to show that the proportional humanitarian cost to Australia was some multiple of *contribution to the total effort*, as the official historian Scott would have put it.[1] The primary goal is to illuminate the war casualty calculation and classification practices adopted by the other belligerents. This approach subsequently highlights the major underestimation in the Australian official records of casualties resulting from injury and illness. Injury and illness make up approximately two-thirds of the 750 000 hospitalisations of the men of the AIF, and yet their incidence has remained under-researched, uncalculated and unacknowledged for nearly 100 years.

The forgotten Butler and his equally overlooked medical services history provided some comparative data for the British Army. He also presented the generalised statistics of both battle and non-battle casualties for the US Army, as well as an overview of French and German casualties. His data are cited here but will also be supported by primary sources where possible. However, owing to limited research resources, primary sources for French and German casualties (the Marin report and Sanitatsbericht uber deutsche Heer)[2] were not researched (*although they were quoted* by Butler and are partially used here) and respected secondary sources were consulted regarding these two countries. Primary source data are provided for Canadian, British and US forces; and while the detail necessary for an adequate comparative analysis may seem large, it is brought together in one table at the end of this chapter to reveal a hitherto unappreciated level of sacrifice suffered by the men of the AIF. Given the size of the task, this chapter does not claim to provide a comprehensive comparison of six armies' casualty statistics, merely an adequate comparative analysis.

It should be kept in mind that at the end of the war, nations did not know their total military human cost. Resources were scarce and priorities lay elsewhere. It was many years after this conflict concluded before medical data were analysed for illness and injury. The timing of the publication of statistics varied from nation to nation, with non-battle and illness statistics usually appearing many years after the release of data on official battle casualties. In Australia's case, such statistics appeared nearly twenty-five years after the war had finished.

The country with the briefest involvement in the First World War, but the most resources, was the first to conduct an analysis of their casualties. Its chosen cut-off date to stop counting their casualties was 31 December 1919.

United States of America

The US declared war on 5 April 1917 but its main troop strength did not begin to be seen on the Western Front for a year.[3] By the end of April 1918, 125 000 men had been sent to France together with an immediately available National Guard contingent of 180 000.[4] Another 1.3 million men were in training camps in the US.[5]

US troops first saw action on 25 April 1918, exactly three years after Australia's first exposure to the war, when a contingent was inserted into the front line at Picardy.[6] Germany was already falling back along large parts of the Western Front when the Americans were first sent into a major *attacking* battle on 4 July 1918 at Hamel,[7] but their lack of training in battle conditions resulted in disastrous mistakes, involving not only their own soldiers but Australians as well, as at that time they were embedded with the Australians under the command of Sir John Monash.[8] It is not widely understood, but the Americans had quite limited exposure to this war. By the end of October 1918, shortly before the war's end, the US had 1.85 million troops in Europe but only 1.39 million had been exposed to fighting in France;[9] and another 2.150 million had not left home, or were in transit[10]—they were just too late. The Americans' official claim of having raised an army of 4 million must be viewed in the light of the fact that *only a third* of that 4 million were exposed to the conflict. In addition, those exposed to the conflict were only involved in fighting for 200 days,[11] albeit in the very different conditions of 1918 compared to the earlier years of the war. With the initially successful start of Germany's spring offensive in March 1918, the war moved out of the trenches along the Western Front as the massive forces swayed one way and then the other, covering ground unimaginable in the previous three years. The exposure of men in the open field increased casualty rates dramatically in this mobile warfare, one soldier's letter described this time as 'a machine gunner's picnic'. In their short time in the field, America's casualties were appalling. Monash was less than impressed with their capabilities. Writing about the 'American soldier' in the context of the commencement of a major assault on the Hindenburg line at the end of September 1918, when Monash had two American divisions under his command, he wrote:

> They showed a fine spirit, a keen desire to learn, magnificent individual bravery, and splendid comradeship. But they were lacking in war experience, in training, and in knowledge of technique. They had not yet learned the virtues of unquestioning obedience, of punctuality, of quick initiative, of anticipating the next action. They were, many of them, unfamiliar with the weapons and instruments of fighting, with the numerous kinds of explosive materials, or with the routine of preparing and promulgating clear orders. They seriously underrated the necessity for a well organised system of supply, particularly of food and water, to the battle troops. They hardly, as yet, appreciated the tactical expediency available for reducing losses in battle.[12]

Butler provides a summary of US casualties, citing the *The Medical Department of the United States Army, Vol XV, Part 2, Medical and Casualty Statistics*. This American publication is extraordinary in the detail it provides in various forms and multiple cross-categorisations (including distinguishing data of 'white', 'coloured', and 'native soldiers'). The most striking feature is the amount of detail concerning the deaths and hospitalisations that occurred in the depots and camps back at home in the US—and it was for good reason. The US had in total more deaths in its home depots than those 'killed in action' overseas,[13] predominantly on the Western Front. Death from diseases of all kinds, not only Spanish Flu (pneumonia claimed 84 per cent of all deaths,[14] of which a proportion was later identified to be the result of Spanish Flu), decimated their ranks, with more deaths at *home* month by month through 1918 and 1919 than those sustained from battle and illness in Europe.[15]

The analysis of American records is made more difficult, however, because the statistics in the US medical records are presented in an idiosyncratic way: they are couched in terms of men on strength at the end of each month. This is essentially a method of approaching wastage, but in reverse. As such, the total number of individuals affected is obscured. It is actually a measure of those 'left over' from losses through death, wounding, illness and injury after *adding* those who were TOS in each monthly period. The choice of this taxonomy is only understandable from a militarist perspective. In other words, the commander was not concerned with those who were affected; he was only concerned with those who remained. For the purposes of this comparative review, this statistical quirk needs to be circumvented. Butler is again not helpful. He states that the mean strength of the Americans in the field was 1 046 533 for the whole of 1918.[16] But when the table Butler has referenced is examined, it becomes clear that this mean figure is the average over 1918 of monthly numbers, from 214 000 at the end of January to 1 816 000 at the end of December.[17] Therefore, the average monthly mean strength in the field cited by Butler is essentially useless. A better estimate of America's army capacity in the field would perhaps be its strength at the end of September and October 1918, which provides a number averaging out at approximately 1.75 million.

In any event, Leonard Ayres, Chief of the Statistical Division of the General Staff, resolved the issue by stating that 1.39 million American soldiers were exposed to this war.[18] Overall, the American Army was to suffer 114 000 deaths up until the cut-off date of the end of 1919 used to calculate its statistics. In Europe, from the beginning of 1918 (in only 200 days of exposure to the war) the American death toll reached 76 700 deaths, over a *third* of them from injury and disease, and US soldiers incurred 210 000 admissions to hospital due to wounding.[19]

In addition, for all of 1918 and throughout Europe, there were a further 90 000 hospitalisations for injuries and 910 000 for illness among the US troops.[20] This occurred in the context of a military exposure of 1.39 million men—over four times larger than Australia's contingent. While reluctant to use the measure of the total number of casualties (that is, deaths, wounding, injury and illness) per 1000 men—more will be said on the reasons for this reluctance in Chapter 8—America suffered 1018 casualties per 1000 men.[21] Australia's equivalent ratio was over 2600 per 1000 men. This data must be put into a time context as well: the period from 5 April 1917 to 31 December 1919 for America, whereas Australia's involvement ran from 6 August 1914 to 31 March 1921, when the AIF was disbanded.

It is revealing to examine the American ratio of the total number of deaths from disease and accident at home and abroad, from their declaration of war on 1 April 1917 to 31 December 1919, to the total number of deaths as a result of men 'killed in action' and wounding. At 1:26, this ratio means that more men died of injury and illness than in battle. This is extraordinary, and is nearly eight times that of the Australian AIF ratio of non-battle death to battle death (0:14). Furthermore, it occurred in less than half the time of overall wartime involvement,[22] a timeframe that would be reduced again if we considered the period of exposure to battle (Australia's conflict exposure of 1295 days contrasts with America's exposure period of only 200 days). Either the US had an incompetent and/or underdeveloped medical service or Australia had an extremely good one. It is contended that the latter was the case, as claimed previously, whereby the application of rapid quarantine measures both in the Australian Army and the civilian population was identified as critically important and practical implementation measures were largely in place. Rapid quarantining saved many lives. It can also be said that the Americans appeared to have had little idea of the relatively poor performance of their medical services in this war. For example, in discussing the causes of death from disease (51 per cent), accident (6 per cent) and battle (43 per cent) among US troops, Ayres observes that:

Some of the outstanding causes of the remarkably low disease death rate in the war against Germany are: (1) a highly trained medical personnel, (2) compulsory vaccination of the entire army against typhoid fever, (3) thorough camp sanitation and control of drinking water, and (4) adequate provision of hospital facilities.[23]

Ayres makes this comment in the context of comparing America's First World War experience to the Spanish War (1898), in which disease claimed five times more fatalities than the fighting; the American Civil War (1861), in which disease deaths were twice the number of battle deaths; and the Mexican War (1846), in which the ratio was seven to one. To be fair to Ayres in relation to his comparison, there would not have been data available from other countries involved in the First World War at the time of his publication. Conversely, however, it beggars belief that he would have been unaware of the rates of death due to illness of many of the other belligerents. If the Americans had a medical performance that was theoretically equal (non-battle deaths to battle deaths) to Australia's during this war, the Americans would have more than halved their losses of 114 000 men to 55 900 men, thereby saving 58 000 lives.

Referring to these non-battle fatalities, it could be argued that, as a third of America's total losses were from disease and injury that occurred at home, these should not be attributable to the war, but rather to poor public health management. Of the 37 422 deaths that occurred in the depots across the US, 2564 were due to accidents.[24] There were 34 858 deaths due to disease, with almost half (16 571) due to influenza[25] and another 9035 due to pneumonia, bronchitis and pleurisy.[26] The term Spanish Flu is not used in the US medical history as it was not defined as such by the end of 1919. However, if we conservatively denote only these defined 'influenza' deaths as attributable to Spanish Flu, this equates to approximately 12 deaths per 1000 fighting force men, with a further 6.5 men per 1000 succumbing to pneumonia. As revealed in Chapter 6, the analysis indicated that the AIF lost the comparative equivalent of 5.2 men per 1000 to Spanish Flu and 4.3 per 1000 men to pneumonia. However, these AIF deaths occurred overseas in the theatres of war. A comparison of these rates with domestic deaths would be more useful. Along with the 100 or so deaths recorded in the MT series, the AIF lost 3 men per 1000 fighting soldiers at home in Australia compared to the US's domestic loss of 27 men per 1000 fighting soldiers. The finding by Shanks et al. canvassed in Chapter 4, drawn from a major statistical analysis funded by the American Defence Department in 2010, was that the AIF had a lower death rate from Spanish Flu than the American Army due to a longer period of exposure to this illness in the war which had allowed some resistance to the disease to build up. However, this seems at odds with the comparative data on deaths at home and abroad of the respective countries. It is contended that the significantly lower AIF death rate was due to the organisation's efficacy of rapid quarantine. By any measure America's medical services performed poorly, effectively doubling US losses.

A final observation is made. The rate of American battle deaths and woundings rose rapidly among the US infantry from 31000 in July 1918 and 30000 in August 1918, to 44000 in September, and then 82000 in October 1918,[27] in this army's short exposure to this war. It would seem that Germany's capitulation saved many American lives.

Britain

The first observation to make on British casualty statistics is that there have been many *books* written comparing British, German and French losses in the First World War. The general tenor of these publications has been *disagreement*. For example, Churchill has argued that the number of German casualties was smaller than that of the British and French,[28] Edmonds claimed that German casualty numbers were higher than those of the British and French,[29] while Oman asserted that the number of casualties were about the same.[30] Significant reviews of these works by Williams,[31] Prior,[32] McRandle and Quirk[33] dwarf the comparative efforts attempted here, but an important point to highlight is this: each of these participating countries uses data on death, wounding *and* injury and illness to describe their war casualties. The numbers vary but the extent of the variability still allows for some valid comparison with Australian figures as variances in impacts for Australia, compared to that of other countries, are so great as to make the variance within German or British statistics of much less significance and therefore importance, for the purposes of comparison with these other belligerents.

The second comment to make about British casualty figures is that there are very limited areas of commonality with the Australian record that allow detailed comparative analysis. As an example of this lack of common ground for comparative purposes, British non-battle medical data were collected from the sample of over 1 million records for the years 1916 to 1920. Similarly, the battle casualty data are confused for comparative analysis as the bulk of them are *corrupted* by the inclusion of British Dominion data, which on occasion even include the major contribution made by India (over a million men).[34]

Individual British soldier Attestation Papers were largely destroyed following bombing raids and fire in the Second World War. The remaining 'burnt' records were digitised by a commercial US genealogical company and can be individually accessed online for a fee. However, large proportions were inadvertently duplicated, multiple times, so they are not suitable for a major statistical analysis.

The British medical statistics were released in 1931.[35] Table 1 in this text, labelled 'Approximate total casualties in the British Expeditionary Forces during the Great War', listed the totals for various campaigns categorised under the headings 'Killed, Died of Wounds, Died of disease or injury, Missing and Prisoners of War, Wounded, Sick or injured'. The final column in the table has a fairly meaningless title, 'Grand Total', which lists the total of *all* of the previous numbers. The important point to make here, however, is that illness and injuries were presented as casualties of the war. Butler provides British *battle* casualties separated according to British and Dominion forces,[36] citing *Statistics of the Military Effort of the British Empire* as his source.[37] These statistics were effective to 31 December 1920 but were revised and released in 1922. They tell us that the UK enlisted 5.7 million service people of whom 5.4 million 'took the field'. They suffered 702 000 killed, or 13 per cent of those who took to the field (Australia's equivalent was 20 per cent); and 1.66 million woundings, or 31 per cent (Australia's equivalent was 68 per cent). When those taken POW are accounted for, the total number of battle casualties as a percentage of men exposed to this conflict rises to 47 per cent for the British Army. This compares to 86 per cent for the AIF. McRandle makes a strong argument for acceptance of the 1924 United States of America War Department calculations,[38] of British, French and German battle casualties. These nominate the British

Empire's (as a whole) death toll at 908 000 and woundings at 2.090 million. When POWs and those missing (192 000) are included, the percentage impacted among countries of the British Empire rises to 59 per cent compared to the AIF level of 86 per cent. However, recalling earlier reservations, adding the three quite different categories of killed, wounding and POW together is only useful as a blunt and limited instrument for the measurement of loss and suffering.

Britain's non-battle casualties, inflated by Dominion casualties (including Australia's), totalled 8.040 million hospitalisations, and the extent to which this number overstates the British-only figure is unknown. With this in mind, and deducting Australia's total, the ratio of men in the field to the number of non-battle hospitalisations is 1:1.35 times, so the actual British-only figure would be somewhat less again. Australia's equivalent ratio of men in the field to non-battle hospitalisations was 1:1.75.

Germany

Robert Whalen produced a powerful piece of scholarship in 1984 detailing the casualties suffered by Germany in the Great War,[39] and this forms the basis for a comparison with the AIF figures. The Germans compiled casualty lists throughout the war in their four war ministries in Prussia, Bavaria, Wurttemberg and Saxony. Then, after the war, a single casualty office, the Zentralnachweisstelle fur Kriegerverluste, was created; however, this office and its records were obliterated by Allied bombing raids during the Second World War.

Germany's fundamental statistical problem was size. The nation had mobilised about 13.2 million men, more than any other belligerent. About 15.6 million men were eligible for military service—that is, between 17 and 50 years of age—and about 85 per cent of them were mobilised. Not everyone was in the army at the same time; usually the armed forces were about 6–7 million strong. Nevertheless, virtually all the men in Germany born between 1870 and 1899 were at one time or another, swept into the military.[40]

However, one factor confounds the accuracy of Germany's casualty statistics, evident in the different treatment of the deaths recorded in this conflict—stated to be 1.061 million by Butler[41] and 2.037 million by Whalen[42]—who cites Urlanis's convincing argument for adjusting the official figures.[43] (These adjustments involved the addition of 100 000 men, who were still listed as missing in 1933 as well as a further 36 000 navy personnel killed in the war, but who were not included in the official death toll). The difference arises from the categorisation and treatment of 'missing and prisoners of war' (Germany's official death toll was adjusted in 1919, 1920 and 1933). In summary, Whalen states that Germany suffered 2.037 million deaths in the war.[44] This represented about 19.4 per cent of men in the field (which totalled 10.5 million), and is similar to the AIF death toll of 20.2 per cent. Quoting Dr Otto von Schjerning, the Chief Officer of the German Army Medical Service in 1922, Whalen also asserts that 4 211 469 men were wounded.[45] And later, citing the 'official Army Medical Report',[46] he claims that there were 5 680 000 wounding admissions. However, the way these data are presented suggests an error possibly including lightly wounded, treated and released—an assertion that is supported by the following two claims. First, McRandle cites the US War Department's figure from 1924 of German woundings numbering 4.216 million.[47] Second, Whalen also cites von Schjerning, from a book written two years earlier, in which the latter states that the number of German wounding 'cases' during the war was 4.807 million.[48] It is this higher number that is used for comparison although it may overstate Germany's woundings number. This represents approximately 460 woundings per 1000 men of the German Army, and compares to the AIF proportion of 680 per 1000 men. It is recalled that Australia categorised shell shock as a wounding. How shell shock was categorised by the Germans needs to be researched, because if they categorised it as an illness, we lose a valid wounding comparison. But there is a potential determination for this and it shall be discussed shortly.

Figures quoted for *rates* of deaths resulting from murder, suicide, accident and illness for the German military are all significantly lower than those for the AIF.[49] The incidence of VD was a fraction of that of Australia's (Germany's rate of 27 admissions per 1000 men compared to the AIF admissions incidence of 178 per 1000 men).[50] The rate of death from disease for Germany was 16 per 1000 men on strength compared to Australia's rate of 28 per 1000 men. In discussing the incidence of disease among German troops, Whalen lists fourteen categories for 19 428 million admissions to hospital during the war, commenting on two of them he states:

After battle injuries, the most common medical cases were stomach or intestinal disorders, not ordinarily thought of as war injuries. The cause of stomach disorder is often difficult to find; it can be caused by poor diet or by excessive anxiety. Venereal disease was the least common medical problem. This was not because cases were unreported; doctors were scrupulous in investigating. Indeed, such careful medical attention is probably the reason venereal disease was a minor problem.[51]

The number of German soldier deaths while a POW amounted to a staggering 55 899,[52] presumably predominantly occurring on the Eastern Front. Whalen also quotes official figures for hospitalisations for illness and injury that equate to a level of 1.39 times the German fighting force. The AIF equivalent ratio was higher, at 1.75—perhaps a bad reflection on the AIF Medical Service's efficacy (for example, its failure to contain the incidence of VD). However, it may mask a worse relative performance. As mentioned earlier, the AIF categorised a hospitalisation from shell shock as a wounding and not an illness (when it was diagnosed as 'shell shock'). Referring back to Whalen's previously quoted hospital admission categories, among that list was the category 'neurological disorders' representing admissions of a mere 3 per cent of the German fighting force; while Australia's equivalent was 30 per cent (see Chapter 6). If it can be deduced that 'stomach disorder' can be caused by 'excessive anxiety' as Whalen supposes and indeed it was a diagnosis of shell shock, this could largely explain the difference in the rates of wounding between the two countries. However, Whalen further complicates the picture by referring to 'stomach disorder' as 'battle injuries'. Comparison may not be possible at the detailed category level of wounding, illness and injury due to the differences in definition, but it can be done in terms of the total number of hospitalisations. The record review and its analysis calculated the total number of hospitalisations per fighting force strength for both the German forces and the AIF in the field.[53] They were found to be proportionally dissimilar (1.85 for German forces and 2.43 for the AIF). Hence, it is now concluded that the AIF hospitalisation rate for wounding, injury *and* illness was approximately one-third higher than that of Germany in the First World War.

Whalen exhaustively documented those post-war impacts as reflected in the pension system and the returned servicemen's influence and demands in this period. The returned servicemen constituted a large proportion of the male population. The disastrous impact of this war on the social fabric of Germany was remarkably similar to the impact seen in Australia, which will be discussed in Chapter 8. Whalen describes the forces that were adding to the financial wreck of post-war Germany, with pension claims increasing, and a pension system that simply could not cope:

> The caseload in the pension offices was staggering. In 1927 some 1 629 000 cases were processed, of which 442 000 were new applications. In 1928, 1 663 000 cases were still being considered.[54]

By 1929 the pension system was broke, literally running out of money.[55] The general public (now consisting of a significant proportion of a new generation of young males in their twenties, who had not served in the war) had come to view the returned soldier as a money grabber, while war victims groups were protesting around the country for better treatment. German society had split. However, it is outside the scope of this analysis to further examine Whalen's scholarship or his argument that this issue contributed to the rise of Nazism. As the 1920s advanced, the waning of the social and political influence of Germany's ex-servicemen began, and the rising melancholia and suicide rates among the country's ex-servicemen were obscured by the rise of nationalism.

France

A soldier record for each of the 1.325 million men who died in service for France in the First World War is available online.[56] Administered by the Secrétariat Général pour l'Administration of the Ministère de la Défense, each record is a single page that includes the soldier's name, rank, date and place of birth, and date and cause of death, and can be accessed by surname. According to Butler, no official medical history of the French medical service has been written, nor statistics published.[57] However, he quotes from a volume published in 1927 by General A Mignon, which states that France mobilised 8.41 million men.[58] The figures on the casualties these men suffered are presented below, each one followed by the equivalent AIF figure in brackets.

The total number of those killed in action, died of wounds, missing presumed dead and died of non-battle causes of disease or injury was 1.325 million, or 15.7 per cent (20.2 per cent for the AIF) of those who fought in the French Army. However, this perhaps understates the true proportion. In 2000, Thomas Compere-Morel, the director of L'Historial de la Grande Guerre, claimed that the French Army mobilised half a million fewer men than was stated by Mignon, at 7.891 million, and that the death toll was slightly higher than Mignon's figure, at 1.327 million.[59] This has the effect of lifting the death toll for France to 16.8 per cent. The proportion of the death toll of those who died of injury or disease is a rough measure of the performance of medical services, and for France this was approximately 13 per cent (compared to 14 per cent for the AIF). Around 3 per cent (compared to the AIF's 1.26 per cent) of French servicemen were taken prisoner, the same number in percentage terms as those seen in Britain and its Dominions (including Australia).

From here, the Butler statistics become questionable. Butler's source, Mignon, states that French casualties due to injury and illness totalled 3.026 million, which is approximately 380 per 1000 men (compared to the AIF's 1720 per 1000 men) of the men who fought, and that 2.3 million, or 270 per 1000 were wounded (in contrast to the AIF figure of 680 per 1000). However, both these numbers significantly understate the true casualty figures as it is contended that their proportions relative to the numbers killed are out of step with those of Germany, Britain and Australia. There is no evidence that France suffered a uniquely and substantially higher death rate proportional (in the order of double) to wounding and illness. It is more likely that hospitalisations for wounding, injury and illness were themselves at least *double* these numbers, reflecting British hospitalisation rates proportional to deaths, and possibly quadruple, paralleling German and Australian hospitalisation rates. McRandle and Quirk cite the US War Department in affirming that wounding for French forces was indeed double Butler's figure, at 4.266 million, and that the death toll was quite similar to the other two sources previously mentioned, at 1.363 million.[60] The total number of battle casualties, including missing and POWs, accounted for 78 per cent of France's fighting force, lying between the British Empire, at 57 per cent, and the AIF, at 86 per cent. There are no equivalent figures for illness and injury to compare to Butler's figures on France.

Canada

Canada's official medical services history was published in 1925,[61] based on a final cut-off date of 31 March 1923.[62] The total number of troops who served overseas was slightly in excess of 418 000. Like Australia, Canada declared war on 6 August 1914 and, as Australia experienced Gallipoli, Fromelles, Passchendaele and the Somme, Canada had major battles on the Somme, Vimy Ridge and during the final phase of Passchendaele. The casualties suffered by Canadian servicemen are outlined below, each figure followed by the equivalent Australian figure in brackets.[63] The number of Canadian soldiers killed totalled 56 638, representing 13.5 per cent (compared to the AIF's 20.2 per cent) of those who served overseas.[64] These deaths included 4960 due to disease and other non-battle causes, representing fewer than 9 per cent (against the AIF's 14 per cent) of the total death toll. Admissions to hospital included 149 732 for wounding, representing 350 per 1000 (compared to the AIF's 680 per 1000) of those who served; and 395 084 for injury or illness, or 950 per 1000 (1750 per 1000) of the total. Once again, reluctantly following the convention of adding quite disparate data together, the total of these casualty numbers produces a total admissions rate of 1290 per 1000 men. Uniquely, among the countries in this comparative study, the Canadian medical historian MacPhail presented this proportional measure by excluding the number of deaths, as should be the case—a view expanded upon in Chapter 8. This measure is just under one half of that suffered by the men of the AIF (over 2430 per 1000).

The Canadian medical services history highlights some strikingly different experiences from those of the AIF. The first observation in this regard is that the Canadian medical officers who served for the whole period of battle on the Western Front never saw a case of dysentery,[65] and throughout the entire war reported just over 1000 cases—a vastly different experience from that of the AIF, for whom exposure to dysentery in the Mediterranean regions cut a swathe through the troops stationed there.

However, CSM was more problematic for the Canadian medical services than dysentery. Around 400 cases of CSM were admitted to hospital, and over half eventually died from this illness, representing

4 deaths per 1000 men.[66] The AIF experience was worse, with the major outbreak in Victoria in 1916 contributing to an elevated rate of 14 deaths per 1000 men.

Another area in which comparisons are worthwhile is in relation to the narrative of the official histories. Butler offers very little discussion on medical advances or treatment strategies during the war. In contrast, MacPhail provides some excellent commentary on improvements in medical treatments that were made during the war, which sheds light on the conditions to which men were exposed during the course of the war. According to MacPhail, the incidence of infectious jaundice[67] was making significant inroads into soldier availability, such that in 1915 all cases were sent to a single hospital in England for the purpose of research into the condition. Interestingly, two Japanese researchers working at this research facility identified its cause in July 1916, and this diagnosis of the cause gives an insight into the conditions experienced in trench warfare. They determined that effectively it was a type of bacteria that was carried in rats' urine which spread the disease, *either directly or indirectly*, to the patient, who further spread the infection in the same way.

Tetanus was another condition whose increasing occurrence led to action. MacPhail records that in March 1916, the British War Office appointed a committee to explore options for a treatment process. Virtually no gunshot wounds were found to be sterile. The preventative surgical process that was adopted, ideally less than 12 hours after a soldier suffered a wound, is particularly illustrative of the consequences of being shot or hit by shrapnel:

> In excising the wound area care should be taken that no incision is carried from infected wounded tissue into surrounding healthy tissue, and instruments used to manipulate wound surfaces superficially and deep, should not be used on surrounding healthy tissue; clean cutting with a knife is better than scissors as less likely to leave bruised tissue behind. All metal fragments and other foreign bodies should be removed and careful search made for detached bone fragments, including those driven into the surrounding soft parts ... When removing the foreign body the fibrous capsule enclosing it should also be dissected away.[68]

The condition called trench foot was notoriously difficult to treat. Continued cold and wet exposure were the principal aggravating factors and its appearance was horrible:

> A mild case showed a brawny swelling; but as the condition advanced the foot became dusky; the toes dropped off by a process of gangrene, and even the whole foot might be destroyed in a very few days.[69]

Through the winter of 1914–1915, trench foot was common. Yet by the following winter it had been virtually eradicated. What was once a disease had become a crime. Strict measures were introduced and strictly enforced, including the rubbing of feet with oil, the daily changing of socks, boots having to be large and well oiled, and puttees having to be worn loose.

Skin infections were suffered by almost *all* soldiers. Lice spread scabies, and any rash became infected in the septic environment. Because of the closer sleeping quarters, lice swept through the ranks and officers were not immune. The treatment of the infestation with powder was useless,[70] washing likewise. It was finally discovered that lice and its eggs can be comprehensively killed off at 20 degrees Celsius above body temperature, and after only ten minutes of exposure to this level of heat. Rooms or huts full of racks and heated with braziers or stoves were found to be the solution, and these Orr huts rapidly spread along the Western Front, named after the Canadian sanitary section officer, Major H Orr, who had made this discovery.

In Chapter 6 the rates of VD in the AIF were revealed and discussed along with a comparison with the Canadian medical services records suggesting that the similar rates of occurrence were due in the main to their soldiers' leave being taken in foreign lands necessitating the resort to professional services. With regard to shell shock, MacPhail had a clear and unambiguous view, unlike Butler. The differing attitudes towards the condition made a profound and tragic difference to the impact of shell shock for the Canadian serviceman, especially as Canadian authorities applied capital punishment in cases of perceived cowardice. As noted in Chapter 2, O'Keefe suggested that the main feature of Butler's views on shell shock was their ambiguity. Evidence of Butler's confused and limited analysis was presented. Not so for Sir Andrew MacPhail. He starts slowly in his discussion of the condition, building upon his views to reach a chilling conclusion:

> Shellshock was a term used in the early days to describe a variety of conditions ranging from cowardice to maniacal insanity. After endless discussion the physicians and metaphysicians, the psychologists the physiologists and neurologists invented a series of names which did not leave the matter much clearer than it was when they found it.[71]

This book referred earlier to over thirty terms revealed in the Attestation Papers. He continues:

> The general statement is probably correct, that in the early days of the war too lenient treatment was accorded soldiers suffering, thinking they suffered, or pretending to suffer, from concussion or fright neurosis, from hysteria, neurasthenia, reflex paralysis, catatonic stupor, or combination and subdivision thereof; and that up to the end it was not sufficiently realised that men who are liable to such condition were not fit for the hard business of war.[72]

This book earlier referred to deterioration in diagnosis and treatment of men suffering from traumatic stress as the war progressed and is evidenced by MacPhail's view. And finally he affirms:

> Hysteria is the most epidemical of all diseases, and too obvious special facilities for treatment encouraged its development. 'Shell-shock' is a manifestation of childishness and femininity. Against such there is no remedy.[73]

This attitude had the most appalling consequences. MacPhail, himself a doctor, does refer to the difficulty of diagnosis, accepting that something like anxiety neurosis did exist in cases when men under some 'supreme trial' might behave in an 'unseemly' manner.[74] But he complains that the task of the medical officer to determine cowardice as opposed to a diagnosis of shell shock, and to then *also* be required to perform the task to oversee the man's death by execution, was a particularly 'unpleasant' and 'haunting' duty.

Summary

The analysis of approximately 12 500[75] AIF soldier records in the three samples taken in this record review (comprising a pilot, the MT series sample and the main B2455 sample of 9604 soldier records) allows, for the first time, a measure of the level of sacrifice among the civilian soldiers of the AIF. By any measure they were decimated. Table 11 summarises the comparisons presented in this chapter of the military human cost of the First World War among a selection of nations involved in the conflict, including injury and illness. It should be emphasised here that the measure of comparison of these nations are for *soldiers exposed to war*, where military personnel not exposed to a theatre of war are removed. This *avoids* the often referenced factor that Britain supplied non combat personnel resources, or a vast military bureaucracy to its dominions thereby exposing proportionately more of the dominions' forces to the conflict.

Table 11: Comparative Total Casualty Statistics—Australia and Other Selected Belligerents©

Column	Deaths % army	% Non-B	Wounding /1000	Illness/ injury /1000	Total Hospitalised /1000	Men millions	VD admissions /1000
USA	8.2	57	150	720	870	1.39	91
Britain	13.0	–	310	1040	1350	5.40	25
Germany	19.4	8	460	1390	1850	10.50	27
France	16.8	13	540	380*	920*	7.89	–
Canada	13.5	9	360	945	930	0.418	158
Australia	20.2	14	680	1750	2430	0.308**	178

* Doubtful.

** Adjusted for 10 000 men mainly in Britain and eligible for only one medal.

Column 1 in Table 11 shows deaths as a percentage of the strength of the armies in the field that were exposed to action. Column 2 provides the percentage of non-battle deaths of the total number of deaths, reflecting a form of a report card on the efficacy of each country's medical services, as most of these deaths were disease related. The performance of Britain and Germany in limiting the numbers of non-battle deaths, mainly from disease, is remarkably similar and shows in relative terms the more moderate performance of Australia's medical services which is comparable to that of Canada. It also underscores the poor outcome for troops from the US, adding weight to the contention that a third of its death casualties were not related to participation in the First World War and should not be counted as such. Rather, it is argued here that this US statistic is associated with poor public health management in America at that time and is therefore unrelated to their war service.

In Table 11, columns 3 and 4 represent hospitalisations per 1000 men in the field—that is, the records of an *admission* to a hospital owing to a wounding, illness or injury—and column 5 presents the totals for these hospitalisations. For many men this occurred several times. The size of the selected nations' *force-in-the-field* follows in column 6, and the last column (column 7) shows the incidence of VD among each nation's troops. The incidence of VD reveals the significant differences in the level of control maintained by the medical services of the different countries, such that the effective performance of the British and German medical authorities produced rates of infection noticeably lower than those seen among the Dominion forces of Canada and Australia. However, it was argued in the previous chapter that as the Dominion soldiers could not return home for leave, their recourse to sexual favours exposed them to a much higher incidence of VD. US personnel were exposed to potential contraction of this disease for a very short time as their service was of such a short duration that their service leave would have been relatively limited.

In general terms, the figures in Table 11 show the magnitude of the devastation wrought on the AIF by this war in comparison to the impact on other nations. This relatively simple comparison displayed here is only a beginning, presenting an accurate estimate of the comparative losses sustained by the men of the AIF. Further research is underway to refine the material contained in the Attestation Papers and endeavour to offer some explanation as to how this terrible loss came about. But the scale of the problem can now be seen. The Australian admissions to hospital due to illness and injury on over 540 000 occasions (or over 1750 occasions per 1000 men) have been forgotten, omitted from our official casualty statistics. The level of wounding has been significantly understated, as have been the levels of death. However, more than this, the data demonstrate for the first time the relative loss and suffering experienced by the men of the AIF. It has largely been overlooked, if it was *ever understood*, that by any major measure Australia suffered, proportionately, *significantly more* deaths, *more* woundings and *more* hospitalisations for injury and illness than the major belligerents the US, Britain, Germany, France and Canada. The rationale for questioning how this came about has now been set. This impact was borne by over 300 000 civilian soldiers who constituted over half of the Australian male population between the ages of eighteen and fifty-five years. The other half of that population, and their relatives, were not involved, and they did not really want to know about it.

And the suffering did not end here—there was more to come.

Notes

1. Miles Staniforth Smith, *Australian Campaigns in the Great War: Being a Concise History of the Australian Naval and Military Forces, 1914 to 1918*, Macmillian & Co, Melbourne, 1919, pp. vi.
2. Heeres-Sanitatsinspektion im Reichskriegsministeriums, *Sanitätsbericht über das deutsche Heer (Deutsches Feld-und Besatzung Heer), im Weltkriege, Volumen III [Army Sanitatation in the Reich War Ministry, medical report on the German Army (German Army field and occupation), in the World War, Volume III]*, 1914–1918, Berlin, 1934.
3. According to Butler (A Graham Butler, *Official Medical History of the Australian Army Medical Services, 1914–1918, Volume III*, Australian War Memorial, Canberra, 1942, footnote, p. 872) the US did incur a small number of casualties in 1917, presumably in small advanced numbers of troops with fifteen reported killed in action and sixty wounded in that year.
4. David Steveson, *1914–1918: The History of the First World War*, Allen Lane, United States, p. 368.
5. United States Army Medical Department, *The Medical Department and United States Army in the World War, Vol XV, Part 2, Medical and Casualty Statistics*, US Army Surgeon General's Office, 1925, p. 17, Table 2.
6. Leonard Ayres, *The War with Germany: A Statistical Summary*, Government Printing Office, Washington, 1919, p. 101.
7. Sir John Monash, *The Australian Victories in France in 1918*, Lothian, Melbourne, p. 64.
8. ibid., pp. 269–272, 283–287.
9. United States Army Medical Department, *The Medical Department and United States Army in the World War, Vol XV, Part 2, Medical and Casualty Statistics*, Table 2, p. 17.
10. Ayres, *The War with Germany*, p. 11.
11. ibid., p. 101.
12. Monash, *The Australian Victories in France in 1918*, p. 265.

13 Americans Killed in Action: 36 694. Deaths from disease and injury in the US were 37 422. (Butler, *Official Medical History of the Australian Army Medical Services, 1914–1918, Volume III*, p. 872, citing United States Army Medical Department, *The Medical Department and United States Army in the World War, Vol XV, Part 2, Medical and Casualty Statistics*, p. 147, Table 48.
14 Ayres, *The War with Germany*, p. 126.
15 United States Army Medical Department, *The Medical Department and United States Army in the World War, Vol XV, Part 2, Medical and Casualty Statistics*, p. 83.
16 Butler, *Official Medical History of the Australian Army Medical Services, 1914–1918, Volume III*, p. 872. In a discussion in the next chapter on pensions, Butler is quoted (p. 959) as stating that the US had 1.39 million as the 'Number of men in Combatant Service'.
17 United States Army Medical Department, *The Medical Department and United States Army in the World War, Vol XV, Part 2, Medical and Casualty Statistics*, p. 17.
18 Ayres, *The War With Germany*, p. 101.
19 Another problem arises here where Butler (*Official Medical History of the Australian Army Medical Services, 1914–1918, Volume III*, p. 872) stipulates 70 552 admissions 'gassed' *and* 210 398 wounded, but the American medical history does not, stating that 210 398 were wounded. Similarly for death from gas of 1221 specified by Butler is not (exactly) included in the American battle casualties. The solution lies in Table 109, p. 1019, where quite clearly Butler has added up all admissions for gassing and presented the figure as a separate item in his Table 7 on p. 872, thereby potentially double counting for gassing in both deaths and wounding.
20 Butler, *Official Medical History of the Australian Medical Services, 1914–1918, Volume III*, p. 872.
21 This is slightly different from the official claim of 987.12 per 1000 (total casualties 4 075 316) concluded in the *Medical and Casualty Statistics*, p. 1183, because it uses Ayres's total enlistment number of 4 million men (p. 11). Despite the minutiae in the medical and casualties tome, there is not one reference in it to the total number of enlistments, only citing strength at the end of each month.
22 The US lost 114 000 men. But of these more than half, or 63 700, were lost to disease (and most, or 37 400, died in depots and bases in America) and injury (the latter only 5500) or 57 per cent of the total toll. States Army Medical Department, *The Medical Department and United States Army in the World War, Vol XV, Part 2, Medical and Casualty Statistics*, p. 1183. The AIF lost 62 300, of which 8700 (14 per cent) were non-battle deaths.
23 Ayres, *The War With Germany*, p. 123, 125.
24 United States Army Medical Department, *The Medical Department of the United States Army in the World War, Vol XV, Part 2 Medical and Casualty Statistics*, p. 147.
25 ibid., p. 135.
26 ibid., p. 143.

27 United States Army Medical Department, *The Medical Department and United States Army in the World War, Vol XV, Part 2, Medical and Casualty Statistics*, p. 1063, 1071, 1081, 1091.
28 Winston Churchill, *The World Crisis, 1911–1918*, Australasian Publishing, Sydney, 1923.
29 Sir James Edmonds (ed), *History of the Great War Based on Official Documents*, MacMillan, London, 1932, in David Freedman, Robert Pisani and Roger Purves, *Statistics*, WW Norton & Company, New York, 1980.
30 Sir Charles Oman, 'The German Losses on the Somme', *Nineteenth Century*, 27 May 1927, p. 294, in Nick Ford and Jeffery Rosenfeld, 'Mild traumatic brain injury and bomb blast: stress injury or both?', *ADF Health Journal*, vol. 9, no. 2, December 2008.
31 M J Williams, 'Thirty Percent: A Study in Casualty Statistics', *Journal of the Royal United Service Institution*, no. 109 (633), February 1964.
32 Robin Prior, *Churchill's 'World Crisis' as history*, Croom Helm, London, 1983.
33 J McRandle and J Quirk, 'The blood test revisited: A new look at German casualty counts in World War I', *Journal of Military History*, The Society for Military History, Lexington VA, vol. 70, no. 3, January 2006.
34 Great Britain, *Statistics of the Military Effort of the British Empire during the Great War 1914–1920*, The British War Office and London HM Stationary, London, 1922, p. 777.
35 TJ Mitchell and GM Smith, *Medical Services Official History of the Great War: Casualties and Medical Statistics of the Great War*, Imperial War Museum, London, 1931, p. 12.
36 Butler, *Official Medical History of the Australian Army Medical Services, 1914–1918, Volume III*, p. 880.
37 Great Britain, *Statistics of the Military Effort of the British Empire during the Great War 1914–1920*, p. 237.
38 McRandle and Quirk, 'The blood test revisited: A new look at German casualty counts in World War I', *Journal of Military History*, p. 675.
39 Robert Weldon Whalen, *Bitter Wounds: German Victims of the Great War, 1914–1918*, Cornell University Press, London, 1984.
40 ibid., p. 39.
41 Butler, *Official Medical History of the Australian Army Medical Services, 1914–1918, Volume III*, p. 868.
42 Whalen, *Bitter Wounds: German Victims of the Great War, 1914–1918*, p. 39.
43 Boris Urlanis, *Bilanz der Kriege: Die Menschenverluste Europas vom 17. [Balance of the War: The Loss of Human Life in Europe from the 17th Century to the Present]*, VEB Deytscher Verlag der Wissenschaften, Berlin, 1965.
44 Whalen, *Bitter Wounds: German Victims of the Great War, 1914–1918*, p. 39.
45 ibid., p. 40.
46 ibid., p. 95. It is not referenced.
47 ibid., p. 675.
48 Otto von Schjerning, *Die Tatigkeit und die Erfolge der deutschen Feldarzte im Weltkriege [The Activity and the Successes of the German Military*

Physicians in the World War, JA Barth, Leipzig, 1920, p. 16.
49 Whalen, *Bitter Wounds, German Victims of the Great War, 1914–1918*, p. 42.
50 ibid., p. 53.
51 ibid.
52 Whalen, *Bitter Wounds, German Victims of the Great War, 1914–1918*, p. 42.
53 ibid., p. 95.
54 ibid., p. 157.
55 ibid., p. 168.
56 French Ministry of Defence, see: <http://www.memoiredeshommes.sga.defense.gouv.fr>.
57 Butler, *Official Medical History of the Australian Army Medical Services, 1914–1918, Volume III*, p. 869.
58 Medecin Inspeceur General A Mignon, *Le Service de Sante Pendant la Guerre 1914-1918 [The Health Service During the 1914–1918 War]*, vol. IV, French Government, Paris, 1927.
59 Thomas Compere-Moral, *L'Historial de la Grande Guerre et le Circuit du souvenir [The Museum of the Great War and the Circuit of Rememberance]*, La Renaissance du Livre, Tournai, Belgique, 2000, p. 33.
60 McRandle and Quirk, 'The blood test revisited: A new look at German casualty counts in World War I', *Journal of Military History*, p. 675.
61 Sir Andrew MacPhail, *Official History of the Canadian Forces in the Great War 1914–1918, The Medical Services*, Minister of National Defense, under Direction of the General Staff, Ottawa, Canada, 1925.
62 ibid., p. 243.
63 ibid., p. 242.
64 ibid., pp. 242, 243.
65 ibid., p. 251.
66 ibid., p. 255.
67 ibid., p. 256.
68 ibid., p. 262.
69 ibid., p. 264.
70 ibid., p. 269.
71 ibid., p. 270
72 MacPhail, *Official History of the Canadian Forces in the Great War 1914–1918, The Medical Services*, p. 272.
73 ibid., p. 273.
74 ibid., p. 272.
75 Comprising 9604 (main sample), 1608 (MT series sample) and 1218 (pilot study), with a total of 12 430 records.

CHAPTER 8

The Post-War Impacts: Those We Forget

'*Dearest Violet*', Isaac Miller wrote in October 1917, '*I had occasion to go forward to where the boys were after the fighting had finished. I would not dream of describing in the slightest degree the awfulness of destruction that came before my eyes. I want to forget all about it. And this is war.*'

Why have the First World War *post-war impacts* been largely forgotten or overlooked? Perhaps we *do* want to forget. This first worldwide conflict saw the use of weapons of mass destruction that evolved through technological advances aimed at improving and refining how to kill and maim. Gas, machine guns, flame throwers, mines and massive artillery bombardments on fixed positions, tanks and aircraft were used against men armed with a rifle and a fixed bayonet advancing over open ground through mud and barbed wire with a cavalry contingent in the rear that was never used on the Western Front. Then, on 11 November 1918, it stopped. The war had finished. People readily took the understandable but narrow view that the killing had stopped and the crisis was over. Many did not consider the wider picture of what the cost of the aftermath of this war actually meant. Yet this narrow view is not sustainable; one cannot stop counting the cost and lives lost in 1918, or in 1921, with the disbandment of the AIF. A *full* assessment of the cost of this war must take into consideration the post-war costs of death and suffering as well. At the time, much of Australia's population knew exactly what this cost was, because over half of all Australian males between the ages of eighteen and fifty-five had been exposed to this war.

Perhaps it can be argued that society's perception of war-related events after the war was that they were less significant than the war itself. It was over; there was a need for the authorities to move the public past this catastrophe, like moving on a crowd silently observing the scene of a terrible accident. Or maybe the war experience itself was so numbing for the authorities, military and political, that the post-war experiences paled in comparison, and hence so too did the need to monitor, assess and report them? In fact, some authorities, upon reflection, chose to minimise the post-war impact. For example, the Australian repatriation authorities adopted restrictive policies governing pension eligibility, although this eventually resulted in a Royal Commission in 1924 which expanded eligibility. Still other authorities tried to erase the impact. The 1921 Commonwealth Census was 'normalised' to remove the distortions of the First World War. The introduction of the statistician's report read as follows:

> The maintenance of uniformity with a series of life tables constructed on the occasion of the Census of 1911 would have required the construction of a table or tables for the decade 1911–1920. The abnormal occurrences, however, of the decade, comprising the war upheaval of 1914–1918 and the pneumonic influenza epidemic of 1919, would result in the experience for the whole decade being the average of experiences very unlike each other and would, therefore, be of little real significance. There would be included in it rates of mortality due either to war or to influenza[1], as well as rates arising in normal times before the war, resulting in a combination of rates not likely to be experienced in the near future. If, of course, war and epidemic were of frequent occurrences there would be no warrant for omitting the data relative to the years in which they occur. In the circumstances it appeared desirable to take a period free from either, and the triennium 1920–1922 was chosen giving a year of experience on either side of the Census year 1921.[2]

These manipulations to falsely imbue reality with a certain 'normality' are not sustainable either, although this is easily said with the benefit of hindsight and the consequential advent *of another* world war. But it should be at the very least considered that in reality the aftermath of this war in Australia was disastrous—overwhelming on both a social and political level. The population was left speechless and divided, the returned soldiers mute. There are very few words in any language that can adequately describe or communicate the mass grief of a community. The best we have to express this grief are—as it is evidenced in France—not words but avenues of trees; monuments in the centre of nearly every small town across this country; honour boards in virtually every church and hall; and silence, as a means of consolation and commemoration. This silence lasts only for a minute, perhaps twice each year. But it is punctuated by 'lest we forget' and 'we shall remember them' all.

It is possible that post-war trauma and suffering did diminish with the passage of time for those who had lost a son or brother, a father or husband. For the families and widows, who lacked even a photo of a grave over which to mourn, the community erected monuments in town centres or public gardens; yet real closure was never achieved and those who mourned simply had to cope. Not assisting this psychological adjustment was the treatment of families of missing men by the military authorities, which was pathetically inept, as will be seen. However, it will be shown that for most of the men who survived, the trauma and loss *increased* after the war ended, present every day for decades for men with mental and physical disabilities, some of whom were partially acknowledged with a small pension, but many whom were not. The suffering increased also therefore for the hundreds of thousands of carers and members of families of these men, infiltrating the very fabric of Australian society for generations. Despite its efforts at 'normalisation', the 1921 Census does bear silent witness to the lost generation of men over the previous decade in the age range of returned soldiers of 20 to 54 years, displayed in Table 12,[3] as their proportion of the population fell by 5, 6 or 7 per cent (20–24, 25–29 and 45–54 years of age, respectively).

Table 12: Proportion of Males in Australia's Population, 1881–1921

MASCULINITY OF POPULATION OF AUSTRALIA, 1881 TO 1921.
(EXCESS OF MALES OVER FEMALES IN EACH 100 OF POPULATION.)

Age Last Birthday.	1881.	1891.	1901.	1911.	1921.	Age Last Birthday.	1881.	1891.	1901.	1911.	1921.
0–4	1.02	1.37	1.23	1.59	1.85	55–59	25.55	16.23	10.22	10.88	7.68
5–9	.90	.98	1.11	1.06	1.28	60–64	23.99	19.45	8.81	7.72	7.19
10–14	.94	1.20	.98	.87	1.09	65–69	22.50	19.31	13.19	5.27	6.95
15–19	1.33	.39	.22	1.49	1.25	70–74	22.23	17.72	16.63	5.42	2.26
20–24	3.49	4.19	.16	2.47	—2.81	75–79	20.04	19.89	13.25	6.69	— 1.97
25–29	12.48	11.80	2.18	3.16	—2.33	80–84	26.35	17.80	7.71	7.25	— 3.93
30–34	12.49	15.53	7.81	3.49	1.23	85–89	28.96	12.31	6.90	—2.11	— 6.87
35–39	15.18	14.83	11.27	4.36	2.17	90–94	3.17	25.42	5.31	—5.16	—11.30
40–44	17.89	16.10	13.29	7.04	2.57	95–99	—5.26	23.97	6.21	—4.65	— 9.79
45–49	20.73	14.76	14.74	10.16	3.42	100 and over	20.00	17.65	.00	5.26	37.50
50–54	24.50	15.27	13.83	12.29	6.24						
						All Ages	7.98	7.36	4.82	3.84	1.66

Source: Commonwealth of Australia, *Census of The Commonwealth of Australia, taken for the night between 3 and 4 April 1921: Volume II, Statistician's Report*, Australian Bureau of Statistics, Government Printer, Melbourne, 1921.

These pointers to post-war impacts open up the questioning of the official practice that stopped counting the effects of the war on 31 March 1921 because the fighting had stopped and the AIF had ceased to exist. A principal reason for this ceasing to account for post-war impacts beyond this date was that it was simply too hard. This chapter will present a means of measuring this post-war cost for the first time, considered by many to be unmeasurable, and will do so in terms of deaths, illness and disability. Fortunately the official evidence we have to work with here, which actually documents this post-war period of death and suffering, is contained in the Attestation Papers of the individual ex-servicemen, in generalised pension data, and in the *Australian Census of 1933*.

But we must first consider a debate that is long overdue, at a national and international level, which addresses the question: when do we stop counting the casualties from the First World War—that is, what cut-off date should be nominated? The extraordinary variability of cut-off dates for this post-war period is evident across the nations, and no two are the same. Deciding on a date requires careful consideration of many complex and confounding interpretations, starting with the distinction between the perspectives of the purely military historian whose interest is in the war itself, and the wastage and availability of men; and of the social-military historian whose interest is found in the impact of war on society more broadly, including civilians and returned service personnel.

These differences of opinion do not end there and are evident in the approaches taken by Major Mitchell's official British medical statistics history and Colonel Butler's official Australian medical services history of the First World War. Neither could be regarded as a social war historian, although Butler's decision to incorporate a detailed examination of the comparative pension costs among the nations involved in the war, for the year 1932, and in Australia up until 1940, provided some details of the generational effects of the conflict—and these data will be utilised extensively for the current analysis as they were not Butler's but were provided by repatriation authorities. On the other hand, Mitchell made the extraordinary decision to skew the official British medical records for the nation of a sample of hospitalisations for illness and injury *two years into peacetime* (1916–1920) and then added the analysis to death and wounding injury and illness for the war years of 1914–1918 to arrive at the publication of the *Medical Services Official History of the Great War: Casualties and Medical Statistics of the Great War*.[4] Why was this done? No supportable reason can be offered. Mitchell also devoted a chapter to an analysis of pensions and decided that a cut-off date of ten years (31 March 1929) was sufficient to capture most post-war influences. Yet no reasoning is provided for this arbitrary decision on the timeframe. Mitchell's decision to offset the date of record by two years was justified, he argues, because it was balanced, as it covered the period of a soldier's transition back into civilian life. It should not be forgotten that the official historians like Butler, Bean, Mitchell, Edmonds and MacPhail did not simply have the power to *re*write history—they *wrote* it. Their legacy is that a very large amount of contrary and factual evidence must be assembled in order to overturn a prejudiced or inaccurate *official* view.

Back in Australia, some historians thought that revisiting this inter-war period in order to make an assessment of the war's aftermath was simply too complex a process. For example, Larsson, citing Michael Mckernon, argues that the reason why the research into post-war deaths conducted by the AWM was dropped was the advent of the Second World War;[5] there was simply not enough room at the War Memorial in Canberra to display the names of the dead from both wars, plus those who died between the wars whose cases in any event still required examination to determine their eligibility to be counted as a war-caused death. Names were collected by the AWM, however, until finally the decision was made to shut down this 'supplementary roll'[6] in 1967 and to revert to the date of the disbandment of the AIF on 1 April 1921. This decision is problematic and deficient; it confines the memory of First World War servicemen who died after this date to their families' generations alone, unacknowledged and forgotten by the nation as a whole.

The series note for the record AWM145, Army 1914–1918 at the AWM provides a concise history of the background compilation of the Roll of Honour, eligibility for entry on which is that a person's death was considered to be war caused and occurred before 1 April 1921. Currently the Roll of Honour contains a record of 61512 names for the First World War. A separate roll, called the Commemorative Roll, contains the names of those Australians who were killed in the First World War while serving in military services *other than the AIF*. This is regularly updated when cases are raised by relatives or researchers and are subsequently proven to be valid. Currently 2168 names are contained on the Commemorative Roll. As is the case with a war-caused death that occurred after 1 April 1921, no names on the Commemorative Roll are included in the official statistics of deaths from the First World War.

It is difficult to accept the distinction being made by their exclusion from Australia's official death toll from this conflict. The exclusion of those on the Commemorative Roll has no logical basis unless the official war casualty statistics for this country are for an Australian military audience only and not the Australian public at large. After all, these men were Australians. It follows *that if* an Australian soldier fighting under AIF command is killed, he is counted on the Roll of Honour. However, an Australian soldier killed under British or New Zealand Army command is commemorated but is not counted in Australia's official casualty statistics. Of the 2168 names on the Commemorative Roll, nearly 1000 of them are categorised as having fought with the British Army, over 700 with the New Zealand military forces, many served with the Royal Air Force or Royal Navy, and nearly 200 died while serving in the merchant navy. The reasoning behind the distinction in classification between these two categories of death contained in these rolls is lost somewhere in the past. This categorisation needs to be reviewed, bearing in mind the intended audience and the education of the Australian public as a whole. The criteria for entry onto the roll may have moved since the previous historical taxonomy.

Post-War Death

It is acknowledged that the exclusion of those who died after 1 April 1921 is partly understandable, owing to the considerable difficulties of determining a war-caused death some years after discharge. There is a way forward, however, in that some very valuable information does exist as a consequence of the 1933 Commonwealth Census[7] which can lead us to a robust estimation of post-AIF war-caused deaths. And this information is to be discussed in this context for the first time below.

However, a divergence to reference some post-war pension data is required before the Census material can be used. Australia's official medical historian Butler reported the data on the deaths of pensioners' data supplied by the chief medical officer of the Repatriation Commission, including the annual death rate of war pensioners from 1925 until the start of the Second World War.[8] All of this material replicates Scott's data to 1935,[9] so we will limit any further reference to pensions post-war to Butler. The death rate of war pensioners sits remarkably consistently at just above 750 men per annum, rising to over 1000 per annum in the late 1930s. These data will prove to be a valuable tool in the analysis presented in this chapter. Of course in these cases the cause of death may not have been related to the war disability for which the ex-soldier was receiving the pension. Conversely, there have been war-caused deaths among ex-servicemen who did *not* receive a pension after the war, for example, in the very sad circumstances of suicide, of which there are hundreds. The issue of suicide is examined further below.

If an assumption is made that *most* of the pensioners listed by Butler died as a result of their war-related disability, over 10 000 additional deaths could be recorded as stemming from this conflict. What did the British authorities do with such data? As mentioned previously, the British medical historian chose a cut-off date of 31 March 1929. Up to that time 120 000 British war pension recipients had died. Mitchell states that, when considering the more disabled classes (levels two and three):

> Broadly speaking, these 120 000 deaths occurred amongst classes two and three, but they were not all either due to or hastened by the disability for which pension was being paid. The extent to which this was so necessarily varied

with the nature of the war service disability, but it has been estimated that in some 60 to 70% of the total 120 000 the pensionable disability was a major factor in the cause of death.[10]

Mitchell does not throw any light upon the basis of this estimation. But if it is applied to the case of Australia's pension recipient death rate numbers, in the order of 8500–9500 ex-servicemen died from war-related causes up until 1939. However, in the absence of any substantiation of this percentage of war-related deaths, it was considered to be too tenuous an assumption to be reliable for use in this analysis.

We can now turn to the 1933 Census, which contained some war-related questions for its citizens for the first time. It shows that 38 000 returned soldiers had died from all causes since their return from war; *but* the Census Statistician's 1938 Report on the results of the 1933 Census went on to say, in reference to these deaths:

> The particulars ascertained from the 1933 census and the results of the special statistical inquiry instituted at Base Records, Department of Defence were referred to Mr F. W. Barford MA., AIA, and Actuary of the Commonwealth Superannuation Board. Although it was not possible from these data to construct a life-table comparable to the Australian life-tables of 1932–1934, it was possible to make some comparison between the two experiences for national and returned soldiers. It was ascertained, as a result of these calculations, that the mortality amongst returned soldiers since discharge exceeds that of a body of males of the same age constitution drawn from the general population by about 13 percent.[11]

This simple statistic, 'by 13 per cent', holds the key to post-war-related death. The actuarial assessment does not count individual men; it counts the death toll among men who saw service and those men of the same age range who did not see service. The difference between the death tolls for these two groups clearly denotes the number of premature war-related deaths. This amounts to an additional number of war-caused deaths over that of the similar cohort of non-service Australian males of approximately 5000 by 1933. The Commonwealth Statistician quotation denotes the applicable period as 'since discharge'. However, if this quotation is taken literally and exactly—specifically, the words 'since discharge'—a problem arises which requires resolution. The problem is that the date of discharge of individuals varied widely from 1915 to 1920 and could not possibly have been practicably accounted for on an individual basis in an actuarial assessment of a comparative cohort. On the basis of this impracticability, 'since discharge' is therefore interpreted as being a reference to the time when all soldiers were discharged, in effect at the end of 1920 prior to the date of disbandment of the AIF three months later. Based on this premise, the number of deaths that occurred *prior to* the disbandment of the AIF can be clearly distinguished from those counted in the analysis of the Actuary of the Commonwealth Superannuation Board, FW Barford, and therefore can be added without overlapping. This is immensely valuable for our purposes.

As mentioned previously, Butler's reported figures of annual pensioner deaths followed a remarkably consistent rate of around 750 men until, coincidentally, 1933. Over the subsequent three years this annual rate rises to approximately 850, and then in the three years to 1939 the rate flattens out at approximately 1000 deaths each year. By annualising Barford's number of 5000 deaths of ex-servicemen in excess of the national male population between 1920 and 1933, we arrive at a war-caused premature death rate of 380 over and above the rate for the similar non-serviceman cohort. This equates to half of the overall annual pensioner death rate in the comparable period recorded by the Department of Repatriation of about 750 per annum. It is reasonable to assume that this relationship that 50 per cent of the annual death rate were war related could, in the absence of any other influencing factors other than the passage of time, be extrapolated to cover another six years to 1939.

In arriving at these figures, for the first time we can conclude that there were a total of around 8000 war-caused premature deaths for the period from AIF disbandment until 1939 and the start of the Second World War. In light of the large proportions of men discharged medically unfit, or the 70 000 plus men who were receiving pensions each year over this twenty-year period, Barford's extrapolated numbers appear too low. The war-caused death rates of British pensioners identified by Mitchell were 'estimated' to be higher, at 60–70 per cent. Nevertheless, Barford was a highly credentialed authority and it is the conservative number of 8000 based on the actuarial analysis carried out by a respected authority that will be used to incorporate post-war deaths in the present compilation of Australian war casualties from this conflict. This represents the first time an accurate post-war death toll has been calculated. It is sadly ironic that the adoption of the timeframe for the calculation of the casualties of the First World War closes with the start of the Second World War. The average age of the returned servicemen at that time was just under fifty years and the youngest just under forty. Of the 200 000[12] First World War ex-servicemen who were still alive at that time, over 77 000 were receiving a pension. With the advent of another worldwide conflict, approximately 50 000 AIF ex-servicemen were still age-eligible for service; but the record review and count revealed that *only a little over 2000* decided to enlist again. This represents only 4 per cent of eligible men who decided to enlist for another war. And only a few of these men saw field service, according to their Second World War service records. It is not known whether this was by their choice, or whether their age precluded assignment to active service. The adoption of the advent of another world war as a cut-off date is sad insofar as this date almost chooses itself, being the only one suitable that is common to all the belligerent nations.

It is important to remind ourselves that these men were not numbers and that post-war suffering took many forms. The mine of information in the Attestation Papers provides a vivid picture of an element of social history and the impact of this war on the citizens of Australia nearly a century ago. Albert Geal (4821) was twenty-seven years of age when he enlisted, nominating his father as next of kin. He was not a bronzed bushman, but a potter, and he lasted twenty days in the field before being listed as missing, last seen 'going over the top'[13] at Fleurbaix near Pozières, not far from Fromelles on 19 July 1916. It was not until a year later, on 29 August 1917, that an inquiry was held which determined that he had been killed. His file was notated 'presumed buried in no man's land'. His father was advised of this finding *two* months later. A death certificate was finally issued on 3 January 1918 and his mother started to receive a pension of 20 shillings per fortnight from that date, nearly a year and a half after her son's death. The matter was not to close there, however. Albert's father was to receive a formal, and what must have been distressing, request from Army Records on 20 July 1921 for any information or letters he may have received since his son had been reported missing. Albert's father responded politely, advising Army Records that *they had advised him* that his son had been killed and that the inquiry heard eyewitness evidence that his son had last been seen 'going over the top'. Albert's parents were again reminded of the tragedy when subsequently they received a Memorial Scroll later in 1921, then a Memorial Plaque in 1922 and, finally, their son's medals in 1924, eight years after his death. Because Albert died before 31 March 1921 he is included on the Roll of Honour and the tragic list of those men missing.

Stanley Percival Carr (2374) was a miner from Kalgoorlie where he left his wife when he enlisted in January 1916. He was gassed in September 1917 but rejoined his unit a few weeks later. Unfortunately, he was again gassed two weeks before the end of the war and evacuated to England on Armistice Day. He was discharged from the army medically unfit shortly after, and eventually died of the effects of gas poisoning on 7 February 1928. Following a written request from his wife to Army Records, on 26 November 1929 she received a Memorial Plaque and Scroll and a copy of the King's message, thereby confirming that her husband's death was war related. But Stanley Carr's file was closed, and he is not on the Roll of Honour.

John Patrick Hoobin (3840) was only nineteen years of age when he enlisted in 1915. He was hospitalised for trench feet late in 1916 and for multiple shrapnel wounds in February 1918, which caused a severe fracture of his femur. He was brought back to Australia on a hospital ship and admitted to a repatriation hospital in Caulfield, Melbourne, in May 1919. A note on a medical report written in September 1920 stated that his femur remained 'un-united' despite eleven operations under general anaesthetic, and that he was bedridden. He was formally discharged medically unfit in May 1921. However, it is unclear whether he was still in hospital at this time, but he still had some involvement with the army as correspondence in 1926 reveals that the army authorities were trying to locate his father to advise him of his son's death. He was thirty years old when he died. A letter sent to the last known address of his father was returned and remains on Hoobin's file. On the back of the envelope someone has written 'moved on'.

Post-War Disability

Robert Whalen wrote of this war in 1984:

> There were no casualties in the Great War. 'Casualties' is an abstraction, a cloak that conceals the fact that millions of human beings died violently between 1914 and 1918. War hurts people and often kills in great numbers, and when war is over, all the people whose lives have been shattered do not simply return to normal. Everyone involved in a war is in some way a war victim. But some can reconstruct their lives more or less; others cannot.[14]

There is another measure related to the records of veteran pensions awarded by the Repatriation Department. It was outlined in Chapter 5 that the 9604 sample count of soldier records would include the recording of the presence in the soldiers' Attestation Papers of the pro forma request from the Repatriation Department to Base Records primarily for a copy of the form B103 or, in lieu, a record of hospitalisations over the soldier's service period. The issuance of such a request indicates that the individual has sought a pension benefit on the basis of a war-related medical condition. In Chapter 5, the example of Francis Gibbs (5569) was provided because he applied for a pension only to have it rejected on the grounds that he was no longer suffering from any ill effects, but was then handed, nine days after the rejection of his pension application, a discharge certificate stating that he was medically unfit. Evidence exists on his file that he applied for a pension on two further occasions in the 1920s. Yet it is not known whether those applications were successful. The point here is that Francis Gibbs felt that he could make an application on medical grounds for some form of recompense or financial support. He was prepared to make that application at a time when even Butler referred to changing attitudes in the general population which were turning against returned soldiers. By the mid-1920s returned servicemen were developing a reputation for being whingers and malingerers. In this regard, Australia's treatment of returning Vietnam veterans comes to mind. Gibbs obviously felt strongly that he had a case to make or he would not have tried to make it, twice. The years in which such applications were made by ex-servicemen were recorded in this analysis and are represented graphically in Figure 7.

Figure 7: All Applications for Repatriation Benefits Post War©

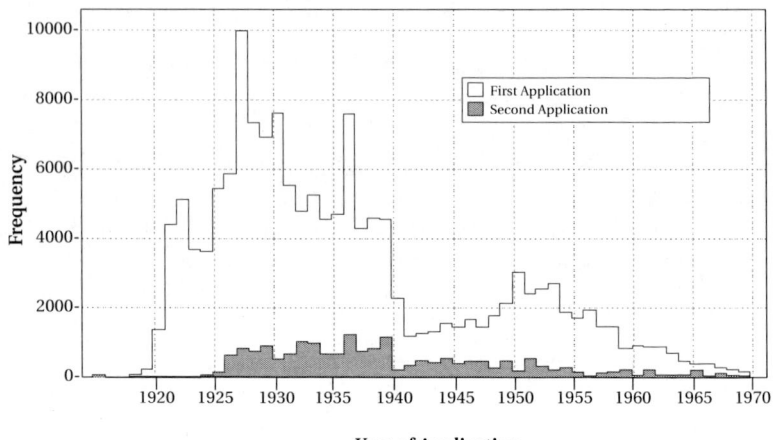

Source: Compiled by David Noonan from Attestation Papers, 2014.

The raw data represented in Figure 7 require modification. Included in these applications are those by next of kin submitted after the soldier had died, which were eligible for funeral expenses assistance. However, only those records that contained evidence of the soldier being alive sometime after the year of his application (for example, if he applied for discharge papers or the replacement of lost medals accompanied by a statutory declaration) was recorded for this analysis.

By the early 1930s it was becoming apparent that a great number of returned servicemen had become virtually unemployable. Some were homeless; many were alcoholics surviving on charitable handouts. This phenomenon had also appeared in Canada, where the government responded with the introduction in 1930 of a special pension for the 'burnt out' veteran. New Zealand followed with a similar form of pension support in 1935, and Australia introduced similar measures the following year:

> In 1936 the Lyons government passed legislation to introduce a 'Service Pension' for returned men aged over 60 and women over 55 years in impoverished circumstances (determined by a means test), those deemed permanently

unemployable and those suffering tuberculosis (whether war-caused or not).[15]

As the dollar amount for this pension was higher and came into effect before the normal age pension, nearly all who reached the eligible age applied for it. This accounts for the spike in 1936 in the graph in Figure 7. Therefore, the years of any apparent application after the ex-serviceman turned fifty-nine years of age were not recorded or collated in the recount process. The statistical software package was able to remove any soldiers who were over this age in the year of application. Thus, for the first time, data on the number of annual pension claims by ex-servicemen in the years 1918 to 1958, after deducting all claims by men over fifty-nine years of age and those who were not evidently alive at the time, have been collated and are represented in Figure 8 below. These claims are therefore based on grounds of ill health or impoverishment. And many of these men applied on multiple occasions.

Figure 8: Applications for non-aged-based pension claims by year©

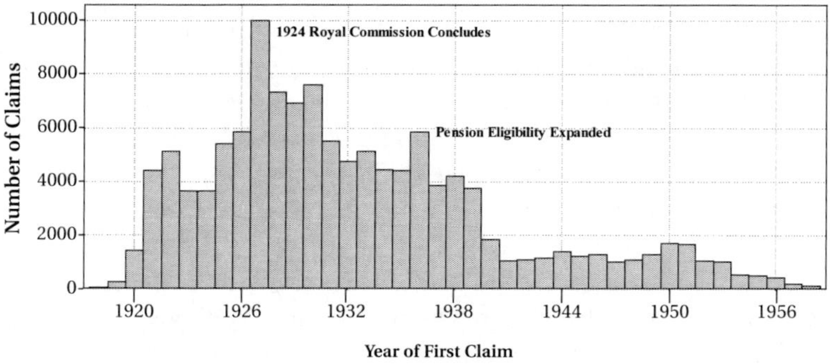

Source: compiled by David Noonan from Attestation Papers, 2014.

These men had returned to a divided country, split down the middle, with many people holding a vastly different view of the war from that reflected in the public celebration of 1914. The conscription referenda had galvanised the public's attitudes. Those who had served, and their families, resented those who had not. The politics had become bitter.

In this disturbed social environment the returned soldier found himself in adversarial combat with the Repatriation Commission, which usually adopted the position that there was no evidence linking the undoubted disease or disability suffered by the ex-serviceman to his war experience. For example, the Commission rejected VD contracted during a soldier's service period as pensionable, until this approach was overturned as a consequence of the 1924 Royal Commission. The data on these applications for a pension presented here provide us with a valuable measure of the extent of the post-war impact.

As discussed in Chapter 6, of the soldiers who survived, over half were discharged medically unfit. This amounted to approximately 130 500 men who, in light of their medical unfitness, could reasonably have expected to receive a pension, particularly as the level of disability that determined eligibility for a small pension in Australia was as low as 5 per cent. However, even in the peak year of 1920, only 90 000 men were receiving a pension. In the years 1916 to 1920, repatriation records show that 37 000 men had their applications rejected. This equates to 127 000 men who applied for a pension (90 000 plus 37 000). Assuming that nearly all men who were discharged medically unfit, like Francis Gibbs, applied for a pension, then this total is quite in accordance with the sample count evidence of 130 500 men who were discharged medically unfit. This is a telling outcome, highlighting that stringent criteria resulted in one third, or 40 000, of those men discharged medically unfit who did not subsequently qualify for a pension, of whom Francis Gibbs was just one.

Another small but significant indicator of the quiet despair experienced by the returned soldier also regularly appeared in the Attestation Papers of enlisted men. Charles Whitelaw enlisted in January 1917 and lasted fifty-two days before he was discharged medically unfit. Charles was not counted in the present analysis as he did not embark from Australia. In April 1931, he wrote to Base Records inquiring as to whether he was entitled to any medals, and enclosed a newspaper clipping, evidently placed by Army Base Records alerting ex-servicemen to the fact that 70 230 medals remained unclaimed. They were comprised of 31 524 British Medals, 33 097 Victory Medals, and 5609 1914/1915 Star Medals. This suggests that tens of thousands of returned servicemen had walked away from this war wanting nothing more to do with their war experience. A surprising number of well over 5000 men who would have almost certainly served at Gallipoli and who had been awarded the 1914/1915 Star had not collected their medals. This represents *a quarter* of all those men who saw service at Gallipoli. Over 30 000 men who had seen service in a theatre of war, as reflected in the award of the Victory Medal, had not claimed their entitlement either. The practice was to send medals in the years 1923 and 1924, as they became available, to the last known address of the recipient, so a proportion of eligible ex-servicemen may have simply moved because their records show returned correspondence and medals. But still so many medals remained unclaimed. Charles was advised that he was not entitled to any medals as he had not left Australia.

Base Records made a concerted attempt in 1936 to write to returned servicemen advising them that they were entitled to a medal and requesting that the recipient return an attached slip informing the authorities of how they would like the medal to be sent to them. Herbert Sharp (4313) received such a letter. He had his British Medal but had not received his Victory Medal. The fact that this slip is on his record indicates that he took the necessary steps to recover it. Another major appeal was made through newspapers around Australia via an announcement that 60 000 medals remained unclaimed in 1941, as evidenced in the soldiers' records. The following ex-servicemen referred to advertisements they had seen in the newspaper when they wrote to request their entitlement: LW Wilkins (7447) referred to the *Hobart Mercury* of 8 November 1941, JF Borger (2351) referred to the *Sydney Morning Herald* of 8 November 1941, and Lieutenant HB Gibson referred to *The Herald* Melbourne of 7 November 1941.

Still a further call for eligible recipients of unclaimed medals is evidenced in the records of Robert Whitelaw (not related to Charles), a porter. In a sign that recruits were desperately needed, Robert enlisted on 5 February 1918 and was embarked on 1 May. The logistics around moving men out of Australia had sped up, but the organisation to get them to the fighting front often had not. He was finally TOS in France on 2 December 1918. In October 1944, prompted by a newspaper article he refers to being published that day announcing that some 50 000 medals from the First World War remained unclaimed, he wrote to the authorities, 'wondering' whether he was entitled to any more medals as he had only received one, the British Medal. He was politely advised that, since he had not been in a theatre of war as he had arrived in France after the war had finished, he was not entitled to the Victory Medal. An aside here is that a striking feature across the Attestation Papers is the extraordinary politeness and deference contained in the correspondence to Base Records and it deserves further research. However, based on the earlier breakdown of the numbers of medal types representing over 32 000 men, this number of 50 000 medals to which Robert refers would represent nearly 25 000 men, one in ten of those who survived the war. Not even their next of kin wanted their medals (possibly 5000 men or one in five of the men entitled to these medals had died by 1944).

In relation to the subject of medal entitlement, there are many examples of disputes between the next of kin over benefits and entitlements contained in these men's files. Phillip Hartigan (148) enlisted as a single man shortly after the declaration of war and nominated his occupation as stockman and his mother as next of kin. He landed with the first troops at Gallipoli on 25 April 1915 but only lasted three weeks when he was severely wounded, evacuated, and died five days later. His mother and sister were promptly advised of his death, something that did not always occur. Within a week of receiving this tragic news, his sister wrote to Base Records stating that no claims from a woman who presented as her brother's wife should be entertained. She explained in her letter that her brother had married many years ago but because his wife conducted herself very badly and had associations with many men, this woman and her brother had agreed to separate four years ago and made no claims on each other. Phillip's sister stated that when his estranged wife found out that he had enlisted, she sought to claim a portion of his pay. Phillip had discussed his circumstances with his commanding officer, and the claim by this woman was rejected.

But Phillip's sister had not finished. She went on to say that his estranged wife was well-known to the police: 'She calls herself Miss Fish the conductor of a house of ill fame and sly grog, and is known as the "Little Wonder" in Exhibition Street Melbourne.' Not deterred, before the end of June 1915, Miss Fish (now Mrs Hartigan) visited a member of the House of Representatives of the Commonwealth Government. Australia's Parliament House was temporarily located in the Exhibition Buildings at the top of Exhibition Street, Melbourne, at that time while Canberra was being built from the ground up. The parliamentarian wrote a letter to the 'pensions department' saying that he had had a visit from a soldier's wife and was asking whether it was correct that Mrs Hartigan had been told she was ineligible to receive a pension. Documents show that she was deemed eligible in early August to receive a pension of £52 per annum, backdated to the day of Phillip's death on 20 May 1915. She was somewhat more fortunate than the mother of Albert Geal (4821), who received half as much from effect of the date of issuance of a death certificate, fourteen months after her son's death. Phillip's mother, as next of kin, was to subsequently receive his three medals, a Memorial Scroll and a Memorial Plaque. Her son's 1914/1915 Star Medal was found at the Richmond tip in 1942.

Butler summarised the details of the war pensions paid each year from 1916 to 1940.[16] He listed by year the number of pensions granted, the number of claims rejected, and the number of incapacitated members of the force receiving a pension and, separately, their dependants. He also recorded the amount in Australian pounds of the annual cost of all pension payments.

The data shown in Table 13 below were constructed from various data obtained from Butler's *Volume III*, in a section entitled 'The Statistics of Pensioning'.[17] Butler chose to present detailed data for a specific single year—1932—but the reason for this choice is unclear, and it does not appear to be connected to the fact that 1933 was the census year. The comparisons made in this analysis are too simplistic to draw too many conclusions, but their value is more in highlighting the comparative proportions of combat troops receiving pensions in the various countries fourteen years after the end of the war. Australia suffered a devaluation of 20 per cent against the British pound on 31 December 1931 and it was this lower exchange rate that was applied to Butler's data on Australian pension expenditure in 1932 to calculate an average cost per pensioner in US dollars, for which a direct exchange rate did not exist at that time. The Australian soldiers' number is in accordance with the findings of this record review rather than Butler's findings. Table 13 summarises these data.

In another table in *Volume III* Butler presents numbers which are unintelligible and undated, and are therefore not cited here; but part of the table purports to show pension expenditure expressed at a rate of pounds *per thousand head of the country's population*. By this measure, total pension expenditure in Australia, contrary to the impression given in Table 13 below, by the cost in US dollars per pensioner, is remarkably similar to that of France, Germany and the British Empire, which in turn had more than twice the equivalent expenditure than that of the USA. This comes about because the US *contribution* in terms of the proportion of its population sent to this war was so much lower than that of the other belligerents. It is therefore claimed that the data in Table 13 provide a clearer view of the relativity of pension costs for each country.

Table 13: Comparative Pension Data of 1932 with Other Selected Belligerents©

Country	Number of men in combatant service	Number of men pensioned in 1932	Per cent	$US million @ 31.12.32	$US/Pens.
Australia	318 000	76 000	24	27.8	368
USA	1 390 000	771 000	55	417.7	541
United Kingdom	4 971 000	481 000	10	231.2	480
Italy	5 600 000	210 000	4	60.8	290
France	7 932 000	1 098 000	14	296.8	270
Germany	12 000 000	820 000	7	290.4	354

Source: Constructed using data obtained from A Graham Butler, Official Medical History of the Australian Army Medical Services, 1914–1918, Volume III, Australian War Memorial, Canberra, 1942, Tables 61 and 67. Pension statistics are for 1932 only.

In order to look at Butler's pension expenditure numbers for Australia and to give the data some context, reference is made to Larsson.[18] She quotes the Australian War Services *Repatriation Act 1920 (Cwlth)* and its stipulation of a weekly pension for a 100 per cent disability which annualises to AU£214 or US$800 per full pension—more than twice that shown in Table 13. The difference from the table arises because so few pensioners have received the full pension. The figure also includes the total administrative expenses of the pension scheme, making the rate received by the pensioner even less. Larsson also makes this point, and highlights that the *full* pension was significantly below the income required to sustain a reasonable standard of living at the time.

Notations were occasionally identified in the soldier records which appeared to refer to a premature or sudden death of the soldier shortly after the end of the war. These deaths appeared suspicious in that they occurred shortly after discharge in circumstances where the soldier was apparently fit or was discharged suffering from shell shock. In order to investigate the possible reasons for such sudden deaths, the death certificates of a small sample of ten men were requested from the births, deaths and marriages registrars of three states. Hence, requests were made for a copy of the death certificates of three men from NSW, three men from South Australia and three from Victoria. The tenth application was made to the registrar of births, deaths and marriages in New Zealand as Robert Hall (6018), who came from Bathurst, NSW, died in New Zealand in 1921. This somewhat surprising evidence that Hall died in New Zealand took the form of a request from his wife for his medals in 1924, in which she states the date of his death and that it occurred in New Zealand.

In each of these cases[19] the death certificates reveal a hidden level of tragedy to an extent that is shocking. One ex-serviceman died of Spanish flu in 1919, and another died in June 1920 where the cause of death for this twenty-three year old was simply marked 'cardiac'. Relating these deaths to war service would be inappropriate although the latter case did seem odd. However, the cause of death of all the other eight ex-serviceman, the last being in May 1922, *was* related to their war service. Three died from TB contracted prior to discharge. Another who was discharged medically unfit suffering from shell shock died in January 1920 from a combination of kidney failure, malaria and cardiac arrest. He is on the Roll of Honour. Of the remaining four, *three committed suicide and the fourth probably did*, although the coroner gave him the benefit of doubt and found his drowning to be accidental. This case is the death that occurred in New Zealand. His death certificate is devoid of all but the most basic information and gives rise to the earlier comment that one of the four deaths was probably suicide. All that was known and shown on the death certificate was the ex-serviceman's name, that his occupation was fisherman and miner, and that he drowned on 28 August 1921. Unknown is his age and any details of his mother, father (both alive) or spouse, how long he had lived in New Zealand, or his usual address. These sections on the certificate were all marked 'Not

Recorded'. The simple letter from his wife sent three years later asking for his medals is all the more poignant. The other cases of suicide were confirmed by coronial inquiries, with the cause of death being drowning, haemorrhage due to a self-inflicted cut throat and poisoning with strychnine. Four of the eight deaths related to war service occurred before the cut-off date for entry onto the Roll of Honour, yet only two of them are on the Roll. There are many more cases of suspicious death such as these ten examples chosen randomly in the record review. This small sample reveals a chilling level of suffering among returned servicemen; eight of these ten men died prematurely due to war service, half by their own hand. This cost can never be fully quantified but it should never be forgotten either.

In returning to the overall review of post-war effects it is to be noted that being discharged medically unfit, receiving a pension or applying for a pension benefit are not mutually exclusive. Francis Gibbs was discharged medically unfit but did not receive a pension as we know. However, his record shows that he made an application for a pension on two occasions. Through the analysis of the collected data, it was possible to remove all those ex-servicemen who were discharged medically unfit. Of those who were not discharged medically unfit, the total number who made a claim for a disability pension amounted to over 76 000. We therefore now have a meaningful measure of the full extent of the post-war impact on the men of the AIF. Of the total of 255 800 men who survived the war, some 206 500 were either discharged medically unfit (130 500) or applied for pension assistance (76 000) before they turned sixty.

Therefore, it can now be claimed for the first time, based on sound, statistically grounded evidence, *that four out of five* of all of the survivors were impacted in some way by disability in the post-war period up until the start of the Second World War. As discussed earlier, some 8000 of them died prematurely as a result of their war service, hundreds by their own hand. But the findings do not end here.

In this search to find out what really did happen to these men, there is one more step that needs to be taken: to combine their whole war experience, both during and after this conflict. And this can be done and follows shortly.

This review of soldier records has endeavoured to provide an example of how the use of statistical analysis using simple random sampling methods can unlock deep historical assessments of *any* event, even if the available records are so large as to be daunting to the interested historian. Statistical analysis is a powerful tool, even in the field of social-historical analysis and narrative. Through these means, this review set out to correct the record via the analysis of over 12 000[20] soldier records, to provide an accurate estimate of the number of enlistments and embarkations of the AIF. It also set out to correct the record by revealing the true extent of the suffering of these men, by producing a measure of hospitalisations for wounding, injury and illness, so long incorrect or absent from the official record. And finally it set out to determine by some measure the pain, death and suffering that these men and their carers had to endure after the end of the war, and for most, the rest of their lives. In the process, this record review, using statistical analysis of soldier records has laid the basis of a new social history of that time with an aggregation of the stories of these men and of those who cared and worried for them. Like the story of Mrs Williams, who lost five sons in this war. Or Mrs Hartigan, who lost her son, her financial entitlements as next of kin and his medals. Or Mrs Sim, who in 1923, six years after her son William's death was told her son's grave was just a head stone and they did not know where his body was, nor did they know where his brother Arthur's body was either. She had previously been advised they had been buried together in the same cemetery. This social history dimension has barely been touched upon in this book but is the subject of ongoing research by the author. The 400 000 cell Excel spreadsheet can be used to record the demographics of these men, and to dissect and reveal multiple facets of their lives. This multidisciplinary study has many stories yet to be told.

The reality revealed by this soldier record and census analysis is that the proportion of Australian soldiers of the AIF who died during the course of the First World War constituted over 20 per cent of all men exposed to a theatre of war, rising to nearly 23 per cent (70 400 in 308 000) when accounting for war-related deaths that occurred over the next twenty years. The death toll was not 60 000 men. Australian soldiers of the AIF suffered a total death toll of *70 400* and all Australian soldiers a total of *72 500*, as shown in Table 14.

It is now also claimed that, of those who survived exposure to this war, effectively *all* were injured, wounded or became ill, some multiple times, resulting in a total of 750 000 hospitalisations during the period of existence of the AIF for the 308 000 men exposed to a theatre of war. By deducting the number of hospitalisations of men who died, it can also be asserted that those who survived were hospitalised on average nearly *three times* each.[21] And it is claimed that *half* (147 000) were wounded, some multiple times. *One in three* of the 255 800 who survived long enough (200 000) were still suffering from a disability more than twenty years later at a level officially deemed eligible for a pension.

Table 14: Australia's Total Death Toll from the First World War

B2455 series count	62 300
MT1486/1 series count	100
Post-war actuarial-based count	8 000
Commemorative Roll	2 168
Rounded total	**72 500**

Source: Compiled by David Noonan from Attestation Papers, 2014.

Through an analysis of the impact of this war in its totality, incorporating this post-war period, the data collected in the record review also produced the following further conclusions—made here for the first time.

Australia's civilian male population offered up 379 000 enlistments to this conflict, 10 per cent less than officially claimed, despite a Royal Commission reaffirming the official number that exists to this day. Of these, 318 000 effectively embarked to arrive overseas and about 308 000 served in a theatre of war—somewhat fewer than the 331 781 suggested by official sources.

The length of time until death did not alter with the risk profile of the soldier. Approximately 5000 men did not survive a fortnight, 10 000 did not last a month. Even if one accepts the general intuitive concept that a younger man would likely take more risks than an older, wiser man, the artillery bombardments did not. Death was indiscriminate, and age and the risk-averse had nothing to do with survivability.

The truth is that the men of the AIF proportionately suffered more woundings, and more hospitalisations for injuries and illness, than the armies of men of Britain, Germany, France, the USA or Canada. During the war Australia's death toll was proportionately greater too, exceeding even that of Germany. Up until Monash withdrew the AIF from the fighting in the first week of October 1918, no longer at fighting strength, by any major measure, Australia's losses and suffering were devastating. And it was visited upon *over half* of Australia's male population between the ages of eighteen and fifty-five years. The outcome of this war came at too high a cost to this young country; it was indeed a pyrrhic victory.

Over half of the survivors were discharged medically unfit, at least 20 per cent of whom suffered from mental trauma. A *further* 30 per cent of those survivors who were not discharged medically unfit asked for pension support at least once in their lives. These combined impacts represent four out of five servicemen who *survived* this war being damaged in some way. Figure 9 below is an attempt to present these numbers in a visual form.

In considering these various proportions of servicemen evidently impacted in some way following the war, and incorporating them along with those who paid the ultimate price into Figure 9, it initially appears that *only 10 per cent* of the men who served in a theatre of war were left unscathed.[22]

Figure 9: The total impact of the First World War©

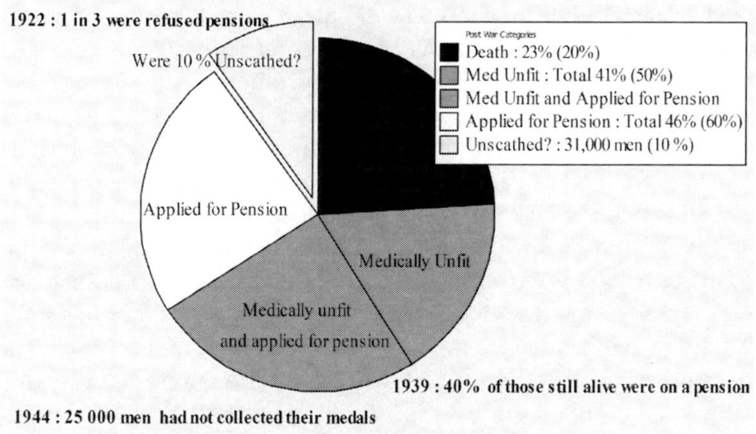

1922 : 1 in 3 were refused pensions

Were 10% Unscathed?

Applied for Pension

Medically unfit and applied for pension

Medically Unfit

Post War Categories
- Death : 23% (20%)
- Med Unfit : Total 41% (50%)
- Med Unfit and Applied for Pension
- Applied for Pension : Total 46% (60%)
- Unscathed? : 31,000 men (10%)

1939 : 40% of those still alive were on a pension

1944 : 25 000 men had not collected their medals

Source: Compiled by David Noonan from Attestation Papers, 2014.

But were they? When these 10 per cent of soldier records were examined and those soldiers who had been hospitalised for wounding, illness or injury were deducted from this remaining segment, the percentage reduces to just over 3 per cent, or *only 11 000 men*, who were apparently unaffected.

But even this may not be the right figure. In this analysis, there was no accounting for the men who walked away, never wanting to have anything to do with officialdom again for as long as they lived. Nor did it cover those who refused to ask for help because of their *pride* and the stigma of shell shock being a *constitutional* weakness, or the *shame* and stigma of *VD*; or those who soldiered on with the stigma of *alcoholism*, to collapse into the care of their families if they had them. Forgotten also are those who took their own lives and will never be identified (as highlighted by the small sample of death certificates uncovered in this analysis), as well as those 25 000 men, or their next of kin (of the estimated 5000 who had died), who by 1944 had chosen not to collect their medals.

In this new light, the following can be stated supported by the factual evidence revealed by this record review.

The appointment of Butler, supported by Bean, was a poor choice and Butler failed in his task of providing this country with an accurate official medical services history of the First World War. Butler's editor-in-chief, Bean, had set a flawed structural brief for the medical services history and failed in his responsibility to effectively oversee this work and its timely and accurate production. It is also contended that Bean's contribution to the official record of Australia in this war is quite limited in this area, reporting on only death and wounding in his concluding casualty statistics (which were inaccurate and over twenty years out of date), and omitting a basic casualty statistic although he knew of the enormity of the incidence of injury and illness. In essence, Bean was a journalist operating under the auspices of military command and the Department of Defence. He was not a fearless public servant as the title *official war historian* would have most believe he was. The soldier Attestation Papers tell the truth of this conflict; and in their aggregation present a very different picture of war and *social history* than that previously relied upon, and which Bean in particular painted in the past. In the assessment of these two large official historical records written by Bean and Butler, in relation to Australia's total casualty figures, neither provides a comprehensive or reliable record, and, it is contended, both fall well short of what may reasonably be expected from an official history of Australia in the First World War.

There is no doubt that an element of both incompetency and conspiracy has contributed to this state of affairs. The larger contributor was incompetency but conspiracy also played its part. This was evidenced in the efforts to present to the world a larger 'contribution' of enlistments than was actually the case. But the impact of these efforts was overshadowed by Bean's omission of the largest component of hospitalisations suffered by these men. The statistic of the proportion of men who had been discharged medically unfit was readily available but Bean did not seek it out. And the disproportional impact upon this nation was best forgotten.

Having said all of that, it is also evident that Bean's version of Australia's experience of the First World War has remained largely unquestioned. Therefore, to return to the question raised at the beginning of this book, as to whether it was conspiracy, incompetency or an unquestioned acceptance of the official record that allowed for this flawed and misleading casualty history record to exist to this day—the answer is that it was all three, each varying in degree in the eyes of the beholder.

Based on a robust, statistically sound, scrupulous analysis in this record review of well over 9604 soldier records, it is claimed here, for the first time, that *all of those* who were exposed to this war were damaged, disabled or died from it. Of course, some recovered, some managed but many did not. We can learn a great deal from this history. But there is still a problem—officially, the plight of so many of these servicemen remains unacknowledged, effectively forgotten. This is contrary to and indeed a breach of this nation's pledge: *lest we forget, we shall remember them*. With its centenary nearly upon us, perhaps it is timely to correct the record and acknowledge the true and full extent of the death and suffering of the men of the AIF in the First World War.

Notes

1. War deaths exceeded Australian civilian Spanish Flu deaths by a factor of five.
2. Commonwealth of Australia, *Census of The Commonwealth of Australia, taken for the night between 3 and 4 April 1921: Volume II, Statistician's Report*, Australian Bureau of Statistics, Government Printer, Melbourne, 1921, p. 326, see: <http://www.abs.gov.au/AUSSTATS/abs@.nsf/DetailsPage/2111.01921?OpenDocument>.
3. ibid., p. 45.

4   TJ Mitchell and GM Smith, *Medical Services History of the Great War: Casualties and Medical Statistics of the Great War*, Imperial War Museum, London, 1931, p. 275.
5   Marina Larsson, *Shattered ANZACs: Living With the Scars of War*, UNSW Press, Sydney, 2009, p. 242.
6   ibid., note 98, p. 301.
7   Commonwealth of Australia, *Census of The Commonwealth of Australia, 30th June 1933*, Commonwealth Government Printer, Canberra, 1933.
8   A Graham Butler, *Official Medical History of the Australian Army Medical Services, 1914–1918, Volume III*, Australian War Memorial, Canberra, 1942, p. 965.
9   Ernest Scott, *Official History of Australia in the War 1914–1918, Volume XI*, Angus and Robertson, Sydney, 1936, p. 888.
10 Mitchell and Smith, *Medical Services History of the Great War: Casualties and Medical Statistics of the Great War*, p. 317.
11 Commonwealth of Australia, *Census of The Commonwealth of Australia, 30th June 1933: Volume III—Statistician's Report*, 1933, p. 398.
12 This was a simple calculation that conservatively extrapolated the 1933 Census finding of AIF soldier deaths since the war of 38 000 or approximately 3000 a year on average to the year 1939, leaving those who were still alive at 200 000. It is probably less than this as the death rate may have risen towards the end of this period of extrapolation, as evidenced by the pensioner death rate
13 His father's words recorded on his son's file.
14 Robert Weldon Whalen, *Bitter Wounds: German Victims of the Great War, 1914–1918*, Cornell University Press, London, 1984, p. 15.
15 Stephen Garton, *The Cost of War: Australians Return*, Oxford University Press, Melbourne, p. 95.
16 Butler, *Official Medical History of the Australian Army Medical Services, 1914–1918, Volume III*, p. 963.
17 ibid., p. 958.
18 Larsson, *Shattered ANZACs: Living With the Scars of War*, p. 95.
19 Frederick Honeybone (2139), Arthur Carr (2051), Francis Davies (8815), Robert Hood (403), Lt. William Geach, Arthur Hooke (3793), Herbert Dwyer (17390, Frank Dwyer (192), John Carter (3369), Robert Hall (6018).
20 This is the total of sampling 9604 records in B2455, 1218 records in the pilot sample, 1608 records in the MT series sample, which gives a total of 12 430 service records.
21 Approximately 246 400 exposed to this conflict who survived were hospitalised an estimated 672 000 times, or on average 2.73 times each.
22 For the sake of thoroughness here is some detail. The aim was to present a very simple graphic so that some overlap is not displayed. The *rounded* numbers to the nearest 500 for the AIF are 318 000 embarked; 308 000 were sent to a theatre of war; 70 500 died (62 500 during the war); 131 000 were discharged medically unfit; a further 76 000 would apply for a pension; another 8000 prematurely died in the post-war period (and some would overlap with the previous two numbers); leaving 31 000 or 10 per cent apparently impacted. Excel allowed access to these files by elimination and

found that 20 000 had been hospitalised at least once, leaving 11 000 (3 per cent) apparently unaffected (the overlap of post-war deaths would have no effect on the validity of this number as it was reached without any reference to the post-war deaths).

Index

37th Battalion, casualties xiv
38th Battalion
  casualties xiv
  officers xiii–xiv
1914–1915 Star recipients 138, 188, 189, 191

accidental deaths 82, 125
active service
  assessing date of commencement (TOS) 94–5
  measuring duration of battlefield exposure 94–6
  time spent 'out of the field' 95–6
Adam-Smith, Patsy 17, 37
Admission and Discharge Books 22, 24, 25, 26, 27, 29, 39, 40
ages of soldiers
  assessment 96
  at enlistment 145–6
  and survivability 146–7, 196
AIF records, analysis of 41
AIF Records Section, compilation of casualty figures 7
Asser, V 25–6
Attestation Papers 2, 25–6, 38, 50, 51, 54, 115, 132, 183
Australian Parliamentary Library, casualty statistics 14*t*, 16
Australian War Graves Commission (AWGC), casualty statistics 14*t*, 18

Australian War Memorial (AWM)
  abandonment of research into post-war deaths 178–9
  casualty statistics 17
  definition of 'casualties' 34
Ayres, Leonard 154, 155–6

B103: Statement of Service (Form) 27, 28, 112, 185
B103-II: Casualty Form–Active Service (Form) 27
Barford, FW 181–183
Base Records (Victoria Barracks)
  attempts to distribute unclaimed medals 188–9
  correspondence with Repatriation Commission 28
battlefield exposure, measuring duration of 95–6
Beaumont, Joan 2, 116 *n*5
Bean, CEW
  brief for medical services history 19, 198
  concerns over Butler's medical history 20–1
  as editor of official war history 1, 3, 4
  failure to refer to Butler's work in final volume of official history 28–9
  publication of official casualty figures 1

support for Butler's writing of medical history 18–19, 20, 29
treatment of Butler's medical statistics 3, 38
Bergen, Leo van 66, 132, 144
Borger, JF 189
Bosanquet, Arthur George 125
Bowlby, Anthony 77
British casualty statistics
comparability with Australian figures 157–8
deaths 158–9, 168*t*
first publication 158
non-battle casualties 159
woundings 158–9, 168*t*
British Medal recipients 89, 90, 108, 138, 188, 189, 190
Bullecourt 117*t*, 126, 126*t*
'burnt out' solider phenomenon 113, 186–7
Burton, Clerke Colquhoun 102
Burton, Gilbert Menzies 111
Burton, S 89
Burton, W 89
Burton, WA 89
Butler, AG
assessment of Howse 23–4
as Collator of Medical Records 18, 23
data on death rate of war pensioners 180
data on venereal disease 65–6, 131, 148*n*19
death 22
discrepancies in his statistics 10–13, 20, 29
Distinguished Service Order 18
emphasis on medical aspects of casualties 36
health problems 19, 21
methodological approach 22–7, 39, 40–1
portrait 19*p*
as regimental medical officer of 9th Infantry Battalion 18
summary of US casualties 153, 154
view of shell shock sufferers 72, 166
work ethic 18, 20
writing of Australian medical history 1, 3, 10–13, 20–1, 22, 29–30, 198

Canada, involvement in war 164
Canadian casualties
death toll 164, 168*t*
disease 164–5
first publication 164
venereal disease 166, 168*t*
Carpenter, Harold Gordon 99
Carr, Stanley Percival 184
Carr, William Henry 127
Carter, Archibald Joseph 105
casualties
definition 33–4
estimates 115–16
militarised definition 37
socio-cultural use of term 37
socio-political use of term 37
see also official casualty figures; official casualty record
casualty categorisation
battle casualties 35
different audiences 34, 35
historians' approach 36–7
medical historians' approach 35–6
military historians' approach 35, 37
non-battle casualties 35, 36
cerebro-spinal meningitis (CSM) 82–3, 84, 122–3, 123*t*, 164–5
chaplains 141
Commemorative Roll of Honour 179, 196
Commonwealth Census 1921 175, 176–7
Commonwealth Census 1933 177, 180, 181
Compere-Morel, Thomas 163
concussion, and PTSD 11, 81
Conference on Venereal Diseases (1922) (Australia) 69–70
conscription referenda 8
Cosgrove, Peter 33
Creamer, Mark 80
Croix de Guerre (Belgium) recipients 140
Cumpston, JHL 68–9, 82, 84

Da Pinna, Les 106
Davenport, Florence 100, 101
Davidson, William 67
Davies, Benjamin Clifford 100–1
deaths *see* non-battle deaths; war deaths

Index 203

'debility', and shell shock 79, 101, 140
dental health 52–3
Depena, Alex 67
desertions, prior to embarkation or between ports 59–60
diseases
 control of infectious diseases 84–5, 99
 deaths from 82–5
 infectious jaundice 165
 major diseases 130–1
 respiratory disease 124, 130
 skin disease 130–1
 see also cerebro-spinal meningitis; Spanish Flu; venereal disease
disordered action of the heart (DAH) 77, 78, 101–2
Distinguished Service Medal recipients 140
Downes, Rupert (Major General) 21
drivers 138
Duncan, Charlie 67
Duncan, George Oliphant 67
Durkin, Joseph 125
Durston, SW 108
Dussell, GH 108
dysentry 164

'effort syndrome' 78
embarkation figures
 1914–1917 8t
 desertions 59–60
 discharge prior to embarking 58, 89
 discrepancies in official figures 11–12, 58
 double counting 57–8, 60–1
 non-applicablity 60, 62, 90, 91
 overstatement in official records 60
 revised by Commonwealth Statistician 11–12, 57–8, 62
enlistment
 age at 96
 promotion of 9–10
enlistment figures
 1914–1917 8t
 ages at enlistment 145–6
 all enlistments distinguished from military enlistments 51, 57
 analysis of MT 1486/1 records 51–7
 'Did Not Shows' 54
 discrepancies in official record 10–11

double counting 54
estimated total 116, 196
failure to enlist statistics 55
home service duties 56
'not applicable' 54–5
officers' ages at enlistment 145
overstatement in official statistics 51, 116, 196, 199
reenlistments for Second World War 183
rejections on medical grounds 52–3, 55
rejections on non-medical grounds 53–4
epilepsy 72, 73
Ewart, Violet xi
Excel spreadsheet 143, 195, 197 n22

Ferguson, Munro 7, 8
Field Medical Cards 24
First World War, total impact on servicemen 196–8
Ford, Nick 81
French casualties 162–4, 168t

Gallipoli campaign 117t, 118, 189
Gallup, George 42, 43
Gammage, Bill 37
Garton, Stephen 72–4, 85, 113
Gault, AK 89
Gavans, Harry 121
Gawley, Edward 93
Gay, George 120–1
Geal, Albert 183–4, 191
German casualty statistics
 accuracy problems 159–60
 categorisation of shell shock 160
 death toll 159–60, 168t
 disease 160–1
 hospitalisations 161
 non-battle deaths 160
 POW deaths 161
 size of army 159
 venereal disease 160, 168t
 woundings 160, 168t
Germany, impact of war on social fabric 162
Gibbs, Charles Earnest 139–40
Gibbs, Francis 112–13, 185, 188, 194
Gibbs, John James 139
Gibson, Albert 130

204   *Index*

Gibson, Benjamin Digby (Capt) 125
Gibson, HB 189
gonorrhoea, treatment 65
Graham, James Joseph 105–6
Graham, Louis 129
Graham, Norman 90
Graham, Robert 138
Grey, Jeffrey 17–18, 37–8
grief 176
Griffith, Samuel 7

Haig, Douglas (General) 118
Hall, Henry Mackie 106–7
Hall, Herbert Joshua 107–8
Hall, James Edgar 108
Hall, John 59–60
Hall, John Richard 137–8
Hall, Philip 122
Hall, Robert 193
Hall, Stephen 126
Hart, Geoffrey John 104–5
Hart, Herbert 104
Hart, James Albert 103–4
Hartigan, Mrs 190–1
Hartigan, Phillip 190
health control systems 84–5
Heney, TW 3–4
hernias 52, 97
historians, approach to casualty categorisation 36–7
Hone, William Alfred 95–6
Honeysett, Joseph (Capt) 127
Hoobin, John Patrick 184
Hood, J 109
Hood, John (19285) 138
Hood, Robert 138
Hood, Walter 137
Hook, Cyril Charles 138
Hook, William 130
Hook, William Bede 138
Hooper, Claude 130
horse-related accidental deaths 82, 125
hospitalisation forms 27
hospitalisations
    of British soldiers 159, 168t
    of Canadian soliders 164, 168t
    changes in diagnosis 98–9
    counting incidences of 98
    estimated total 127–8
    of German soliders 160–1, 168t
    for injuries 130
    multiple hospitalisations 98, 100–1, 128–9, 136
    of officers 143–4
    for shell shock 101–2, 127, 127–8, 144
    total estimate 135–6, 168t, 195–6
    understatement in official records 127, 136
    of US soldiers 155, 168t
    for venereal disease 65–7, 68, 109–10
    wounding as criterion for 97
    without cause 98
    see also non-hospitalisations
Howse, Neville (Major General) 18, 19, 20, 21, 23
Hughes, Billy xiii, 7, 9

illness
    battle-related 97, 98, 136
    major diseases 130–1
    non-battle-related 98
    see also diseases; venereal disease
Imperial War Graves Commission 18
imprisonment, of soldiers 90–1
infectious diseases, control of 84–5, 99
influenza 78
Inglis, Ken 4
injuries see war injuries
Ireland, MW 123–4
'irritable heart' 77, 78
isolation camps, and control of infectious diseases 99

Landon, Alfred 42, 43
Larsson, Marion 2, 178, 192
Lewis, Milton James 68, 69, 83
Lindstrom, Richard 72
Literary Digest 42–3

McCarry, CE 108
McFarlane, Alexander 80
McMullin, Ross 33
MacPhail, Andrew 131, 133, 164, 165, 166
Marin report 151
medals
    eligibility for 189–91
    unclaimed 188–9
Medical Case Sheets 24, 25

medical examinations for war fitness,
    failure statistics 10–11, 52–3, 55
medical historians, approach to
    casualty categorisation 35–6
Medical History Advisory Board 20
Medical Inquiry documents 27
medical statistics
    data sources 24–6
    publication by Butler 1, 3
medically unfit discharges
    definition 103–6
    estimated total 139
    and pension eligibility 194
    percentage of survivors 139
    reasons for 139
    for traumatic stress or shell shock
        103–8, 139–41
    without hospitalisation 137
Memorial Plaque and Scroll 91, 92, 184
Meritorious Service Medal recipients
    138, 140
Mignon, A (General) 162, 163
Military Cross recipients 111, 127, 137
military historians, approach to
    casualty categorisation 35, 37
Military Medal 109
military psychiatry, history of 77
Miller, Donald xii
Miller, Harry xii–xiii
Miller, Isaac Pearce xi, xiii, 174
Miller, Norman xii, xiii
Milton, Rod 80
Ministry of Pensions (Britain),
    destruction of Australian records 22, 23–5
Minitab 63 $n5$, $n7$, $n9$, 116 $n2$, $n4$
Mitchell, TJ 177, 178, 180–1, 183
Monash, John
    on capabilities of American soldiers 153
    losses suffered under his command 117t
    reputation for looking after troops 119–20
mumps 84, 99
murders 125–6

National Archives of Australia (NAA)
    B2455 series of soldier records 44, 46–7, 51

MT 1486/1 series of solider records
    41, 45–6, 51–7
'non applicable' category
    for embarkation figures 60, 62, 90–1
    purpose 89
non-battle casualties 35, 36, 98
    see war injuries
non-battle deaths
    accidents 125
    cerebro-spinal meningitis 82–3, 84, 122–3, 123t
    murders 125–6
    pneumonia 124, 125
    POW deaths in captivity 127
    Spanish Flu 82, 83, 85, 102, 123–4, 125t
    suicide 120–2, 123t
    total estimate 120
    tuberculosis 82, 125
non-hospitalisations
    discharged medically unfit 137
    safest occupations 108–9, 136–7, 138
    wounded but remain on duty 97
'non-ulcer dyspepsia' 78
nurses, miscategorised in records 54

Office of Works (Britain) 25
officers
    captains-in-the-field 143
    chaplains 142
    competence 141
    death rates 142–3
    differences from other ranks re
        details in records 111
    discharged medically unfit 110–11, 139, 144
    hospitalisations 143–4
    medical professionals 142
    promotions from the ranks 141–2
    and signal technology 142
    statistics of those that served in AIF 142–3
    struck off strength discharges 73–4, 79, 129, 144
    under-reporting of shell shock 73–4, 79, 111
    under-reporting of VD 67
official casualty figures
    basis of 5

comparison of various sources
  14–15*t*
cut-off dates 177–9, 183
discrepancies 10–18, 22, 29
first publication 1
lack of scrutiny 13
in military terms 7
overstatement of enlistment figures
  51, 116, 196, 199
total battle casualties for 1919 6–7,
  6*t*
total published in 1921 5*t*
total published in 1933 5*t*
underestimation of injury and
  illness 127, 136, 151
official casualty record, creation of
  3–10
O'Keefe, Brendan 18
Orr, H (Major) 166
Orr huts 166

Passchendaele 117*t*, 118, 126*t*
pension applications 112
  increases due to the depression
    113–14
  rejections 185
  statistics 186*t*
pension eligibility
  conflicts of interest over 23
  and medically unfit discharge 194
  restrictive policies 175
pension expenditure, comparative data
  for 1932 191–2, 192*t*
pension records 38
pension system, claims for assistance
  38–9
pensioners
  death rate 180
  number at outbreak of Second
    World War 183
population, proportion of males 1881–
  1921 177*t*
post-traumatic stress disorder (PTSD)
  71, 80, 81
post-traumatic stress syndrome (PTSS)
  71, 79, 80
post-war deaths
  death rate of war pensioners 180–1
  ex-servicemen not on pension 180
  total war-caused premature deaths
    182–3

post-war disability
  comparative pension data 191–2,
    192*t*
  extent of 194, 196
  introduction of Service Pension
    186–7
  pension applications 186*t*, 194
  pension eligibility 185, 188
post-war impacts
  attempts to minimise 175
  ceasing to account for 177
  generational effects 178
  grief 176
  ongoing suffering 176
  total death toll of war-related deaths
    195–6
post-war suffering, quantitative
  assessment of 28, 38–9
Pozières 117*t*, 118, 126*t*
'premature senility', and shell shock
  78, 107, 108
Prior, Robin 33, 94
prisoners of war 109, 126–7, 161
public health, standards and responses
  in Australia 83, 84–5

quarantining, use by military medical
  services 84–5, 157

random sampling methodology
  accuracy of 43–4
  for B2455 series of soldier records
    46–7
  for MT series of soldier records 45–6
  selected sample sizes 47
  trial or pilot count 45
recruitment, 1918 conference 7–8, 9
Repatriation Act 1920 (Cwlth) 192
Repatriation Commission
  correspondence with Base Records
    (Victoria Barracks) 28
  requests for Form B103 112
respiratory disease 124, 130
Returned and Services League (RSL),
  concern over 'burnt out' solider
  phenomenon 113
rheumatism, and shell shock 105, 110
Roll of Honour
  arbitrariness of cut-off date criteria
    91–3
  eligibility for entry 179, 184

Index 207

Roosevelt, Franklin 42, 43
Rosenfeld, Geoffrey 81
Royal Commission for Assessment of War Disabilities, 1924–1925 (Aust) 70, 74, 175, 188
Royal Commission into Department of Defence Records, 1918 (Aust) 7–9
Royal Commission on Venereal Diseases, 1913–1916 (Britain) 68

sample surveys 42–3
sampling methodology
   flaws in official medical service histories 39–41
   random sampling and sample size 43–4
Schjerning, Otto von 160
Scott, Ernest 151
   failure to refer to Butler's work 28
   publication of official casualty statistics 1, 3, 4–5, 29
   work on *Vol XI* of Bean's official history 3–4, 29
self-inflicted injuries 97, 121
'senility', and shell shock 78–9, 107, 108
Serle, Geoffrey 119
Service Pensions
   application statistics 187–8
   introduction 113, 185–6

Sharp, Doug 125
Sharp, Herbert 189
Sharples, Reginald 61
Sharrock, Ottawa 92–3
shell shock
   Australian Defence Force 80, 81
   Canadian approach to 166–7
   definitions 71, 80
   differentiation between physical and mental effects 71, 75–6
   difficulties of assessing incidence 70–1, 76
   difficulties of diagnosis 72–3, 76–7
   and discharges as medically unfit 103–8, 112, 139–41
   and execution for cowardice 166, 167
   expressions denoting condition 76–9
   hospitalisations 101–2, 127–8, 144
   as misnomer 79–80
   as a moral problem 72
   Maudsley Monographs 77 n26, 78
   number of AIF compared to British sufferers 72
   origins of term 71
   predisposition to 72, 75
   recognition of condition 71
   treatment 74, 75–6
   under-reporting for officers 73–4, 79
   under-reporting in official records 127–8
   as 'wounding' 101–2, 160, 161
Shephard, Walter 92
Shephard, William 108
Shepley, Percy Phillip 97
Sheridan, Dennis Patrick 125
Sheridan, Henry Bradley 125
Sherman, Walter 67
Sievers, William 90
Sievwright, Herbert 93
signal technology, implications for officers 142
Silva, John 130
Sim, Arthur 195
Sim, William 195
Simcock, GE 89–90
Sinclair, Percy Raymond 109–10
Sinclair, Peter 67
Sinclair, Samuel Edward (Capt) 111–12
Sinclair, Wisbey 126–7
Sing, William Edward 140–1
skin diseases 130–1, 166
Smith, Staniforth 5–6, 7
Somme 117t, 126t
Spanish Flu (H1N1 virus)
   efforts by Australian Medical Corp to contain outbreak 85, 123
   impact on AIF 82, 83, 85, 102, 123–4, 125t, 157
   impact on American forces 82, 83, 85, 123–4, 154, 156–7
   impact on Australian non-indigenous population 83
   public health measures in Australia 84–5
   Shanks, Dennis et al 83, 157
   worldwide impact 84
Spanish War 156
Stanley, Peter 64–5

struck off strength discharges 73–4, 79, 129, 144
submarine guard duty 140, 141
suicides 120–2, 123*t*, 138, 193–4
survivability
  age and risk profile 146–7, 196
  safest occupations 108–9, 136–7, 138
synovitis 96
syphilis
  among general population 69
  certificates of cure 70
  treatment of soldiers 65

tetanus 165
traumatic brain injury 81
TOS (taken on strength) 94, 96
Treloar, JW (Capt) 18, 21
trench foot 166
tuberculosis 53, 92, 93, 113, 125, 193
Tucker, Thomas George 20, 21

United States
  involvement in war 152–3
  performance of medical services 155–6, 157
United States casualties
  death toll 154–5, 168*t*
  deaths from Spanish Flu 82, 83, 85, 123–4, 154, 156–7
  hospitalisations for injury and illness 155, 168*t*
  incidence of venereal disease 133, 168*t*
  in Spanish War 156

varicocele 53
venereal disease (VD)
  AIF efforts to control spread 131
  associated stigma and delays in treatment 67
  Butler's data 65–6, 131, 148*n*19
  certificates of cure 70
  condom availability 134
  estimated total hospitalisations 132–3
  in general population 69
  hospitalisations for 65–7, 68, 101, 109–10, 132–3
  impact on war effort 134–5
  incidence among officers 143
  incidence in British Expeditionary Force 133, 168*t*
  incidence in Canadian forces 132, 133, 166, 168*t*
  incidence in German forces 133, 160, 168*t*
  incidence in US Army in Europe 133, 168*t*
  Langwarrin 58, 131 *n*19, 132
  legislation to control spread 69–70
  official statistics 131–2
  public health concerns 68–70
  and rejection of enlistment application 53
  statistics 64–7, 70
  suspension of pay for sufferers 65, 67–8
  treatment 61, 65, 67–8, 70, 134–5
  under-reporting 69, 132
  under-reporting of officers affected 67
Victoria Cross recipients, incidence of VD 64
Victory Medal recipients 89, 138, 188, 189, 190
Villers-Bretonneux 119
vision problems 72–3
Voluntary Ballot Enlistment Scheme 9

war deaths
  after discharge 92–3
  Australians killed under British or NZ Army command 179
  of British soldiers 158, 159, 168*t*
  by campaign 117*t*, 118
  of Canadian soldiers 164, 168*t*
  comparison of Australia with other belligerents 168–70, 168*t*
  of French soldiers 163, 168*t*
  of German soldiers 159–60, 168*t*
  ratio of non-battle to battle deaths 155
  recording of 91–5
  time between TOS and death 144, 147
  total estimate for AIF 120, 168*t*
  total estimate including post-war deaths 195–6, 196*t*
  understatement in official records 120
  of US soldiers 154–5, 168*t*

Index 209

see also post-war deaths
war injuries
  accidental incidents 96–7
  of Canadian soliders 164
  hospitalisations for 130
  readmissions for previous wounding 97
  of US soldiers 155
  wounds from exposure to battlefield conditions 97
  see also post-war deaths; post-war disability
War Office Medical Research Committee (Britain)
  report on shell shock 74–6
  as repository for Field Medical Cards 24
war woundings
  of British soldiers 158, 159, 168*t*
  of Canadian soliders 168*t*
  criterion of hospitalisation 97
  estimated total number of AIF hospitalisations 127–9, 168*t*
  of French soldiers 163, 168*t*
  of German soldiers 160, 168*t*
  multiple 128
  official statistics 127
  soldier remains on duty 97
  understatement in official accounts 127
  of US soldiers 155, 168*t*
  see also post-war deaths; post-war disability; shell shock
Ward, Frank 89
'washer-woman knee' 96
Webber, Charles William 89
Webber, David 89

Webley, Ivan 149*n*33
Webster, John (11) 93
Webster, John (2206) 93
West, Clement 102–3
West, Ernest Albert 101
West, Hugh 109
Whalen, Robert 159, 160, 161, 162, 185
White, Brudenell (Brigadier General) 19, 20
Whitehead, Fred Furness 101
Whitehead, James Francis 99–100
Whitehead, LT 89
Whitehead, Vernon J (Major) 110
Whitelaw, Charles 188–9
Whitelaw, Robert 189–90
Wilkin, Francis Charles 96
Wilkins, GE 108–9
Wilkins, George Hubert (Capt) 137
Wilkins, LW 189
Wilkins, Robert 125
Wilkinson, Alfred 137
Wilkinson, Henry 129
Williams, RC 91
Williams, Reg (3167) 137
Williams, Reg (5432) 90–1
Williams, Reginald Samuel (98) 140
Williams, Richard 122
Williams, Sydney (306) 130
Williams, Sydney (2462) 130
Williams, Thomas Arthur 129
Williams, Thomas Conwell 149–50*n*34
Williams, Thomas Peter 61
Winter, Jay 34
woundings *see* war woundings

Zwar, Bernard 64, 65